FORGET ME

Balestier Press
Centurion House, London TW18 4AX
www.balestier.com

Forget Me:
Madame Qian Xiuling—The Belgian Schindler
Original title: 忘记我
Copyright © Xu Feng, 2021
English translation copyright © Kyle Anderson, 2023

First published by Balestier Press in 2023
Published by arrangement with Yilin Press Ltd
through Beijing Gliese Culture and Media Co Ltd

A CIP catalogue record for this book is available from the British Library.

ISBN 978 1 913891 45 9

All rights reserved. No part of this publication may be reproduced, stored in a retrieval system or transmitted in any form or by any means, electronic, mechanical, without the prior written permission of the publisher of this book.

FORGET ME

MADAME QIAN XIULING

The Belgian Schindler

XU FENG

Translated by
Kyle Anderson

BALESTIER PRESS
LONDON · SINGAPORE

"Forget Me."

How can history be forgotten? The evening drum and morning bell still resound within my ears.

Qian Xiuling

PROLOGUE

A Phone Call across the Chasm of Time

2002, late autumn, 4:00 pm, Beijing Time; 10:00 am, Brussels Time.

The telephone rang exactly as scheduled. A gentle, old voice came across the receiver in a perfect Jiangsu Yixing accent:

"Hello! This is Qian Xiuling."

"Grandma Qian! How are you? I work for the local television station. I've recently been in touch with your family, hoping to arrange a phone call with you to share your thoughts with your local countrymen."

"Local countrymen ...?"

"That's right, Grandma Qian. Whatever comes to mind is just fine. Everyone misses you greatly and wishes to hear your thoughts and voice."

"Ahh ... But, I've been wandering abroad my whole life. The

thing I most feared to hear again was this word: 'countrymen.' It's best that I keep my thoughts to myself."

"Isn't there anything you wish to share with them?"

"I miss my hometown. And I wish to return to it. But I'm too old now and can't easily move around. I can't possibly return now. I wish everyone the best, though."

"Alright, Grandma Qian. You take care! When we get the chance, we'll go and see you in person in Belgium."

"Alright, then. Can you actually come and see me?"

"Of course we can!"

"Ok. I'll be waiting for you in Brussels, then," she crisply laughed.

However, we could never make our schedules work. There were always a thousand reasons we couldn't meet up. And then the old lady finally passed away.

This unfulfilled wish was put off for 16 years.

CHAPTER 1

Jerome and Stories from Grandmother's Hometown

There are a lot of ways a story can veer off once it has begun. I like the saying that if the opportunity is right, you just might find what you're looking for.

But frankly, I don't dare start off with such unreal expectations.

It was early autumn last year when I met with Jerome. I had received a lot of gentle warnings before that moment: when praying for those you count on to lend a hand, it might be that help only arrives from the world of spirits.

"Chasm" — this key term contains so much. There is an old saying that people on opposing riverbanks are of two different minds. Perhaps only heaven knows how they take their separate forms.

And, yet, Jerome brought with him a veritable key. Despite the fact that he didn't share it with me at the time, he did at least allow me to take a small step forward. He allowed me to spy the first door that I wished to open.

When you think about it, people's fates are intertwined. Suppose for a moment that if a well-known international photographer hadn't invited Jerome to shoot scenery in an ancient city on the banks of the Yellow River, I would have never met him at all, pushing off our encounter to some far distant future. That deeply treasured memory inside of me would have had no way of germinating.

But Jerome is somebody who does things in his own way.

Every time he came to Shanghai, he would never use WeChat or text-messaging to let his friends know he had arrived. In fact, he practically never used cell phones at all.

Once in a while, he would send a written mail. That really had nothing to do with any physical attachment to handwriting per se. This would, of course, leave his loved ones waiting impatiently by the computer screen for some heavenly messenger to deliver something as simple as "I've arrived. If you've got some time, let's meet up." This didn't seem to bother him at all, though. This kind of person possesses a valiant sense of intuitive wisdom. They follow fate wherever it leads them. Maybe they believe that fate is a kind of magic? It can pluck two completely unrelated people from the sea of humanity and place them side by side to work their way through the twisted landscape of life to form a brand new relational node.

Who is Jerome, anyway? He is the eldest grandson of Qian Xiuling. Who is Qian Xiuling, you ask? Google her! You'll find over a thousand webpages of descriptions and records.

On that day, we had decided to meet up downtown near the Hailun Hotel on Nanjing Road. Jerome and his wife showed up right on time. I originally believed that as Qian Xiuling's eldest grandson he would need to be at least mostly Chinese. However, sitting across from him it was obvious that he was 100% a middle-aged, European man.

It was extremely difficult to track his origins from his face. This wasn't the typical task of following a winding path to an origin, but more like one of blood is thicker than water. So, I imagined Jerome's grandmother, an old, silver-haired woman seated at the head of his genetic line.

A century ago, she was a bright-eyed, pearl-toothed young maiden, heading out from the Qian family estate called Wang Po Qiao Pan in Yixing, Jiangsu, squeezing through a crush of people on a Shanghai dock to board a Sphinx cruise liner heading for Europe.

Her origins were nothing really to write home about. The fact that she had obtained a dual-PhD in chemistry and physics at the age of 22 didn't necessarily touch anyone outside the bubble of her own experience.

About 70 years later, though, people from her tiny hometown suddenly received some revelatory news about her: thousands of miles away in Belgium, she had saved over 100 hostages, instantly becoming a national hero from afar.

The aura of that event was pretty powerful — the townsfolk for some time averted their eyes from it. They seemed adamant about still calling her Uncle Xi (Jiangnan people are used to interchanging "uncle" with "aunt"). They always believed that Uncle Xi's was similar to the case of the scientist Madame Curie. After all, when Uncle Xi was young, that's all she could talk about.

However, Jerome had this to say about his grandmother's identity: "Perhaps grandma didn't even know who she was supposed to be then. It usually happens that things don't go according to the whims of our vulgar plans. But in that moment of need, divine intervention appeared, throwing obstacles in her way, and rigidly removing her from the path of becoming a Madame Curie, a female PhD and master of chemistry and physics, to becoming the manager of three separate Chinese restaurants."

Jerome visited China countless times. It could have been that he was his grandmother's favorite grandson. His first Leica camera was a gift from her. She had wanted him to take it to China to document people's local lives and customs. Sometimes, she would laugh out loud looking at the photos he brought back to her. Other times, she would retreat to the kitchen to hide the tears streaming down her face.

Grandpa Gregory Perlinghi was a doctor. He wasn't a very attentive one. Grandma always said he was a kind of a pushy good-for-nothing. But his Greek and Russian genes were strong. It was an all-or-nothing thing where he was incapable of changing any of his little habits — what he ate and drank, even how he expressed himself and the clothes he chose to wear. Nobody would say that this was due to his culture, though.

Whether at the dinner table, in the living room, or in the kitchen, grandmother's sphere of operations was extremely limited. Nobody liked eating her Chinese spring rolls or wontons. Waffles, cookies, hamburgers, roasted fish filets, and steaks were the preferred items on the local menu. There was no real place for her to use her Chinese language either. Her French and Belgian were quite good, but she still dreamt in Chinese — with a heavy Jiangsu accent at that. Inside the house, though, her words did hold immense weight. How she disciplined the children was certainly Chinese-like. If forced to use only one word to describe her method, I would say "severe."

Jerome would often listen to his grandmother telling traditional Chinese stories about Goddess Nuwa mending the heavens, Chang'e's flying to the moon, stealing a bell while covering one's ears, viewing the sky from the bottom of a well, and many others. Her storytelling seemed to sprout wings, lifting Jerome's little heart on a ride through the blue skies, crossing expanses and oceans within the bounds of little idiomatic proverbs. To say that Jerome was China-fied at an early age might be pushing it a bit. But the first time he arrived in Shanghai, the first thing grandmother made him do was to buy a particular map of the city. She told him that that map represented the city she grew up in as a young girl. She loved its enchanting quality. Grandma wanted Jerome to walk down every lane on that map with his own two feet — not drive around it. Every time Jerome completed a street, he would mark it red on the map. After three months of walking, he carried a pile of crinkled, red-coloured maps and a thousand plus photos back to show her.

> "Unfortunately, you didn't make it to my place of birth. It's a little village on the banks of the Taihu Lake." She found it hard to conceal the regret in her praise. "That's OK for now, though. Maybe looking at these other scenes in the photos will help to chase away the sleep."

Grandmother's words felt like a fragile still frame of a place frozen in time at the bottom of Jerome's heart. Then one day, he instantly realized that grandmother's hometown, that little village on the banks of the Taihu Lake where she was born, was itself a living part of her. This was a large part of his grandmother's story that had been missing from his comprehension, mainly her childhood and teenage years. Now he had returned to China once more, and this time he was extremely intent on hearing more about grandmother's hometown.

As we talked, he demonstrated a look of such imaginative concentration that it seemed like he was actually hearing the waves of the Taihu Lake lapping the shores of the tiny village. Within those moving waters, he was listening for the delighted giggle of a child playing on the beach. He could no longer deny the sound of his grandmother's childhood there.

During our dinner at the hotel, the word "hometown" turned into a kind of main entree — no, not an entree — an entirely new spread of dishes.

CHAPTER 2

That Old Bridge of Fate

Staring at that old bridge from a distance under the setting sun made it look like the skeleton of a dinosaur. Some call it the hunchback of Wang Po.

This name "Wang Po" must certainly refer to an old woman, certainly not the matchmaker from the Golden Lotus story, though. There are a ton of these old women characters in Chinese folk wisdom. They shuffle around in three-inch lotus shoes, bustling along the raised banks between rice and vegetable fields. In reality, their stories are nothing spectacular, nothing more than the running of a household or the carrying out of menial tasks. But when they do strike, they touch a raw nerve in the agricultural societies surrounding them, turning them into instant successes and household names in an age of want.

Legend has it that this Wang Po was an upright, virtuous woman whose original name was Yangshi. She was known for her exquisite needlework. She was also referred to as Queen Yang. Her husband passed away at an early age and she diligently observed that rule of widowhood, raising her son on her own. They say that her child at some point fell into the river and drowned. She cried so much that she nearly went blind. After a time of mourning, though, she decided to apply her best efforts to build a bridge over the river running alongside the village street. This might have been because she often walked along the riverbank, seeing children going to school and ferrying across the water. Perhaps in a daze she felt like her child was still among those children, or, better yet, perhaps she feared that those children, just like her son, might be swept away by the roiling waters of the river.

Ferrying across the river will always make people feel worried at times, whenever the wind is blowing or rain is falling, or whenever the captain is sick or the hull is leaking. That long wait for the children is always nerve-wracking.

People would watch Wang Po's two, tiny nimble feet flit over the raised banks between the fields, her silhouette vanishing into the horizon. Where would she go, they wondered? Nobody knew for certain. Sometimes she would disappear for quite a long time and then suddenly return on some gloomy evening, laden with a heavy rucksack, hovering around a dark road in the village. Some said they'd seen her braving the streets in a nearby village, begging for food. She, of course, denied those allegations. In fact, she was only ever walking rural roads she wasn't familiar with to tell folks she'd never met about how her child was suddenly swallowed by the river. Naturally, the longer her story ran on, the bigger it grew, until by the end of her tale she was calling for the construction of a new bridge as she wiped the tear stains from her face. She'd then confidently declare she was there to collect funds to construct that very bridge.

Nobody ever knew how much she collected in donations, begging for money outside the village. But after just a few years, a limestone arched bridge was stretched like a bow over those rushing waters, flanked by mulberry trees and blooming oilseed rape flowers. Old records have left no trace regarding Wang Po's contributions to the bridge's construction, but the legends of her exploits circulated through the vast countryside.

In almost every generation, a lonely remote village needs some inspirational story to motivate and console its people. Dynasties quickly rise and fall, years fly by, but Wang Po has not yet vanished into the chasm of time. Her memory is engraved by the elements onto the head of that bridge. In old China, this was one of the ways that praise was publicly conveyed. It might visually disappear without a trace, but there is never a time when it does not remain. Can you control the mouths of the people? They might never find enough to eat, but you'll never succeed in controlling the stories that come out of their mouths.

Naming the Wang Po bridge after her was not the culmination of the story, though. It would go on to form the character of an entire region.

Later generations did become skeptical about its origins. The construction of the bridge was understood as a benevolent act of the Yang family, so why was it attributed to Wang Po? Researchers went on to verify this with some explanation. During the period of the Taiping Heavenly Kingdom (1851–1864), rebels revolted and the army tracked down and executed the Eastern King Yang Xiuqing. They then killed every last Yang they could find — STAB — STAB! Naturally, Yang Po decided to change her name to Wang Po.

They say that Wang Po never got the chance to see the

completion of the bridge. It was rumored that she might have departed earth the very night the two sides of the bridge were to be connected. Local people said they never actually discovered her remains. All they ever found was a pool of dark blood sitting before the bed of her rundown hut, red stains splotched on her quilt. Some said she left behind a pair of broken old cloth shoes on the bank of the river. Everyone instantly knew what that meant: she had gone in search of her son.

More than a hundred years later and Wang Po's Golden Lotus gait was still vigorously shuffling its way through folk stories. Sadly, the Wang Po Bridge was left tottering on the edge of collapse, corroded and beaten down by the weather. A series of endless conflicts brought one disaster after another upon the once affluent Jiangnan region. A starving populous region wasn't expecting Wang Po to trot out those old tales and repair her bridge.

In Wang Po's village of origin there was a household named Qian. The head of that household was called Qian Shengxiang, a county-level student who did everything he could to try and pass the imperial examination. Legend has it that during the essay portion of the examination he wrote down the benevolent act of Wang Po's bridge project and swore that after he had established himself, the first thing he would do was to dedicate a large portion of his annual salary to renovating and securing the stability and safety of the bridge. The county student Qian Shengxiang passed over the bridge every day to go into town. It stood there as a witness to his long days of strenuous study. The odd thing, though, was that he never gained a position at court like his classmates. Instead, he returned to his childhood path of becoming an educated farmer, inheriting his grandfather's property and estate. He loved the earth and the rural landscape and understood the hardships of farming and the travails of the common worker.

Plowing fields is a bedrock principle; studying is the cultivation of the human mind and spirit. In studying ancient books, he discovered the hidden machinations behind the state bureaucracy. That's why an intense dislike for the deep cesspool of politics grew within him. The poet Tao Yuanming's collection of poems soon turned into his essential reading, resting at the side of his bed.

If you want to swim upstream to discover the ancestors of the Qian line, it is a long, long journey. In the ancestral hall of the Qian family, there is a shrine to the ancient Qian Liu with his portrait and tablet. During the Five Dynasties and Ten Kingdoms periods (900–960AD), Qian Liu undertook a massive enterprise in Hangzhou's Lin'an county: the very founding of state of Wu Yue in Southern China. Previously, during the late Tang dynasty, Qian Liu followed Dong Chang to repel rebels and protect his home, laboring tirelessly up the ranks to the Zhenhai Military Governorship. Afterwards, as a consequence of Dong Chang turning on the Tang Emperor, Qian Liu was called upon to subdue Dong Chang, from which he acquired the Zhejiang Eastern Military Governorship. He gradually came to occupy the 13 prefectures of the two eastern provinces that constituted the center of Hangzhou at the time. One after another, the central plains dynasties (Tang, Late Liang, and Late Tang) bestowed upon him the titles of King Yue, King Wu, and King Wu Yue. He reigned for 41 years, and was consecrated with a Great Ancestral Temple, endowed with the posthumous title of Solemn Martial King, and interred in the King Qian Mausoleum.

Such an imposing family tree branched out in sundry directions, eventually touching Qian Shengxiang, who moved to northern Zhejiang and settled the old Yang Xian residence. This in itself was a rather complicated and twisted affair. The lineage is recorded in the ancestral hall and keeping it up to date was a generational responsibility. The glory of their Great Ancestor, Qian Liu, was customarily hidden by Qian Shengxiang's family. The reason for being so tight-lipped about it was not merely to avoid the appearance of vanity but to avoid generating envy or a feeling of rampant destruction.

Qian Shengxiang chose an auspicious, beautiful springtime day to light the first fireworks celebrating the groundbreaking of the Wang Po Bridge. There was a firmly observed custom in the village: every benevolent act must link the name of the doer to their great deed, thus broadcasting their fame near and far. There were some who suggested Wang Po Bridge be renamed the Shengxiang Bridge, but Qian Shengxiang summarily rejected the proposal. He had no desire to rework the stone tablet at the head of the bridge. It wasn't that he disliked leaving a record of his name as much as he felt that this kind of public display would be a terrible dishonor to the figure he so highly cherished in his heart: Wang Po.

Qian Shengxiang was unlike others in many ways. For example, he didn't keep multiple mistresses like so many others with wealth did, nor was he a chain smoker or a heavy drinker. Regrettably, though, such a clean, respectable lifestyle didn't ensure him a longer life. He lived to the age of 43, the prime of life for a man to undertake major exploits. The new burial spot in a corner of the Qian family plot marked the imperial exam candidate Qiang Shengxiang's early departure from life. It also was a testament to all that there was no necessary connection between good deeds and great achievements and luck and longevity.

Qian Xixun was Qian Shengxiang's second son. Among all the members of the Qian family, Xixun was the most erudite, sharp, and productive, not to mention the best at forming relationships and karma, while also maintaining his father's air of tempered management. Where he differed from his father, however, was in how much more he emphasized culture's role in one's personal development.

He and his wife bore three sons and two daughters. Ten fingers tie hearts together, but he alone admired his second daughter named Xiuling. Not only was she witty, but she possessed a talented flair for an extraordinary memory. At the age of three, she was already memorizing Tang poetry and adorably penning calligraphy. During the peach blossom flood season, Qian Xixun would often hold her tiny hand, crisscross through the raised paths between the green fields, and linger alongside the rushing waters passing beneath Wang Po bridge.

Why did Wang Po leave the village to beg for money elsewhere? Why didn't people in her own village assist her? Xiuling was stressed over this so much that she lost her appetite, imagining that Wang Po was still out there begging for help.

Xiuling pointed to the massive stock of rice in their storehouse: "Why didn't we just give some of this to Wang Po!?"

CHAPTER 3

The Qian Family Ancestral Hall Utopia

Why didn't they just divide it up among Wang Po and poor people like Wang Po? This indeed was quite a problem.

In Chinese villages, whether in the north or in the south, behind every rich man there are at least a few hundred poor ones. Sustained hunger can turn a person's face bluish, and his or her eyes green. It's a popular concept that the poor work on behalf of the rich man — it's because of them that the rich man gets fat. We were later informed that this was referred to as exploitation and being exploited. Actually though, the relationship between the rich man and the poor man was never that cold, particularly in the Zhejiang region. From the Southern Song dynasty (1127–1279) until the present, a system of permanent tenancy had prevailed. This permitted the tenant farm the right to cultivate the landlord's land on a permanent basis. In this specific context, this system delimited the baseline of their dealings. To be frank, though, as long as the tenant farmer cultivated the landlord's land, the landlord couldn't run him off it. In fact, even if the tenant farmer couldn't pay his rent, the original owner of the land couldn't do anything to him. Within the social structure of the village, the landlord's powers were hampered by all kinds of controls, especially when some of those tenants were his own elders or relatives. During the celebrations of Chinese Lunar New Year and other traditional festivals, the landlord would kowtow to them and give them gifts, and in ordinary times there seemed to be no difference in status between any of them. If you had to search for a discrepancy, it was the issue of literacy. If you insisted upon entering the details of their lives, you would quickly discover that the life of the rich man was on the whole not very luxurious and the poor man's day was not without its comforts and dignities.

Because of the immense fame Qian Shengxiang earned from repairing the Wang Po Bridge, the accomplishments of his son Qian Xixun in the village seemed almost nothing to write home about. Compared to his father, he spent more time lingering over his books every day. It was as if he possessed a scholarly disposition. In such an ordinary village, that made him especially stick out. He would often go into town to participate in activities that the villagers couldn't quite grasp and make friends with people whose heads were filled with all kinds of new terminology. If we were to create a timeline and place him on it after 1919 in China's Republican Era (1911–1949), we would see that he brought back more than just a few fashionable terms from the town to his village. There was the entire concept of the May 4th Movement or the New Culture Movement. Qian Xixun's meager frame stretched along the dikes between the fields in the setting sun. Sometimes he made his trip on a speed boat. In the middle of autumn, he enjoyed standing on the bow and looking at receding bleak shorelines under the great dome of heaven. The stern was always piled up with stacks of his books. Nobody knew how those books and farming had anything to do with living the way he did at home.

Qian Xixun also enjoyed a position in a civil organization, the president of the local Cherishing Characters Society. As the name implies, it was an organization for enthusiasts who cherished language. The group had only one main objective: no paper with writing on it or utensils for writing were allowed to be carelessly discarded. In terms of a standard, whether it was an outdated old newspaper, or even a little note with some writing, it had to be properly preserved or handled. The village expert would go from door to door to collect the samples and then send them to the local temple for proper disposal.

Even an illiterate who couldn't recognize a character had a kind of reverence for the language. This type of implicit value system had influenced the everyday life of these people living for centuries on the relatively peaceful plains of Zhejiang.

When approaching middle-age, Qian Xixun surprisingly decided to establish a school in the village. Naturally, it was for free schooling. Every child in the village, whether rich or poor, was required to attend and learn to read and write. While implementing his near utopian idea, he ran into some difficulties — not from the families but from their illiterate countrymen. A lot of villagers believed that education was a luxury and they wouldn't dare to accept it. Though everyone recognized the generations of good deeds provided by the Qian family, they felt that schooling in the village was like an unattainable stairway to heaven. There were some who also feared being ridiculed by others as they struggled to read their lessons. Besides, this would just delay their duties in the field. One of the particulars included Qian Xixun visiting one of his family's old tenant farmers. He asked the household's 11 year-old child why he wasn't coming to study. The old tenant farmer responded for him: "He's 11 now. He can't eat for free anymore. It's time to get down into the field and do some work like the cattle." Qian Xixun lost his temper. He ordered him right on the spot to hand over years of unpaid back rent unless he sent his child to school.

The original schoolhouse was located inside the Qian family Ancestral Hall. Usually that place was tightly secured, opening only for New Year's offerings to forebears or when other solemn events took place. But now the door was flung wide open, and instead of an open spacious hall, it had become a crowded classroom with 20 or so children from all walks of life. Qian Xixun felt a real sense of accomplishment from all of this. His family noticed that the halo he walked around with shined even brighter than it had standing in his wheat field during a bumper harvest.

Mr. Gao was someone Qian Xixun had invited from the city to teach for six cups of rice a month. Mr. Gao had a rather small build, but his voice was sonorous. It made people feel empowered. The resonant tember of his voice when he read out loud was sufficient to pierce the thick, heavy walls of the Qian family's Ancestral Hall. It swirled above the vast open fields. Qian Xixun appreciated Mr. Gao, because he was gifted at teaching cultural classes to different kinds of students at the same time. In other words, he could, under the same roof, use different teaching methods and content to cater to students of varying ages and capacities. The drama all unfolded under the ancient eaves of a house in a particular Zhejiang village within an anti-rote learning environment. Mr. Gao would start at the crack of dawn and work diligently, honoring his trade to the extreme. This was no doubt because of Qian Xixun's high expectations. However, privately, the extra red envelope Qian Xixun would hand him was always quite full. The sound of children reciting text transported Qian Xixun's spirit to a different place.

If we had been able to spy in on the classes in the Qian family Ancestral Hall and have a look around, we would have discovered a little girl seated in the front row. That was Qian Xixun's beloved daughter, Xiuling. She was calm at times, then lively at others. Mr. Gao had some preconceived notions about her at the beginning. She was rather energetic, not the especially quiet and bashful type of girl. But he learned to see her differently very quickly on account of her intelligence. She could with little effort stand up and answer every kind of question Mr. Gao could put to her. If you were to say that Mr. Gao's multiple teaching method was like climbing a staircase, then in Xiuling's case, she was using a bamboo pole vault to soar over every railing he set up.

This frankly amazed Mr. Gao. We came to find out that Qian Xixun would bring home reading materials from the city containing knowledge a great deal more profound than what he was teaching her, and Xiuling would sneak around reading her father's books at his bedside or pillow. This was no secret to the Qian family, though. Qian Xixun was indeed quite a strict father, but in this one thing, reading, he never set up any boundaries. Naturally, he did his best to keep the *Golden Lotus*, *Story of the Stone*, and *Romance of the West Chamber* and other such romances hidden and well out of her reach.

I will attempt to paint a picture of the childhood and youth of this precocious rural reader, Qian Xiuling. She was robust, sharp, sincere, cheerful, extremely intelligent, and eager to assist others. Without a doubt, the backdrop of the multilevel instruction of the Qian family Ancestral Hall cannot be overlooked as a strong influence upon her later studies. However, that narrow hall was, in fact, unable to contain the appetite of Xiuling's informed wit. She quickly tired

Qian Xiuling in her childhood

of Mr. Gao's instruction. Though she would never drowse off or disturb the order of instruction, Mr. Gao discovered numerous times how she would secretly read popular novels just as he was passionately introducing a new chapter in his text. One time, Mr. Gao made her stand on her feet and recite Zhu Geliang's "Former Paragons of Virtue". Qian Xiuling recited it in one breath, not skipping a single word, then shyly asked Mr. Gao: "Would you also like me to recite the 'Later Paragons of Virtue'?" Mr. Gao was stunned: "We haven't studied that one yet. Can you recite it?" A second later, Qian Xiuling was clearly and loudly performing the piece:

> The emperor realized that Shu Han and Cao Cao could not exist alongside one another. The monarch's kingdom could not easily flourish in one location, thus he appointed me to go and subdue Cao Cao by force. Taking the emperor's perception of this, and estimating my talent, it was known at the outset that I would be going up against an enemy that was stronger than me. But, not crusading against the enemy would likely also result in the defeat of the emperor's kingdom. The choice was to sit and await death, or to take the initiative and bring the fight to the enemy. As a result, the monarch dispatched me without hesitation to fight the enemy.
> The officials received their orders, then tossed in my sleep and ate with little enjoyment. In order to reach the north, I had to first conduct a campaign against the south. So, in the fifth month, we crossed over Lushui and entered a barren landscape. Food was scarce, providing just one meal every two days. We were not thinking of caring for ourselves, however, but of protecting the monarch's power that could

not be preserved in its current location in Shu. Thus, we braved many perils to fulfill the monarch's last wishes. There was, however, some dispute about the wisdom of the scheme. By coincidence, the enemy had grown weary from suppressing a rebellion on their western border, and also struggling to fight back Sun Wu's invasion on the eastern border. *The Art of War* requires that you take advantage of an enemy to launch an attack when they are in difficulty. It was the opportune moment to immediately march on the enemy! What occurred, I will now solemnly narrate below: The wisdom of the ancestral emperor can compare with the sun and the moon. The experience of the monarch's strategic advisor was vast and his stratagems far-reaching, but he still needed to pass through great peril. Bodies are wounded and great calamity is encountered before peace can be achieved. Now, his majesty cannot compare with the great ancestral emperor, neither can his strategic advisor with Zhang Liang or Chen Ping. His thought was to use a war of attrition to win victory over his enemy and then establish peace across the land. This was the one point that I did not grasp ...

Mr. Gao's shock occurred on a bright and sunny morning in the middle of the 1920s. In his most grave tone of voice as the village's teacher, he recommended to Qian Xixun that if he wished for his little princess to reach her potential that he must send her from the Qian family Ancestral Hall as quickly as possible. She needed to go to the city — and not the small town of Yixing, either. At the very least, she needed to go to Suzhou — that's right, Suzhou, where she could pursue further study and open up doors of endless possibilities to her future.

At that moment, a new character arrived on the scene. He was someone Qian Xixun had become friends with in the old town, a certain Wu Zizheng. The Wu family was the most distinguished family in the old town, and Wu Zizheng was scholar of the highest reputation in the late Qing period. He and Qian Xixun understood each other very well — they were thick as thieves, as they say. This was no mere casual acquaintance of a year or two. The Wu family was running more than half of the shops on Gingko Alley in the old town at that time. And in the surrounding environs, the family had well over a 1,000 mu of estate land. He very much enjoyed the clean, rustic manners of his friend Qian Xixun, and the fact that he didn't put on pedantic academic aires. He had a son, Wu Chongyi. He was of a similar age as the beloved Xixun. One time while drinking, the two of them concluded a pact to have the children marry each other. The fact that the two children had never seen each other and might not develop affections after growing up didn't seem to matter much to them. As they say: the will of the parents and the word of the matchmaker have always been from ancient times the basis of children's marriage.

The young Xiuling's blossoming academic cleverness became a common topic of conversation among Qian Xixun and his friend, Wu Zizheng. In Zizheng's opinion, Xiuling was still quite young and should first go to a girls' middle school in the county to study, and then later go to Suzhou with little delay. Qian Xixun sensed a bit of vague self-interest leaking out of Zizheng. He knew that Wu Zizheng was playing very close attention to the future of his daughter-in-law: if she was studying in the county town, that means she would be right outside his front gates. From Wu Zizheng's perspective, she could still study a little, learn logic and reason, cultivate an elegant manner — all good things. But, if she were to go directly to Suzhou to study, that would be well beyond the reach of his family's influence. If other issues crept up, things would be hard to bring back under his control. Qian Xixun felt similarly about the whole thing. To be honest, he didn't really wish to see Xiuling be too far away from him either. His daughter was his daughter, after all. Despite the fact that his friendship with Zizheng didn't hinge upon his daughter's arranged marriage, a gentleman's word is binding. He didn't want this once in a century happy occurrence to be derailed by a miscalculation.

Wu Zizheng was the supervisor of the county town girl's middle school. According to standards, the supervisor had the authority to control the number of students enrolling in the school free of testing. However, Qian Xixun actually insisted that Xiuling take part in the rather intense competition of examinations to enter the program. As a result, his little darling comfortably succeeded in entering the program as the number one pupil based alone on her test score.

 At present we have no way of obtaining records of Qian Xiuling's time studying at the county girl's school. We have found some information on it in the Qian family's incomplete genealogy, however. From this we have a witness of some influential people she met during her short time there. Among them, the most important was her older male cousin, Qian Zhuolun. Zhuolun was a great deal older than Xiuling, 23 years old. Though they were technically from the same generation, their difference in age made Xiuling feel that he was sometimes more father-like and sometimes more brother-like. Zhuolun was obviously not as stern and dignified as a father, but he did go to great lengths to care for his favorite little sister. At that time, Qian Zhuolun's family had already migrated from their ancient home in the Wang Po Village to Academy Street near the northern gate of the county town. Qian Xiuling would often leave her female dorm on the weekends to go and eat a sumptuous meal at her "older brother" Zhuolun's home.

Zhuolun was currently studying at the Armed Forces University and Xiuling liked to listen to strange tales and anecdotes about the military school. At the time, Qian Xiuling's personal idol was not the legendary bridge-builder Wang Po, but a scientist working at the edge of the world named Madame Curie. Her older cousin used to love the ancient eliminator of evils Zhou Chu, but now he was infatuated with the French General Napoleon. The demanding military school life often prevented him from returning home, but if there was a possibility, he always tried to enjoy a rare gathering, and the crisp and melodious chatter of Xiuling was always a present at those joyous events. For example, they would draw straws and recite Tang poetry in competition for a first batch of roasted sweet potatoes or gingko fruit. Xiuling would always proudly exclaim: "Man, am I stuffed!" She also had another closely related cousin, Zhuoru. He was known as a quick-witted prankster. He was studying at the county high school at the time. At every gathering, he would provide his own programming, most often some gender-bending performance that put everyone in stitches.

One time, Zhuolun purchased a magazine from a bookstore in the Nanjing old city with some content on Madame Curie. He wrapped it up and gave it to Xiuling as a present. Little could he have guessed that the magazine would not only fascinate her but that it would change the course of her future. One day, she suddenly approached Zhuolun to discuss a serious topic: She wanted to go to Suzhou to study. Rumor had it that the Jiangsu Provincial Suzhou Girls Middle School was situated among the new bridges and old alleyways of the Suzhou old city. The school's architecture had that classical flair of the traditional Suzhou style. They said that the ambience felt very new, and that the school uniforms were sharp.

Xiuling responded without the slightest hesitation: "I'm not scared!"

Zhoulun laughed. That was the defining feature of a member of the Qian family. He even responded saying he would personally go and see Uncle Xixun to lobby on her behalf. One of the movements he especially loved to perform was to use a finger to point at his tongue. When Zhuolun was younger, his tongue would grow sores, and according to the village doctor's knowledge, those needed to be sliced off. Some people gasped — this man was a genius. Only a rotten tongue could cut one's future short. Surprisingly, God was watching over this saucy-tongued youngster and Dr. Yang, a Shanghai doctor from a teaching hospital, ended up saving the boy's tongue. Following his recovery, Zhuolun was enunciating clearly and speaking eloquently and fluently. One time, he was with his younger brother and sister when he joked that he had only one disappointment in his life: not living up to his tongue's potential.

Nobody knows just how Zhuolun convinced Uncle Xixun, but in just that one visit, Qian Xixun agreed. Xiuling's father threw open the windows onto Xiuling's unexpected wish. The only thing he blamed her for was why she hadn't come and asked him herself. It might have been that one of Qian Xixun's nerves had been struck by the youthful vigor of his nephew Zhuolun. Furthermore, a reason children often do not realize, the noble son of the Wu household was also going away for his studies. Qian Xixun didn't want his daughter to fall behind the son of that other family.

Later, Xiuling spotted a freshly-written scroll by Zhuolun on her father's desk:

Centuries of merit are gained through the highest achievement of study.

Her father was quite praiseworthy of the progress in Zhuolun's calligraphic skill. Though his nephew had joined the military, he still nurtured a classical soul, returning to the inkwell on a daily basis — never breaking that connection with letters. Deep down, he was a scholar. His calligraphy possessed the manner of the famous calligrapher Wang Xizhi's work, exuding care and skill that did not match his age, while simultaneously not losing its youthful freshness.

However, her father also wrote a note of his own to Xiuling. He wanted to take his daughter into the city to visit the Wu household on Gingko Street. It would only be a simple visit. Speaking frankly, though, he wanted Xiuling to know quite early that she was a member of the Wu family. Nonetheless, he was adamantly turned down by Xiuling. Her reasons were that since young men and women should not be in contact and because she was not of a marriageable age that she had no business going to another's household.

Before leaving for Suzhou, Qian Xiuling returned one last time to the Qian estate. She departed out of the east gate of the old city, passed over a little wooden bridge, walked through a tiny fishing village on the lake called Sanlidun, past the Wuli Temple headed eastward for a few miles until she finally arrived at the tottering Wangpo Bridge. We can't know what she thought about as she stood there on the bridge watching the water slowly flow to the east.

Perhaps she had some vague expectations for her future. The old Qian estate in the background made the moment serene. Whatever awaited her, she didn't believe it would completely cut her off from this place. Every vague, impractical fantasy appeared in the mirror of her mind. Her hurried steps couldn't keep pace with her youthful longings. Her base mood was cheerful, though occasionally she experienced an indescribable melancholy.

She paid a formal visit to the always encouraging Mr. Gao. She suddenly found herself getting emotional. Mr. Gao had become very thin, and his incessant coughing and flushed protruding cheek bones made one worry for his health. While speaking, sweat beaded up on his forehead. Mr. Gao faithfully maintained her father's personal insistence on a free education at the Qian family Ancestral Hall Combined Academy. Her father's silence was not like it was in the past. Xiuling sensed that it was not just about sadness in parting, but a bit of concern as well. What would come as a result of stepping over this threshold? Nobody could know. Xiuling's engagement to the Wu family son was a monumental commitment in her life. But she had an independent personality, and her brilliance had already begun to show. Her kind-hearted, timid mother very rarely voiced her opinion in the large household. She was rather like a silkworm, knowing only how to ceaselessly work on her string. Her mother spoke to her privately, telling her how her father hadn't been able to sleep for days now. Some unknown intuition was nagging at him that his precious daughter's wings were not like ordinary people's. If she wanted to fly, there was no stopping her.

"Ling, you really want to fly?" her mother embraced her, tears welling up in her eyes.

"I'll come back, Mom, to pay my respects to you and Father."

However, decades later when she recalled these events, she said:

> In the end, I wrote an essay about leaving Yixing county in my youth. It made me feel like a little bird taking off into

the sky. While waiting for my return at some point in the future, I was already wishing that the ways of the world and I had transformed."

CHAPTER 4

Huangpu River, Only You Understand Me

An old photo flashes by on a documentary by Jerome's sister Tatiana:

It's a group photo of the Datong University's women's basketball team taken during the Republican period, sixth month of the 18th year. A group of budding beauties is wearing athletic gear in the style of the period. They're organized neatly in a single file line. Their soft complexions frozen in time span half a century. There are absolutely no discounts on this yellowing photo. The third one on the left with the round face, smiling but showing no teeth is Qian Xiuling.

But didn't she go to Suzhou? So, what is she still doing in Shanghai?

Calculating from the calendar, the 18th year of the Republican period is 1929. Qian Xiuling should be 17 years old in the photo. She had already finished her studies at the provincial girl's middle school in old Suzhou, taking just two years to complete a three-year curriculum. Skipping a grade was nothing new to Qian Xiuling. To merely say that she was a child endowed with a gift for study was actually to overlook her exceptional work ethic.

A pale blue long-sleeve shirt, dark blue shorts, a clean-cut bob, Bailish shoes, and a school badge in white script over a blue field on her chest were the fashionable standard of female students after the May 4th period. A slim-fitting skirt contained her slender, tall frame, but couldn't contain her soaring thoughts. Qian Xiuling would later leave a photo album to her granddaughter Tatiana. There was only a single photo in there having to do with Suzhou.

There is a very tall chimney in the background and a factory paired with it below. She is standing on the riverbank with the factory in the background. The river is clear. It's a representation of the strength and contradiction of industrialized civilization in old Suzhou. It's not entirely clear what factory this is. For a May 4th New Woman like Qian Xiuling, this kind of towering chimney signified both science and civilization at once. Compared to the Huqu Pagoda, Humble Administrator's Garden, or the Heavenly Scale Mount and other kinds of historical sites, this location possessed more the spirit of its time. She appears calm in the picture, her hair is stylish — bangs permed evenly above the eyebrows. She is wearing a loose, open black leather jacket over a hidden twill woven skirt. Glistening high-heels adorn her feet. If you compared this to a photo of when she was younger and living in that small village in Zhejiang, you would realize just how completely her rustic roots had been obliterated. Sophistication driving fashion at the time washed over her entire being.

The photo has the power to prop up the story of what's to come for her. She was a paragon of studies and virtue. Her math scores were

*Qian Xiuling at Jiangsu Provincial Girls'
School in Suzhou*

outstanding. In the standings of the Provincial Suzhou Girl's Middle School, Qian Xiuling led the way every time. The crucial point was that Shanghai and Suzhou were too close together. This great Asian international capital opened up a world of possibilities every day. It was an adventurous paradise for dreamers of all kinds.

At the time, Qian Xiuling's "older brother" Zhuoru was already studying professional metallurgy at Shanghai's Jiaotong University. The shadow he left behind constantly spurred on his younger sister's desire to study hard and rise to the top. Besides, Xiuling knew the next step in her brother's plans: to sit for exams and become a European top ten student at Belgium's KU Leuven.

Remote Europe. In Qian Xiuling's heart at that time, that once vague idol had already become crystal clear in mind. That idol was Madame Curie. Since the moment Zhuolun had gifted her that magazine with the descriptions of Madame Curie's achievements, Xiuling insisted on tracking down every trace of her in the news. And every time there was a report or news out on her, Xiuling would grab some scissors and cut the story out and insert it into her scarpbook. She even knew all the papers that Madame Curie had published in recent years and what her achievements were. Secretly she wished that she could find her way closer to Madame Curie, and then a little bit closer.

Qian Xixun all at once had to provide for two children to study in Shanghai. That amounted to quite a bit of pressure on him. There was incessant fighting between warlords in Zhejiang at the close of the 1920s — human disasters were heaped onto natural ones as crops in the rural areas failed year after year and every form of destitution was on display. Nonetheless, Qian Xixun's determination to support his children's studies never once wavered. His close friend, a future relative by marriage, Wu Zizheng, had produced three university students in his household, and all were studying abroad. He had watched with his own eyes as Wu Zizheng sold off acre after acre of good agriculture land outside the city to provide for his little brother Wu Dayu's and his nephew Wu Chongren's studies in France. And then there was his son, Wu Hongyi, Xiuling's betrothed, who had already tested into Belgium's KU Leuven.

Xiuling wanted to go with her brother Zhuoru to KU Leuven to study as well. Zhuoru was the first one to have brought this up with her father.

As brother and sister, they ordinarily fought, but when it came to big issues, they always arrived at a natural understanding.

For a while, Qian Xixun found it hard to make a decision. Initially, the issue was the amount of tuition. Just the cost of preparatory courses at Leuven for a year came to 1,000 silver dollars. That was truly expensive. In the Yixing old city, the monthly income of a police officer was only a few silver dollars. You could raise a large household with that amount. Qian Xixun supported his son to go abroad for his studies, something obviously influenced by the example of his friend Wu Zizheng. However, with regard to Xiuling's prospects, he still harbored some reservations. A daughter is a father and mother's precious treasure — what was she doing traveling so far away from them?! How different was it really from staying and studying in China anyway? Besides, Xiuling was going to be a part of the Wu household in the end. Xixun was torn by the pain and worry of the situation, and just dealt with it by pushing it out of his view.

On her side of things, Xiuling easily jumped through all the necessary hoops. It took very little effort for her to test into Datong University's preparatory school. The university was a very well known private institution. In the world of higher education, the saying went that "The north has Nankai, and the south has Datong."

She would watch as passenger vessels belched smoke as they ever so slowly docked along the Huangpu River. People of all different skin colors exited the ship's hold. She imagined that a thin, old lady was headed straight for her on the deck. Her silver hair, broad forehead, peaceful gaze beneath light eyebrows, and firm lip line was the very image of the woman she had traced a million times over in her mind: Madame Curie.

All of a sudden, she realized that she had grown much, much closer to Madame Curie.

She would often watch the riverbank and calmly sort out her innermost thoughts. She wouldn't do that from inside any of those fashionable storefronts, though. This was one of her hobbies at the time. She felt that it was only the breaking ripples of the Huangpu River that understood her and that could engage her in a dialogue.

She was always following Madame Curie closely. That year, Madame Curie turned 62 years old. It was in the fall when a lucky Chinese university student, a Tsinghua University physics graduate named Shi Shiyuan, was selected by Madame Curie. He entered her lab to research actinoid radiation chemistry. Qian Xiuling found this out reading the news. Her heart thumped in her chest. That student was so lucky! At the same moment, she was struck by an inspiration: "Thank you, Brother Shi! You're blazing the way for your younger sister to stand at the Madame's side. I'll be right behind you!"

That year, there was another Chinese student named Zheng Dazhang who directly received guidance from Madame Curie. Her daughter, Eve Curie, actually came to China for a visit and wrote a piece called "Interviews in Wartime China." She wrote about the Jiang Jieshi and Guangxi warlord conflict, the seizing of the Zhongdong railway line by the warlord Zhang Xueliang, the northwestern general Song Zheyuan, Sun Liangcheng and his 27 soldiers defying Jiang Jieshi, and the beginnings of war between Jiang Jieshi and Feng Yuxiang's northwestern forces. And then she wrote about all the turmoil that this had caused in Chinese society.

At the end of the piece, Eve Curie spoke about how Madame Curie deeply respected and was very concerned about China's students.

It was only a few short sentences, but those words were like huge banners painted into her heart.

As long as there was even the tiniest bit of news on Madame Curie, the woman's image would never slip from Xiuling's vision.

For example, Wang Weike, a Chinese translator, after returning home from hearing a lecture given by Madame Curie at the University of Paris had this to say about her:

> When she lectures, her voice flows like a tranquil river. There's a musical quality to it like the sound of a pipe organ floating on a distant breeze. Her enunciation is precise but not extravagantly so — light, not stiff. Her opinions are authoritative but not oppressive. She can take an uninteresting physical chemistry formula and insert it into a kind of fantastical world, like a child's fairytale.

These substantive additions to Qian Xiuling's "Madame Curie Collection" scrapbook were in absolute direct proportion to her yearning to be with Madame Curie in far-away Europe. A girl with such dreams and goals spent every day on striving to bring them about.

Compared to her character in middle school, Xiuling was much more enthusiastic and bolder. She enjoyed physical activity and basketball was her first choice. Despite the fact that she wasn't tall, she could run very fast and her jumping ability was outstanding. People called her "Sofia the Pointguard." Anything that had a competitive aspect to it she willingly joined. She had an especially stable psychological disposition. Her marks in math and science were exceptional, as well as her English composition and speech. Her instructors and classmates all looked up to her.

One day, Xiuling received a letter from her father, urging her to return home that weekend. She shared the letter with Zhuoru. Zhuoru grimaced back: "Most likely to meet a certain somebody! And you probably know who that is." Xiuling thought about it, embarrassment coming through her expression: "I know. But times have changed, right? Aren't we the masters of our own fate now?"

The words came from the sincerest depths of her being. They frightened Zhuoru.

Qian Xiuling didn't obey her father's request to return to the old Wang Po Qiao estate that weekend, but she did write a letter back to him.

In the letter she explained that final exams were coming up at school and she really couldn't break away. At the same time, she also mentioned for the first time to her father how it was her dream to become one of Madame Curie's science pupils. She wanted to go with her brother Zhuoru to Belgium to study at KU Leuven.

Qian Xixun felt an unexpected disappointment waiting for his daughter to return home on the appointed weekend. On this rather ordinary weekend, Wu Zizheng was bringing his son Wu Hongyi to the Wangpo Bridge Qian family home for an official visit, so there was some trick to it. Wu Hongyi had already matriculated as a student of KU Leuven in Belgium and was on winter vacation visiting his family. Though the boy's visage wasn't particularly handsome in Qian

Xixun's eyes, he possessed an air of culture and refinement, the quality of a well-educated person. He seemed somewhat introverted, not speaking very much — in fact his words felt a bit clumsy. He appeared to be one of those men set on burying themselves in their studies.

Qian Xixun had only seen Wu Hongyi when he was a child, but he still felt quite satisfied in his future son-in-law. He was honest and considerate and utterly polite. He only seemed to be lacking somewhat his father's sharp speech and wit.

At the meal, Qian Xixun brought up how both Zhuoru and Xiuling wished to study at KU Leuven in Belgium. Wu Zizheng praised their plan. In fact, he supported Xiuling's thinking. If she was able to test in, then she and Hongyi would be able to see each other every day. It would be a fine way for them to take care of each other. After drinking a bit, he even suggested that the Wu family help pay for her expenses to study overseas: "Then there would be four study abroad students under our Wu roof!"

Qian Xixun obviously politely declined his offer.

Zizheng's natural show of strength wasn't at all ill-intentioned. But his rustic scholar, independent streak made Qian Xixun incapable of accepting charity, even if it was from a close friend. Even if in the accepted sense of the notion Xiuling was the future daughter-in-law of the Wu family, she was still a maiden of the Qian household. If the well-off Wu family was selling its land and property to provide for their children's education abroad, why couldn't the Qians do the same?

One thing was perfectly clear to him, though: if they wanted to accelerate the engagement between Xiuling and Wu Hongyi, there was no better way than to agree to let Xiuling join him in Belgium for her studies.

They had to dispel now all disagreements from the past. Any

reason that might influence Xiuling's studying abroad had become an obstacle to the development of their children's affections. Wu Zizheng would say at the time: "Wait, so you're telling me that not only do you not want to give money to your daughter to study with my son to nurture their relationship, but that you don't agree to letting me sponsor her either? What is it you're exactly trying to pull here?"

One's friends can become one's enemies. That's a dangerous situation to court.

Sell the land. That's what Qian Xixun decided.

Normally, guarding every inch of land handed down by one's ancestors is the fundamental responsibility of every virtuous son. Only for funding studies would any mainstream society excuse and even support the selling off of home and property, painful as it is. In fact, that act on the contrary might become a kind of encouraging folk example spread far and wide. Qian Xixun believed firmly that even in the unseen world of the spirits, a host of his dignified and sacred ancestors would tacitly praise his decision.

From that moment on, his mind was made up. Not only did he agree, but he began to actively encourage Xiuling to go to that nation far, far away. She must sit for exams at KU Leuven. In his letter to his daughter, he pretended to accidentally bring up Wu Hongyi's studies at KU Leuven and praised the boy for being so intelligent, indicating to her how she should consult with him moving forward.

Xiuling closely studied the letter a few times. She finally teased out an important meaning: "the Wu family's son." In recent years, her father had been using this term more and more. It felt like it was actually a way of calling this fact to her attention: don't forget that he is her husband-to-be. For a woman receiving a modern education, she had always just treated the term as some kind of rumor. But with the passing of the years, that rumor became fuzzier and fuzzier. In fact, she never had even measured up the man. What kind of man was he? How tall was he? Was he good-looking, or not? That's right. Even though she was at that age women yearn for love, her imagined Mr. Right was someone who matched her own understanding and aesthetic sensibilities, not some reincarnation of what her father indicated.

Naturally, she couldn't have known about how in her hometown Wu Zizheng and her father raised their glasses filled with homebrewed *Gangmianqing* rice wine to her and the Wu family son's future courtship at KU Leuven, their love and wedding festivities, beautiful children. etc. A long time ago, her simple life focused only on study limited her imagination of what her father was up to. What was that ageing father of endless compassion thinking? She really hadn't a clue .

Her horizon of study in Shanghai was not that long, since she had already set her mind to sit for exams at KU Leuven in Belgium. The homework she spent the most energy on now was English and French. Though extra time after school was filled up with basketball, and rehearsals for a small role in the school performance of Shakespeare's Twelfth Night, her brain was swimming in English and French vocabulary.

But there was something that couldn't be ignored: her older cousin Qian Zhuolun had come to Shanghai on official work business and had invited Xiuling and Zhuoru to eat with him in his spare time at a small, seedy tavern not far from the Cheng Huang Temple.

Nobody in the family had imagined Zhuolun would develop so quickly. This first-rate graduate of the army academy was promoted in succession from sergeant to company commander to battalion commander, gaining the respect of his superiors. During the Northern Expedition conflict he had distinguished himself over and over in a myriad of battles. At such a young age, he was selected to go to the armed forces command center to take up a staff officer position as deputy department head, bearing the epaulet of a rear admiral. Word had it that he had won the favor of the Commander-in-Chief and had become one of the top aides in the armed forces command center. His advisory work was outstanding, turning the command center into a center of intelligence.

Qian Zhuolun had arrived in Shanghai on official business. The receiving party most certainly attached great importance to his visit. The reception was no small affair, everything was arranged according to the rules of the game. Zhuolun was put up in the city's most luxurious hotel — even a young major general requires proper treatment. However, one day he declined all of the prepared activities, changed into civilian clothing, got on a rickshaw, and quietly snuck away down one of the Yuyuan Garden alleyways. The tavern was called Yellow Wine and that is precisely what it smelled like. They had mildew dried veggies, non-greasy red braised pork, a pan-fried, lucid, fresh and tender croaker fish, and small wontons in chicken stock — all Xiuling and Zhuolun's favorite dishes. Watching his younger cousins wolf down their food made Zhuolun laugh.

Being there with Zhuoru and Xiuling truly relaxed him. He enjoyed hearing them spout off about this and that, and really didn't say much. He never liked to show off or impart great wisdom from on high. When he was relaxed he liked to drink, putting him in that most splendid realm of feeling a little tipsy. They passionately discussed a number of things that beautiful evening together, things they wouldn't remember decades later. When it was time to part, Zhuolun gave each of them a picture of himself in military attire signed by his own hand. The photograph accompanied them both on their journey abroad. His image possessed a calm expression that defied his young age. He looked satisfied but dignified. As they left, Zhuolun took great care to remind Xiuling that he was there for her at any time, in any predicament.

That year on a foggy day in November, Qian Xiuling and her older brother Zhuoru boarded the Sphinx cruise liner for Marseilles, France. France was very close to Belgium. The two of them had selected one of the best ship lines available at the time.

As the ship pulled away, Qian Xiuling felt no sadness. She knew that she had just begun a new chapter in her life. Her emotions all felt brand new. A flock of noisy river gulls flitted by and rose high into the sky, gradually disappearing into the dense, creeping autumn fog. That's when Xiuling finally cried. A spiritual finger had touched a scene that she would never forget in her entire life.

It was the night before she was to leave home and a stranger had shown up to pay a visit. Her father didn't seem to think the guest's arrival was strange. He even unexpectedly arranged to have their conversation take place in his study, not where he usually hosted guests in the parlor. Xiuling's room was right next door. She was seized by an indescribable curiosity and walked over to the study where the door remained unlatched. The lantern light flickered giving the scene a dazzling feel. She stood there for a bit and then understood everything.

Her father had just sold over six hectares of land.

It was their family's most fertile nighttide plot, close to the lake. The nighttide plot was so named because of the rising evening tides of Taihu Lake that irrigated the farmland in a vapor of diffuse droplets. During the day, the hot sun dried up the spongy earth, a cycle continually repeated that made the humid soil perfect for growing sweet and crisp radishes, sticky and soft lily roots, and all kinds of lush and oily greens. It was a fertile and beautiful land.

The plot was her father's favorite, hanging often from his lips.

Qian Xiuling and Qian Zhuoru studying abroad in Belgium together

Every sentence he spoke seemed's to smash Xiuling's heart like a mallet. "If it weren't for my daughter's needing to study abroad, I wouldn't sell the land even if you lopped off my head!"

Her father and the guest seemed to be arguing in whispers over the price of the land. In the end, the guest threw down his last words: "It's not actually I who am buying the land. I'm doing it on behalf of somebody else. The price is already low, but if you, good sir, do not wish to let the land go, I believe it is best I take my leave."

Xiuling noticed a twitch in her father's face. In the dusky light of the sun, her father's face loomed for a moment vague and gloomy.

She began to cry and no matter how hard she tried to stop the tears, they kept on flowing. She couldn't sleep that night. Her beloved parents had paid a high price to support her study abroad.

The next day, she went into her father's study to say good morning: "Daddy, I promise to always honor you."

Her father smiled with grace and affection. The sunshine shone through the bronze-colored wood window panels. The warm light froze his smile in time, as bright and soft as silk, a memory that she would carry with her for her entire life.

She had originally supposed that at a moment like this her father would certainly bring up the "Wu family's son," maybe even use the arranged marriage as a condition for study in Belgium. But, her father never said a word about it. Nonetheless, this didn't relieve the suspense she was feeling about the situation. She knew that her father valued trust and honor more than life itself. The matching of his daughter was a constant source of anxiety for him.

As expected, Zhuoru told her that just before they left, her father had exhorted him to create opportunities between Xiuling and the Wu family's son to develop their feelings for each other.

On the day they were to leave home, their father deliberately went into town to take care of some business. He didn't leave her with even one word of advice. Perhaps it was painfully clear to him that his children already understood everything and that harping on it would become a bother. Of course, what was most important to him was that he didn't reveal how fragile he felt inside. If a father with a hardened exterior and soft interior were to watch his children fade away into the distance under his own eyes, there was no guarantee he wouldn't start crying uncontrollably.

The sobs of their mother creaked and buzzed like a spinning wheel. She left Xiuling with these words: "If you truly try to honor your parents, make good with the Wu family's son."

She was shaken to her core. She could hardly believe it! She finally realized that her father and mother's generation really did elevate honor, trust and promises over life itself.

She replied to her mother that they would speak of it again once she arrived in Belgium. After all, how could she discuss such a crucial topic when she hadn't even met this person yet? But she promised to herself that she would do her best, almost like she was making a promise to help someone out with a difficult task. She had certainly heard that interior voice telling her: "I can't make promises over a blank piece of paper, dear father and mother."

Time moves like the tides: waves that wash the shores by day, become vapor that dissipates across the highest peaks and lowest valleys.

The deck was full of people standing around. The passengers were still waving to the shore as it receded in the distance. Some were wiping their eyes, and some were happily bouncing about the deck. The gradually fading line of the buildings on the Bund far away became a deep backdrop behind her journey to the west.

CHAPTER 5

Amnesiac Maurice — Luckily We Have Nurse Basta

Please inform Mr. Xu from my grandmother's hometown that I have located the sole surviving hostage that grandmother saved so many years ago. The man is 103 years old. Mr. Xu should come with all speed. May the Lord bless and protect him!

This was the email that Jerome and his wife sent to his relative, Mr. Xu, in Shanghai, three days after returning to Belgium.

That dinner at the Hailun Hotel had helped Jerome form the first feelings of trust towards me. His original plan was that he and his wife were to return to Chicago in the US. Thank heavens he was still in Shanghai at the time when a member of his family sent him the news.

As Jerome is Qian Xiuling's eldest grandson, the family had a few family heritage issues that they urgently needed his opinion on. He needed to return to Belgium right away. An opportunity to help requires sometimes that we respond to seemingly disconnected things. This good news dropped like a free-falling gift from the heavens into my lap. I had to use all of my power to hold onto it. To say that I was overjoyed at that moment actually doesn't do the feeling justice. Unexpectedly accompanying it, though, was a sprawling sense of worry, since the night before receiving the news, I had strangely dreamt that that 103 year old survivor had suddenly passed away for some reason. My heart was still wildly thumping as I awoke, my ears still echoing with the prayers for Mr. Mo in the chapel.

Please allow me to temporarily address you in this way, Mr. Mo. You must wait for me. That is right — at some point I will suddenly believe completely. I could clearly hear the promise of an aged voice in the air. Moreover, I could sense that there was an old woman in the spirit world remaining completely still as she managed the entire event. She had led her grandson Jerome to hurriedly go and seek that lone survivor, Mo, and make him patiently wait. She knew that there would be someone from the younger generation from her hometown that would diligently heed her call to return to Belgium to make an inquiry.

October 11th, 2018 — clear skies. A Chinese husband and wife quietly walked into Ecaussinnes, a small city not more than 70 kilometers outside of the capital city of Belgium, Brussels. My wife and I were both carrying video cameras with the purpose of recording even more precious footage. We passed through quiet streets until we finally arrived at the Ecaussinnes train station, the site where Jerome had agreed we would meet. At 9:00 am, Jerome arrived on his train.

Standing beside us was an older gentleman, tall, grey-haired, with a ruddy complexion. His gaze was fixed on the passengers exiting the train. Jerome stepped down from his car carrying a load of heavy camera equipment. The old man jogged up to him, face beaming with elation, extending both arms to embrace Jerome.

The occurrence of so many historical moments has no portent. This man with such graceful bearing was named Raymond Mueck. He was introduced to us by Jerome, amicably greeting us with a nod of the head. He then drove us to a nursing home in the suburbs of the small city. On the way there, Jerome told me that Mr. Raymond's daughter was one of his classmates in junior high school. They had both stayed in touch over the years. One time while they were chatting over the internet, he had mentioned to her how his grandmother, Qian Xiuling, had helped to save a number of hostages in the past. Without hesitation, she remarked that she believed her father had spoken of this and that in a nursing home in Écaussinnes there still lived someone whom his grandmother had helped save. At the time, Jerome simply ignored the comment, imagining it couldn't be true. But his old classmate went back to her father to get more proof, and then quickly responded to Jerome in another email: "It's true, Jerome. There is still someone living whom your grandmother saved. That person turned 103 years old this year. Apparently the Lord is smiling down upon him."

You can imagine the level of emotion Jerome experienced when the news was first confirmed. He told me how as a photographer he was beside himself for nights waiting to rush toward Écaussinnes and immediately capture this 103 year old man on film.

The curious thing, though, was how Mr. Raymond knew that a 103-year old survivor saved from the holocaust was still living.

Jerome explained that it was because he was a local undertaker.

In the small city of Écaussinnes, when somebody passed away their burial was generally handled completely by Mr. Raymond, including religious rites, cemetery plot selection, interment, and all its related procedures and rituals.

"So, he was familiar with everyone inside the nursing home."

Jerome innocently smiled as he spoke those words. A familiar, deep meaning suddenly surfaced in his expression, connecting his spirit with his grandmother's. That goodwill brimming in the countenance of Qian Xiuling's photographs was extraordinarily similar to her grandson's smile. It made Jerome feel more familiar to me than he really was.

It turned out that Mr. Raymond possessed a title of even greater importance, but Jerome didn't speak of it.

My heart began to beat wildly the moment I stepped foot into the nursing home. It was quite the peaceful place — so tranquil it felt like the air had congealed. There were old folks scattered about on various seats, their soft conversations barely forming tonal fluidity. Once in a while, a nurse wearing a large white gown would come over, moving in her soft-heeled shoes, not making a single sound, as if she were walking on clouds. One of the old folks sat up straight in his wheelchair, not moving a muscle for quite some time. He looked like a stern sculpture until I approached, and then he suddenly raised a hand and amicably greeted me. It startled me, actually.

In a remote, narrow but clean apartment on the second floor was an old man with a shiny bald head and a healthy-looking expression.

It was apparent that Mr. Raymond was a frequent visitor here. He stooped down and gently kissed the man to say hello. Jerome was quickly setting up his recording equipment. A rather heavy-set, middle-aged, female nurse walked into the room. Her name was Basta. She spoke with a clear, crisp tone, and got straight to the point. Through translation, I learned from Mr. Raymond's and her conversation that the 103 year-old man on the sofa was named Maurice. He had been the mayor of Ecaussinnes for close to 20 years. They said that as mayor he never once rode in a car. Even when he attended meetings in Brussels, he did so on foot. It was unbelievable! This was most likely one of the reasons for his remarkable longevity. Perhaps he didn't stand out at the time on Qian Xiuling's list of rescued hostages, but the tenacity and miraculous nature of his survival to the present had made him the lone survivor on that long, long list of the saved hostages.

This is an appropriate time to narrate his account. Jerome had already removed the lens on his camera. Nurse Basta rapidly fired off her story like a machine gun, making me feel her odd excitement at having a Chinese guest come from over 3,000 miles away to interview her. She then crouched down and whispered into Maurice's ear the name of Qian Xiuling. The expression on Maurice's face wasn't what we had expected. It didn't seem surprised or excited. Instead, he only showed us a friendly smile. He tranquilly received the clay pot gift I offered him, obediently put on his suit, and sat down close to Jerome's lighting hood to let him snap a few photos. But there was never much of a reaction when Qian Xiuling's name was brought up. The corners of his mouth trembled slightly. His voice was extremely quiet. Basta became a bit worried. She repeated it more loudly in his ear. Maurice seemed to be struggling to remember something. Maybe the events of the past seemed to be too far away, like a kite flying too high in the sky. The poor old man didn't have enough energy to drag it back down from the heavens. It was obviously a difficult moment for him — his efforts were failing him. A kind of heavy regret turned into an ominous premonition in the midst of that unbearable silence. Time ticked by second by second, minute by minute. The air in the room

Qian Xiuling's grandson Jerome and the 103-year-old man Maurice

seemed to thicken. Maurice apologized to me as he shook his large head, and then let it droop down.

Nurse Basta deftly measured his blood pressure, then consoled him with a few words. She then told us that Maurice's condition wasn't great today. He had obviously forgotten those events from the past. At his age, forgetfulness was a common occurrence. But his vitality was formidable. Who is to say that tomorrow he wouldn't remember those things from before?

My forehead was sweating for a few short minutes. A discerning person would have pierced right through my cool demeanor at a glance to see my emotions surging like the tides! We had come to a courteous impasse. Old man Maurice looked quite tired. One thing was for sure: he temporarily was incapable of answering any questions about Qian Xiuling.

Maybe the sound of that name echoing in his ear made him recall that familiar stranger. He almost seemed to know who she was. But he couldn't remember her face clearly. It was as if he was searching for it in a small, tightly sealed box, one whose lock was covered in too much rust. No matter how hard he tried, he couldn't open it up. Life was too long a journey for him. Some of the stops along the way had already crumbled beyond recognition. An old, rundown excavator was doing its best to dig through the ruins of his memory, kicking up dust that whispered to him the uselessness of his efforts.

So, it was now time for much needed rest and calm. The mirage and call of memory were like the rolling thunder on the horizon dragging him into a swamp of exhaustion.

"He's tired. Let's let him rest for a while."

Nurse Basta's smiling words left us with a shred of hope: if only Maurice was in a good state, he might open and activate those long lost memories of the past. Of course, who knew when exactly such a miracle would occur?

A chill ran up my spine. Our good luck had quickly evaporated out of the blue.

However, Jerome maintained his composure. He said that he had a feeling that old Maurice was already standing at the threshold of his memory. He believed that some power in the world of spirits would help him to cross over and tell his story.

Mr. Raymond kindly asked me if there was something else he could help me with.

I hurriedly removed a photo from my shirt pocket and asked him, "How can I find this Jean Dujardin?"

Mr. Raymond looked over the photograph and sighed regrettably, making a gesture across his chest with three fingers: "Three years ago he succumbed to a heart attack."

My heart sank.

Mr. Jean Dujardin was the old mayor of Ecaussinnes. He had come to China on a special visit to Yixing county, and made a number of friends from Qian Xiuling's hometown.

Whenever her name was brought up, there was one phrase he never failed to utter:

"If it weren't for Mother Qian, I wouldn't be here."

He possessed high emotional intelligence. On his recommendation, Ecaussinnes and Yixing county formed a sister city partnership. At that time, a delegation from Yixing paid an official visit to Ecaussinnes as well. He received his guests from China at a banquet held in his own home.

A friend of mine, Mr. Chu, who had served as secretary for the county and had accompanied the delegation, told me before leaving for Belgium that I must find this warmhearted Jean Dujardin.

But I had already gotten off on the wrong foot. A deep sense of loss seemed to be sticking to me.

That evening, I ate with Jerome. He excitedly remarked during the meal that in his entire career as a photographer no kind of international honor would have made him happier than getting to film that 103 year-old survivor saved by his grandmother. He went to say that sometimes bursts of creativity must come from the spark of something unexpected. A Chinese husband and wife suddenly appeared on the scene — life had actually given him a clue. A door opened for him as he was grasping at it. Its significance far outweighed the wrapping up of a one-off film production. He sighed that most of life is wasted looking forward to the next thing. Very rarely do we look behind us. The magic of film is that it captures life and renders the moment unforgettable. He then asked me if an author's words feel the same?

I completely agreed. Jerome was right to be content. As a photographer, he shot images of things that were satisfying. He used the appropriate lighting to help him interpret and construct historical ambience. The shadow of Maurice's large head filling up his weather-worn face and slightly blank expression recounted the state of a centenarian who had lived much too long. From there, people's boundless imaginations could take off. Writing, on the other hand, required an expressive method needing Maurice's own words. He needed to use his voice to transmit his thoughts and feelings. Even if it was all chatter and meaningless words, it was still much stronger than silence. Although history had decided earlier that he would be a hostage saved by Qian Xiuling, that was only one aspect of his identity. As a figure captured in writing, he could use language to lead us back to that historical moment.

Jerome was a good conversationalist and keenly perceived that I was doing my utmost to hide my great disappointment. He consoled me saying that I needed to believe in God's power — that he wouldn't let such a devout soul fall into despair.

Jerome took a phone call during the dinner. It was Mr. Raymond. Jerome hung up and let out a sigh, drawing the sign of the cross across his chest. That afternoon, there was another 95 year-old resident at the nursing home who passed away.

The phone call gave me a profound sense of worry.

Jerome offered some advice that it would be better to go some other place to have a look than pointlessly wait around in Ecaussinnes — perhaps KU Leuven. That was an extremely important place to grandmother.

"You know anyone there?" I asked.

He shrugged, and then shook his head, smiling. "God will assist," he assured me.

We chose a Chinese restaurant for our dinner that night. We wanted to demonstrate our gratitude to Jerome, so we ordered a table full of dishes. Jerome willingly accepted the gesture. However, he didn't eat that much — he was constantly offering us food. This wasn't supposed to be the way foreigners demonstrated their friendship, though. Mid-way through the meal, he got up and went out for a spell. We thought he must have gone to wash his hands. Surprisingly, he had gone and pulled the Chinese move of paying the bill before the meal was done!

Perhaps, in social interactions in western society this was a rare phenomenon. We had agreed upon it early that we would pay for the meal. It wasn't an issue of money. Jerome assumed the role of the Chinese patriarch. He obviously had absorbed deeply the influence of his grandmother. This wasn't a trait he was shunning, but something he actually took pride in. He said that he was only five when he learned to use chopsticks. In fourth grade he would bring his classmates to his grandmother's restaurant to eat. She taught him everything she knew about Chinese etiquette and behavior.

The greatest significance of that dinner was that Jerome had laid out a new route forward for us: we were to travel to KU Leuven to try our luck. Over here in Ecaussinnes all of our original hopes had been dashed by the passing of Jean Dujardin. Wasting time waiting around for old man Maurice to finally open his lips was unrealistic. Perhaps we could uncover some new possibility by going to KU Leuven to search for traces of Qian Xiuling.

Our translator, Mr. Peng Fei was from Shenyang. He understood our plight. KU Leuven was a place he obviously knew very well. He brought up a very practical question that stumped me, though: KU Leuven itself was spread out over an entire old city — 30 plus colleges scattered across its different districts.

"We have no particular place to start, so how are we going to look for traces of Qian Xiuling?"

Was impulsively rushing into KU Leuven city sure to become another error in our journey through Belgium? Regardless, I firmly believe that it's only on the road where you find your way. As long as you go out there, you'll learn what is actually going on. Even if you get a taste of defeat, it's never as strong as all other tastes.

It was time for Jerome to say his goodbyes. It was nearly time for him to return back to Chicago in the United States. He said to me: "Keep contact with Maurice's nurse, Mrs. Basta. In the instance that the sluice to Maurice's memory opens up, she will contact Raymond first thing. Then, the always attentive Jerome asked our translator Mr.

Peng Fei for his phone number. He didn't use a cell phone himself, so he told Mr. Peng Fei that he would promptly send his phone number via email to Raymond.

In other words, if by chance Raymond's phone number were to suddenly appear on Mr. Peng Fei's cell phone, then a miracle had just occurred.

You couldn't not admire Jerome's appropriate way of handling affairs. When it was time to part, he extended both hands and gave me a hug, asking me what else I needed from him.

Watching him walk away, I felt a sinking sense of loneliness.

CHAPTER 6

KU Leuven:
Qian Xiuling Waits in the Classroom

The bell of St. Peter's Cathedral rang long and deep, bending our ears toward it, stirring up in our innermost beings the ripples of tranquil rumination. Leaves slowly drifted down from the paulownia trees on the side of the road, rocking quietly in the wind, synching with the rhythms of the bell. An old-fashioned buggy slowly passed through the clean alley. The crisp clopping of horse hooves beat a clipped and elegant pitch over the patinaed cobblestone road. It reminded us of some medieval scene at sunset. A flock of plump, ashen pigeons took off into the sky from the red tiled roof ridges, painting a lonely arc across the hidden recesses of the horizon. This was a classical, relaxed Belgian afternoon in late autumn. Little tables were arranged row upon row along the street. Comfortable smiles blossomed in the steam of the afternoon tea and coffee they enjoyed. The shine on the foreheads of the cafe goers unexpectedly paired perfectly with the sheen of the cobblestones. Though it was no birds-eye panorama of the old city, I could still feel the elegant, lingering pulse of it from within its winding alleys.

However, walking briskly through the boulevards and alleyways of Leuven's old city, a feeling of blind confidence is gradually diluted by a kind of unfamiliar, vacuous feeling. Every tall building on every alley is part of KU Leuven. A group of university students will suddenly burst from their class onto the ancient lanes, bicycles underneath them turning into fervent instruments of release. These favored ones form a group and rush forth like the tide, their youthful vigor washing away the grime of the ancient, worn-down architecture, leaving a cloud of hormones in their wake.

We turn down a tranquil road and unintentionally come across yet another dusty, solemn, towering college building. There are no trappings on its high walls, only a line of unobtrusive but clearly crafted Arabic numerals greeting the eye: 1425. These must have been crafted by an artist 600 years ago. Looking up at them, one recognizes the deep and humbling mark of the ages. The Chinese name of the university is quite long: The Dutch Leuven Catholic University. 1425 was a jubilee year of the Catholic Church. Pope Martin V ordered the establishment of the university on February 9th of that year. The majority of the professors recruited at the time were from the University of Paris, the University of Cologne, and the University of Vienna. The great sixteenth-century intellectual and researcher Desiderius Erasmus taught at KU Leuven. In 1517, he established three language colleges where Hebrew, Latin, and Greek literature were researched, transforming KU Leuven into the center for humanism at the time.

In the minds of Chinese, ambience is everything. Who lectured and what teachings they founded all add to the ambience of a place.

What pen he used, what lectern he leaned on, even what cup he drank from — these all convey a certain flavor. Of course that ambience must be transmitted by that person's followers for generations. Penning the history of KU Leuven with an ancient quill on parchment naturally conveys a fuller sense of the times. You know, even Adrian, who was full of creativity, once taught here as well; Lipsius the philosopher was an instructor there for years; the origin of KU Leuven's scientific tradition, the mathematician Frisius, educated many future scientists here, like the cartographer Mercator, who invented map drafting methods, which are still in use; the botanist Dodoens and the father of modern anatomy Vesalius both studied and lectured here. People now barely speak of the stories these people left behind. Their inherited philosophies and formulas no longer warm up a room. Instead, Father Time enjoys leaving ice cold statues among the warm living. There, only on a pedestal stamped in apparently solemn words are the deceased's life and accomplishments recorded. Only on their foreheads and lips corroded by time can we attempt to activate our limited imaginations to estimate the deepest riddles of their hidden past.

  Which college was Ms. Qian Xiuling studying in at the time? The records only barely show that she had matriculated in the Department of Chemistry. So, where was the Department of Chemistry located back then? Circling such a massive university city made us feel more and more at a loss, like bad weather was continuing to follow us around. We really had no idea where to go to search for traces of Qian Xiuling. We would time after time hastily enter a mysterious and silent college with its bright and tranquil ambience, clearly meant to repel strangers. Our translator, Mr. Peng Fei, had an idea that we should go to the KU Leuven administrative offices to try our luck.

Naturally, we hadn't any idea where the KU Leuven administrative offices were either. Mr. Peng Fei's forehead was beginning to sweat. He kept on stopping people along the way, asking them for directions. We were led on foot down a few city blocks until we came to a rather small, ancient building.

"There is no perimeter wall here in the traditional sense of the term. Any place with a door you can freely enter and probably not be interrogated by anyone. The sense of freedom here is as real as fresh air. However, you cannot take photos or film." These cold standards were delivered from the smiling mouth of a healthy young woman at the university's Information Desk. Being laden with all of that camera equipment made us feel like we had just been caught red-handed.

There were two long halls with tightly closed leaf doors. Occasionally someone would emerge from the hall, almost without a sound, and the leaf would gently swing closed behind them. Once again, quietly. At the far end of the hall was a spiraling staircase, exquisitely inlaid with dark gold patterns, which led to the second floor. The place was like a giant auditorium, dark red seats bobbing like pomegranate seeds on a rippling lake. The podium furnishings were solemn and dignified. In front of a row of high-backed, genuine leather chairs loomed a sumptuous, glossy lectern, delicate flowers carved around it on all sides. There was a smooth and graceful elegance to it all.

But, what did all of this have to do with Qian Xiuling?

At this very moment in time, I can meditate to complete the historical scene that was unfolding before my eyes. According to our sources, the young Qian Xiuling's opening ceremony was held in this very auditorium. On that day, she wore a blue qipao with white jade flower patterns and a purplish-red cardigan. She was carrying a thick notebook and sitting between her classmates. As a KU Leuven preparatory student, she sailed through her first oral and written examinations, speaking fluent French. Those who knew her all recognized that this rather reserved but lively Asian girl whom none could resist had an innate gift when it came to testing. If you were in the same lecture hall as her taking class, there was no way you could ignore her. She wasn't the kind of student to wait for the instructor to pose a question, but was always waiting for her opportunity to interrogate. It wasn't that she was intentionally trying to show off either, it was just that her train of thought moved so quickly, keeping pace with the instructor. Sometimes she would even rush ahead of the teacher. She would sit next to the window, her little face flushed, sweat beading on the tip of her nose when class ended as if she had just completed a 5,000 meter race.

They were always seeing this Asian girl with the round face beaming back at them. If you look into her face, you would observe two tiny dimples in the corners of her mouth. She nearly always appeared to be happy, like no trouble had ever found her. The fact of the matter was, though, that it had. Nobody paid much attention to her outside of class when her hidden troubles would grow. But that was nothing, just a Chinese boy that she didn't like — her childhood betrothed, Wu Hongyi. Dislike in itself is like a bitter medicine: even if it does have its benefits, it's nearly impossible to stomach once, let alone for an entire lifetime! You were better off dropping dead!

At this point, I must retell the first time Qian Xiuling met Wu Hongyi. The day that she and her brother Zhuoru arrived in Marseilles, France, Wu Hongyi was already there to welcome them. It was unclear how he ever found out what cruise line they were coming in on. They had run into a typhoon along the way and were forced to spend a couple of extra days bobbing on the Pacific Ocean. When

Xiuling stepped off of the deck, the throng of passengers almost separated her from her brother. But she quickly noticed someone tall pull him aside. The person was raising a small wooden sign way up high with boldly written Chinese characters: "Welcome, Ms. Qian Xiuling and Mr. Qian Zhuoru." Qian Xiuling felt a surge of warmth inside when she first read the wooden sign.

The warmth meant so much more than you meet an old friend in a distant land. Her line of sight passed to the dark face of the young man holding up the wooden sign. Suddenly a faint but sharp hole opened up in her heart — she remembered who this was. Originally there was no hope, so likewise there was no disappointment. But when she looked at him a second time, an instinctual feeling of rejection flooded over her entire body. In that exact moment, everything was decided.

He had a dark long face. When he talked, he displayed a mouthful of big white teeth. It made him look a bit foolish, really — nothing like a sharp boy from Zhejiang. He was extremely honest, his thick lips were always trembling, like he had difficulty expressing himself. Maybe it was nerves. His two blank eyes didn't dare look directly at her.

She used the excuse of sea-sickness to politely decline Wu Hongyi's invitation to dinner. She also knew that he had waited around the dock for two days and one night to properly receive her and her brother. Whatever his fault was, he was sincere. What was the big deal about eating a meal together? But no matter how hard she tried to convince herself, every time the words came out of her mouth they were always the same: a graceful decline. She saw the disappointment flash in his eyes. This was what she had expected. Zhuoru clearly wasn't putting up with it any longer. He pulled her to one side and quietly but firmly warned her: "What are you doing?!

This isn't how the Qian family acts! You need to listen to me!"

She was forced to accompany them both into a buggy. The roof of the buggy was ancient. It had a thick gold velvety texture, a patinaed copper armrest with an extremely bright luster. The horse hooves clacked against the street, sending out a crisp echo. It made her think of some plot from Emily Bronte's *Wuthering Heights*.

Climbing into the buggy, Zhuoru intentionally dilly dallied, hoping to make Xiuling and Wu Hongyi sit next to each other. He was going to take another buggy close behind them. Xiuling quietly obeyed out of a sense of propriety. As Wu Hongyi awkwardly sat down next to her, she caught a faint whiff of men's cologne. It made her feel ill. Whatever nerve that struck, Xiuling's stomach began to turn. She was in a great deal of pain trying to hold back the desire to vomit. Wu Hongyi just sat there not being able to do anything about it. His empty, helpless expression made Xiuling feel like she was in a comedy sketch. He was a kind person, but he wasn't suited for me, she thought. It was the kind of conclusion that could not be changed, and that first encounter stepping onto foreign soil had made it all the more certain.

Their old buggy driver had a grizzled, star anise-shaped beard and was wearing a black western-style hat. Whenever he cracked his whip, he would politely speak to her. His French was mixed with Dutch, though. It was hard for Xiuling to understand him and her gaze wandered back to Wu Hongyi. He was still in a daze. But he finally got an opportunity to translate. The driver and he were chatting. His French pronunciation was accurate, though his tone seemed a bit flat. He stole a look overcautiously at Xiuling as she listened. The buggy drove them through the old upper city hall square and the main cathedral before entering a bustling drinking alley. Xiuling smelled the overly fermented wheat of beer. The scent made her think back to the golden fields as far as the eye could see along the borders of the Wang Po Bridge. The smell of wheat in the wind had an irrepressible charm, intoxicating every farmer who plowed those fields. She pictured her father and mother thousands of miles away incessantly worrying, and their seemingly right and proper hopes that they had placed on her and her older brother. But, but... She didn't want to think about it any longer. In her view, she could go against anything she wanted, anything except her own heart and most sincere feelings.

The welcoming dinner was obviously nothing special. Though richly prepared and meticulously thought out by Wu Hongyi, Qian Xiuling could only draw a blank when trying to recall the evening. Wu Hongyi was studying economics. He was a hardworking student, but he wasn't very good at expressing himself and he hadn't scored any extra points with his and Xiuling's relationship. At the same time, he was also quite obedient. His parents' commands were like a double-edged sword hanging over his head. To be quite frank, the first time he laid eyes on Qian Xiuling, he liked her instantly. She had a graceful and gentle demeanor. She possessed the quick and lovely qualities of a Jiangnan woman with a perfectly-balanced sense of style that set off her bloom of youth. It made her adorably attractive. The only negative thing was that she remained a bit aloof, not saying much of anything, as if she were a cold, distant moon suspended above the horizon. He shared all of this with his father in a rather frankly written report about his impressions of things. His father admonished him that Qian Xiuling was his betrothed at a young age. He shouldn't cower and shrink away, but on the contrary take every opportunity to insist with a persistent, manly spirit.

But that situation was far from the reality of things. After that first meal together, Wu Hongyi never again invited Qian Xiuling out to eat. Not only were they not studying in the same college, but they weren't even living in the same city block. He clearly understood why this was the case. She said she was always very busy, and although they would occasionally run into each other, they would only nod back and forth like acquaintances. He sensed that she was almost trying to actively shun him. When she wasn't in the classroom or her dorm, she was locked away studying in the library. He went to speak to her brother, Zhuoru, hoping he might be able to start up some new opportunities for contact between them. He even wrote her a note, inviting her out on a date, and gave it to Zhuoru to deliver to her. But in the end, Zhuoru hastily apologized and only returned a litany of excuses for her not being able to attend. If Zhuoru had only openly spoken with him, telling him that his sister didn't like him, that would have been the end of it. But Zhuoru kept on hoping that Wu Hongyi would stick with it and give it his all, and this only trapped the boy in a distressing and hopeless situation.

Qian Xiuling's mind was occupied day and night at the time with how to pass all of her tests and officially become KU Leuven's top student. However, she couldn't avoid one very real problem: her and her betrothed's relationship. Her father came right out with it in one of his letters to her, asking her what was going on. His tone was quite serious — she guessed he was getting some pushback from Wu Hongyi's side in China. She thought long and hard about her response. This was a big issue, and she wasn't going to deceive her father. So, she decided to be just as frank with him and reveal her own feelings on the matter: the match wasn't right–she had no feelings for him. She hoped her father would dissolve the marriage on her behalf.

After the letter was sent off, she continued to feel secretly nervous. He would obviously be livid when he read it. But a quick pain was better than a long one — it was no good dragging this all out.

She didn't discuss any of this with her brother, Zhuoru, since he was always swinging back and forth between her and her father. She needed to take care of her own affairs.

At this point, we can't avoid addressing the issue of Qian Xiuling's tuition. "Very expensive" is merely a general concept. One year's tuition was in total 14,000 Belgian francs — that's 1,000 silver dollars in Republican money. Zhuofu was already a proper KU Leuven student studying mining and metallurgy. His tuition cost a little more. At the end of each month, the Qian children would eagerly wait for their remittance to come through the post. Sometimes, the mail would get delayed and the children needed to scrape their pennies together to get by. For the most part, that was the life of being a Chinese student abroad. One time, the Qian children had spent every last bit of their living expenses and their tuition remittance still hadn't shown up. Qian Zhuoru went to Wu Hongyi and borrowed 100 francs. Qian Xiuling knew what he had done and blamed him for doing it. Zhuoru responded that ultimately he was one of their own. Xiuling then really blew up: "If that's how you really feel, then from this point on, I'm going to starve myself!"

When the remittance finally arrived, the first thing they saw was the letter from their father. Qian Xiuling had an ominous feeling as she tore open the flimsy envelope. In the past, her father's letters were always quite long, filled with every kind of admonition and reasoning, twisting and turning to deliver his messages. But this time, there was surprisingly only one page in the letter. She scanned it rapidly. Every character written there was full of extreme disappointment and resentment. She could clearly see both how enraged and helpless he was feeling — unable to cry in his frustration.

The final lines of the letter surprisingly read:

> This ridiculous decision is disgraceful and rebellious. You have disregarded your father's entreaties, obstinately adhering to your own path. If you mastered 10,000 scrolls of learning, what benefit would it offer you now? You can yet recognize the damage you have done to your father and family's reputation, change course and repair your mistake. Or, you can quit your studies, and promptly return home, for your father will no longer assume the responsibility for paying your tuition.

His hand was obviously trembling from the anger he felt. The final characters where all crooked. Xiuling imagined the corners of her father's mouth twitching as he finished the letter.

Immediately following, Zhuoru received a telegram from the old Jiangnan city:

"Your father has suffered a severe stroke."

Both Zhuoru and Xiuling felt the sky collapsing on them at the same time.

For a while, this simple, unsophicated pair of brother and sister didn't know what to do. Xiuling washed her face in tears for a few days. If the cost of her decision was her father's life, well she would rather die. But death would be too easy and silly an exit. Her life on earth had only just begun. Her tolerant older brother had up until that point finally understood his sister. He knew that this decision was really hard for her. According to both of their values, betraying one's heart was both the hardest and the most inappropriate thing to do. People should be loyal to and hold fast to their own feelings.

Furthermore, in Europe where freedom to love reigned, bringing up a childhood betrothal arranged by one's parents was cause for derision. And since Xiuling had already taken this step forward, her brother saw no reason not to support her.

In the end, their decision was for Zhuoru to ask for a leave of absence to go and formally speak to their father.

Originally, she wanted to accompany Zhuoru back to China. There were some things that if she said herself to her father their effect would certainly be different. But she thought better of it in the end. If she initiated the journey home, the door that had opened up for her to study would slam shut forever. The worst thing about it all was precisely what he had written in the letter about cutting short her student tuition. It was then that Xiuling's stubborn character trait suddenly began to swell. She wasn't going to turn back now and one of the biggest reasons was her proximity to Madame Curie.

A month later, Zhuoru returned from China. The news he came back with was even worse than what she imagined. Father had fallen gravely ill. His terrible situation was due in large part to the pressure he was getting from the Wu family. In all honesty, the Wu and Qian families had already had a falling out. What was once a close friendship had ended up in the severing of all ties because of a marriage split. Qian Xixun had given the letter his daughter had written to Wu Zizheng. He who was usually quite cultured abruptly flew off the handle, calling this a grave shame and humiliation. How could he possibly face his family and friends where he lived? Actually, though, the pressure Qian Xixun faced was in no way less than Wu Zizheng's: not only did he fail to educate his children in a proper way, but he had broken faith with a friend. Both he and Zizheng played critical roles in their respective corners of society, and they both cared much about Others' opinions.

There was one detail that Zhuoru didn't dare to tell his sister. Their father's stroke occurred during a visit to the Wu family outside their village. They had exchanged words and their father stormed away in a huff. While walking out and down the Wu family's stone front steps, he suddenly tripped and ran into one of their stone lions, knocking himself out cold.

Regardless, Xiuling's actions had led to a rupture between the households. There was another crucial point as well and that was the matter of Xixun already having sold his beloved 7 hectares of prime land. And the actual customer was surprisingly Wu Zizheng.

His original plan was to wait until Wu Hongyi took Qian Xiuling as his wife to then take the 7-hectare contract and offer it back as a betrothal gift from the Wu family to Qian Xixun. He was hoping that news of the deed would spread far and wide around town. But now that everything was going up in smoke, Wu Zizheng suddenly could no longer hold the investment, telling everyone about the scandal in his anger and declaring that the land was already worthless and that if anyone wanted it, they could take it. He'd sell it for practically nothing. Sacrificing himself in this tragic way was meant to place him a little higher on moral grounds, but it actually just made things more difficult for him. It was like throwing away his escape ladder. Moreover, the original owner might drown in the froth of public opinion as well.

However, everyone around was keen on those wanting to push Xixun underwater; Wu Zizheng must be behind it all. The drama of the sudden cheap sale of some lucrative land circulated in a number of local versions. The heavens bore witness that it was Wu Zizheng who could not swallow the affront. The way he viewed it was that the Qian girl had violated a marriage vow and so she must have certainly received her father Qian Xixun's tacit acceptance. In all these years, the Qian maiden had not seen his son even once. Each time someone from the Qian family would make up some excuse and reason to avoid the issue. Wu Zizheng indeed harboured an evil heart, yet Qian Xixun was unaware of it until then. What vexed Qian Xixun, however, was that his daughter simply did not agree to be with the Wu boy and she didn't have another suitor in mind. Sure she was thousands of miles away still, but the matter was far from resolved. He could still attempt to sway her. The details of the land sale had, in fact, dealt him a heavy blow. He never supposed that Wu Zizheng would be so devious. Whether or not they became relatives by marriage, Xixun desired to be on the good side of public opinion. Obsessing over it turned his heart cold.

Xiuling sobbed, feeling guilt-ridden at first for her father's circumstances, feeling like she could never atone for her crime. But after settling down, she realized that she still couldn't bring herself to do what her father had asked. Even if it meant her death, she couldn't be with someone that she didn't like. Her classmates noticed that her usually smiling eyes had grown puffy and red, and that a sullen look like a black cloud had cast its darkness over her fair skin and cheery face. There was no one to listen to her story, all her pain and trembling churning in her heart.

But she quickly recovered and pulled herself together. The two basic facts laid out for all to see were: (1) Xiuling had not submitted to her father and the Wu family's pressure, and (2) she had resolutely applied for and won a Boxer Indemnity Scholarship.

The so-called Boxer Indemnity referred to the payments that came from the Eight-Nation Alliance massacre on Chinese soil in 1900. The declining Qing dynasty government a year later was forced to sign the Boxer Protocol of 1901. Just one single reparation equaled

450 million silver pieces. Among the ranks of the Great Powers was the little pellet-sized country of Belgium. At the time, they had only sent one squadron of a dozen or so soldiers to join the war, but the gains won were truly outsized. In all, they collected 8, 484, 345 pieces of silver.

After all was said and done, though, this money was tainted. It made a number of those countries that pocketed it feel like they were in the wrong. Some things are like that. Space needs to give way to time. Around 1925, the United States, Russia, France, English, Belgium, Italy, and other nations decided to return these inexcusable indemnity funds. Some of those nations in order to save face actually recruited Chinese study abroad students as a way of returning the money, using their value systems to influence an entire new generation of Chinese youth. This inevitably turned into a deeply significant program.

The Belgian government also made a face-saving commitment to reallocate China's "indemnity funds" to construct in Antwerp the world's most luxurious train station and use what remained to establish a special scholarship aimed specifically at Chinese study abroad students. Of course, the students first had to pass through a laborious testing regime. If they passed, they earned the scholarship and avoided any student tuition fees and their most basic physical needs were guaranteed to be met. A sudden change in her fortunes forced Qian Xiuling to go down this road, but could it have been the work of figures in the world of spirits as well? She loved to take tests. Ever since her time in the Ancestral Hall through her studies in the county city, Suzhou and Shanghai, testing was her very best friend. She put out the effort to study, and the test results had never once let her down.

She passed the test. In her preparatory cohort, she was the only government-funded student. She told others afterward that that was the most difficult test she had ever taken and the most unrestrained testing environment she had ever experienced. She answered questions for two whole hours on a testing sheet that was as long as a scarf. She was writing so furiously that her hand shook and cramped up. She knew that she was crossing a gorge at the bottom of which rushed a raging torrent. When she left the testing center she felt especially relaxed. She looked up at the blue sky and suddenly heard a familiar voice, as if it was floating down from the heavens. He seemed to stagger stubbornly toward her, his words sticking in her ears: "Well done, girl!" Tears came gushing out of her eyes — it was the voice of her dear father. She was convinced that despite their falling out that he still loved her just as deeply as she still loved him. Nothing could ever change that. In her most critical time of need, how was it that she heard his voice, though? She couldn't believe that that instant was a figment of her imagination.

She could picture her father Qian Xixun experiencing the worst torture of his life. Nonetheless, from her limited, simple experience, she still couldn't understand why her father and Wu Zizheng, men who had been friends for decades, would end up doing what friends should never do over the issue of one marriage. Zhuoru explained to her that a prominent family's honor doesn't rest on a single person but involves the reputation of an enormous clan. The ancestors of the Wu family would under no circumstances accept that a broken betrothal would fall upon the Jiangnan old city's most honorable family. All public opinion supported Wu Zizheng in demanding an explanation from the Qian family. Xixun had no recourse but to throw open his arms and ask for forgiveness and be labeled by the Wu family as shameless.

Wu Zizheng was rather impetuous. In an intense atmosphere he whipped out the deed to the 7 hectares of farmland not to humiliate Qian Xixun but to make it clear that he was willing to do anything, even sacrifice himself, to make this marriage happen. But the act cut Qian Xixun deep, like the fuse of a bomb had just been lit. It was like an explosion in the sky which made the courageous and excitable Qian Xixun collapse to the earth. His best friend had stuck a dagger in him when he was defenseless. Rumors in the shops along Wang Po Bridge told of a Qian Xixun whose body had completely broken down. Standing up and walking around had become a serious challenge for him. At the time, Mr. Guo, the most famous doctor in the old city, was seen making frequent trips to and from the Qian house on a speedy sailboat.

Though the doctor told nobody anything, people could still decipher from his furrowed brow that Qian Xixun's physical condition was deteriorating. When winter arrived, Mr. Gao died of illness and the Qian family Ancestral Hall Combined Classroom was temporarily closed. People generally believed that Qian Xixun wouldn't be able to hang on much longer either. They spoke of him as a light being snuffed out too early, a man dying before his time. A man who couldn't recover from his sickness eviscerated the spirit of the Qian estate village. The locals secretly regretted the cold fog and insipid light of the coming winter, casting a cheerless, bleak tone over the ancient estate.

Criss-crossing the classroom hallways of KU Leuven gradually made us feel like we'd entered a labyrinth. Thank heavens for my faithful wife: she had walked to the end of a classroom corridor and turned to enter an empty courtyard where she found an old, large tree to rest on. As she lifted up her head, an almost hallucinative image materialized in front of her, passing through the panned glass of an adjacent classroom. She suddenly saw a familiar, stunning black and white photo hanging on the wall. She yelled out: "I can't believe it! It's Qian Xiuling!"

She was right. It was that widely recognized photo of the young Qian Xiulin. She looked graceful, with slightly curled hair and slender eyebrows. Her subtle smile with the corners of her mouth slightly upturned gave the impression that she was good at reading others. Her forehead exuded with the gentle temperance of an Asian woman's understanding. She wore a fitted Chinese style cotton jacket with bright floral patterns, giving off a very freely-flowing Chinese air.

She was calling to us from the wall, as if to say: "Wow! It's about time! I'm thrilled to see my people have finally shown up!"

There were a number of other photographs lined up beside that one. They must have been pictures of other outstanding peers from KU Leuven. We didn't pay much attention to them, but hurriedly called our translator, Mr. Peng Fei, to the front of the classroom door where Qian Xiuling's photograph was hanging. The door was shut tight. Inside, it sounded like there were voices speaking softly. I asked Peng Fei to knock on the door. He hesitated for a moment. Perhaps it was because he had been in Belgium for so long that he was so considerate of local standards and expectations. I repeated the request and he finally gathered up the courage to knock on the door. A crack quickly opened in the doorway. A middle-aged man with curly hair and glasses stuck out half of his head and politely asked Mr. Peng Fei something or other. Mr. Peng Fei explained with a few more sentences and the man shook his head, turning down the request. Mr. Peng Fei softly said a few more words. The man finally shrugged his shoulders and let us enter.

Mr. Peng Fei quietly told me that the man had refused the request when he first spoke. Classes were in session and they were all at work. But Mr. Peng Fei braced himself and kept on with his explanations: this was a couple from Qian Xiuling's hometown in Yixing, China. They only wished to see the picture of her and then would quickly leave. After hearing that, he agreed.

It was a rather narrow classroom. It contained three work desks where one male and two female instructors were seated. They were all in the act of staring at their computer screens, busily working. The two female teachers never even lifted their heads. I took out my cell phone, activated the video feature, and began filming. The male instructor chuckled kindly and quietly mumbled for a moment. I asked Mr. Peng Fei what he had said. Mr. Peng Fei said that he was quite humorous and had said that filming inside was not allowed, but because it seemed like God had brought us here, who was he to deny us. Besides, Madame Qian Xiuling had already bestowed a good deal of fame upon KU Leuven. He had no reason to not warmly welcome her fellow countrymen.

He indicated that that rule we had learned about at the main information desk applied everywhere. Wherever you were inside the campus, it was forbidden to take pictures or film.

Mr. Peng Fei said that this room was now being used as an administrative office. The man who had allowed them to enter was called Marc Wylie. He seemed to be the person in charge there.

"Please forgive my impulsive and ever more demanding requests — I obviously am not here to merely shoot a video and take a few pictures. I want to verify firstly, whether this was a classroom where Qian Xiuling actually studied; and secondly, whether there is a memorial room or other recognition hall of Qian Xiuling's achievements."

To the first question, Marc Wylie said he couldn't be certain. But he spoke with quite a bit of confidence that it was probably the case that she had studied there. The way he carefully weighed his words made him seem like an authoritative spokesperson, fearing that his original intent might be blown out of proportion by an overeager reporter. He said that that classroom was certainly the oldest one at the school. Furthermore, it had belonged to the Chemistry Department. At the time Qian Xiuling was studying at KU Leuven, there were only a handful of students in the Chemistry Department. There were probably only four from Asia at the time, and Qian Xiuling was the sole female student. There was no doubt that this was the cradle of the world's top scientists. The pictures on the wall displayed the Chemistry Department's most outstanding alumni.

"Qian Xiuling was clearly an exception. She was awesome, and always had been. There was no other in the entire school who could compete with her on examinations. But she actually never became a scientist. It was a bit of a disappointment."

As for the second question, Marc Wylie just shrugged his shoulders, opened his two long, slender hands and softly spoke a few words to Mr. Peng Fei.

Mr. Peng Fei related this to us: "In Belgium, it didn't matter if you were a monarch or a person renowned for an achievement, nobody had their own memorial hall. What the nation most detested was people worship. Outstanding alumni of KU Leuven were numerous and the highest form of treatment they received was to occupy a place as a photograph on the wall of a classroom they once studied in."

Marc's words proved that that room was most likely a classroom Qian Xiuling studied in back in the day.

Immediately, an indescribable excitement came over me. If I could have managed it, I would have carried her away with me.

Every single tile under our feet, every ancient chandelier hanging from the domes in the corridors, and every stairway banister polished to a high gloss suddenly took on some of Qian Xiuling's essence.

The deep, serene corridors all of a sudden echoed with the sound of her footsteps. Her fashionable, burgundy low heels; her cloth, tax stamp decorated backpack that easterners seemed to love slung over her shoulder; her bob haircut; her glistening, jet-black pupils; her arching half-moon smile; and her moon white slim cardigan outlined the contours of her mature, full bosom. She had sat down in the front row of that classroom ninety years ago, with a peaceful gaze and focused expression. You could see her pencil writing furiously, her little, unadorned fingernails flashing like shells. She walked blithely with a smile, and spoke in the gentle manner of the Jiangnan people. If you could have heard her sing, you would have been captivated as well — not by the song per se, but by the intensity of her bearing.

From 1929 to 1934, all the stories of Qian Xiuling studies had been compressed by the ruthless machine of time into a few introductory sentences. And the style of these words was rather bland. They had the effect of causing the reader to admire her, but they obviously lacked warmth and color. For example, when she was 22 she received her doctorate in Chemistry and shortly thereafter collected her doctoral degree in Physics. This was all to be celebrated, but that would merely make known once more that she was the top student, something nobody was shocked by. Besides piling on more rhetoric about her intelligence and diligence was already becoming tiresome. In fact, there was a particular detail hidden in the autumn of 1931 that confirmed her stubborn character. But how does one pass through the external armor of time to embody an undying obsession?

One day in the lab, her advisor Mr. Wilson unintentionally mentioned how he had visited the radium research institute in Paris set up by Madame Curie. There were more than 20 researchers working there, all immensely privileged to be working underneath Madame Curie. Without a doubt, Mr. Wilson enjoyed his delightful conversation with Madame Curie.

Qian Xiuling plucked up her courage and asked if he might introduce her to Madame Curie, even if only at a far distance. Professor Wilson said, "The Madame is quite busy and already well over the age of 60, and her body is not in the best of shape either. If you are merely curious, it's best not to go through the trouble." Qian Xiuling replied, "I have worshiped her since I was a child. If you can arrange for me to see her, even if only for a single minute, it will be the experience of a lifetime for me." Professor Wilson especially liked this student from Asia, including her Eastern-style persistence. He thought that rebuffing such a beautiful request was unwise, and furthermore Qian Xiuling was his most excellent student. So, Professor Wilson sat down and wrote a letter of introduction especially for Qian Xiuling. As a result, one beautiful Sunday morning, Qian Xiuling and her classmate Hu Gemeng boarded the train to Paris, France. There exist no credentials to prove the identity of this Hu Gemeng. But one thing was for sure: she was a female and a close friend and classmate of Qian Xiuling. When they arrived in Paris, they made a beeline for Madame Curie's workshop. Then the disappointment arrived: one of the sweet-tempered workers told them that Madame Curie had left for Warsaw, Poland. A newly established radium research institute had been set up there and they were waiting for her to arrive to direct the opening ceremony. As for when she was supposed to return, the worker had no exact idea. Madame Curie's travel itinerary was only under her own secret control.

After reading Professor Wilson's letter of introduction, the worker permitted them to enter and visit her office. The worker apologized that unfortunately the entrance to the laboratory was locked, and the key was with Madame Curie. They took a photo together in Madame Curie's office. Many years later, Qian Xiuling gave this yellowing photograph to her grandson as evidence of the regrettable story.

She turned around and left Madame Curie's workshop, not realizing that she would only ever just miss meeting her childhood idol. At the time, she was certain that she would return there and see her. The train back to Belgium was laden with her unspeakable regret, its sonorous rhythm abruptly turning gloomy and heavy.

CHAPTER 7

Hurry and Call Two Buggies

Moving forward, Qian Xiuling's unavoidable emotional problems quietly emerged for all to behold.

There were men who pursued her, naturally. The everyday fresh air circulating in KU Leuven was always laden with a generous dose of pubescent hormones. In many of the things Qian Xiuling would later write, she mentioned a certain Ge Lixia medical student who ultimately became her companion. She talked about two men pursuing her at the time, and how she hoped to select one of the wooers soon. However, in the documentary filmed by Qian Xiuling's granddaughter Tatiana, *Was My Grandma a Hero?*, there is a rather touching scene where the lead actress from the soap opera, *A Chinese Woman at Gestapo Gunpoint*, Xu Qing, is chatting with Qian Xiuling in her own living room. Xu Qing gathers Qian Xiuling's silver hair and playfully asks her:

"So, mother, was it your husband chasing you, or you chasing your husband back then?"

A smile flits across Qian Xiuling's face and she bashfully shrugs her shoulders.

"Ah-hah. So it was you who initiated?"

Qian Xiuling proudly tosses her shortly cropped hair and curls her lip: "Uh-huh!"

This is a rare moment that captures Qian Xiuling at her most carefree and romantic. The scene drags us back onto KU Leuven's campus in 1932. Qian Xiuling was the top student in the Chemistry Department and her good name had already begun to echo within the small classrooms and serene hallways. Her silhouette was often seen shuttling back and forth within the ancient, palatial and majestic library. Her back attracted all kinds of well-intended interpretations. Though it often led to the diplomatic rejection of a courageous suitor, the admirer at least was afforded the opportunity to enthusiastically speak with her, hanging on her every word. Qiang Xiuling's style was not to pay attention to how others saw a person or thing, but rather to put weight on how she felt about them. Within her emotional sphere, as long as she liked someone, she had no problem walking straight up to them. That was not the traditional Asian female's way of doing things by waiting idly around for a frog prince to turn up.

From a lot of the available historical photos, Gregory Perlinghi from her university days looked quite distinguished and refined, having the air of someone with noble gentleman's blood. The Russian and Greek genes he inherited from his parents made his blue eyes always appear compassionate. The unperturbed temperament he acquired as a clinical medical student made his prudent mannerisms contradict his young age. People's earliest memory of them was at an open evening party where Qian Xiuling was seen dancing with a student from the medical department. They danced to a waltz. After the song, they promptly disappeared from everyone's line of sight. Decades later, a black and white photo emerged of the two nuzzling in a pine forest. Qian Xiuling's granddaughter Tatiana found it in an album and brought it back to light. Qian Xiuling was openly expressing her happy and blessed state for later generations to see. Gregory Perlinghi was always outside of her laboratory waiting for her, carrying a bouquet of dewy violet roses and her favorite snack, a delicious baked waffle. Little did everyone know, they had already been in contact with each other well before then. It wasn't an intentional arrangement, only a chance encounter that God could only arrange.

It was a lazy Sunday afternoon and Qian Xiuling was near the campus doing some shopping on a small street. On the corner of a small bar, a group pressing tightly in a circle drew her attention. She stepped up to see what they were looking at. It was an old man who had fallen over. An unfamiliar young man was also stretched out over him giving him mouth-to-mouth resuscitation. The old man's face looked pale white and his lips were purple. Those who knew the man said he was a tramp who would come by the bar and eat others' leftover beer and food. The young man's face was covered in sweat as he worked hard to resuscitate the man. Some of the students who knew him said he was a medical school clinical studies student. His name was Gregory Perlinghi. Her first impression of his look wasn't panicky at all, but nimble and controlled. She busted through the crowd not to see what was going on but because she was deeply concerned for someone who was said to be teetering on the edge of life. Who knows how much time passed but with eyes still closed, the right hand of the old man twitched a little. Then his eyes finally opened and his mouth let out an indistinct groan. One of the bystanders exclaimed: "He's back!"

In that instant, perhaps Gregory received a kind of divine premonition. He tossed the sweat from his brow, turned around and saw the nervous expression of Qian Xiuling for the first time. He shouted at her without thinking:

"Hurry! Call a buggy!"

Qian Xiuling trembled. She really didn't know how she squeezed out of the throng of people to stop a buggy on the street. She did feel quite honored, though, to have just been ordered about by someone who had saved another's life. Later, she planned on riding the car to the hospital to lend a hand. She had unconsciously become the assistant of the old man's resuscitator. But the car couldn't accommodate three people. The medical student looked at her as he was holding the old man. Her heart suddenly felt the rush of a peculiar emotion. Leaning over and saving that man, he had been so calm and steady — his look both cool and fervent. This was the first time that Qian Xiuling had even paid any attention to a man. She sensed masculine vigor in his strong arms. She didn't know his name, but she was convinced that she would see him again.

The next day, his picture was hung on the university's bulletin board. A talented, third-year medical student saved the life of a vagrant in the street. In the minds of westerners, the medical professional is an angel sent down from God. She remembered his name: Gregory Perlinghi.

They would often run into each other after that on the way to the library. She initiated the greeting, bringing up her impressions of that day when he saved the man. She made no attempt to hide her fond feelings towards him. She was calm and not the least bit confrontational. He listened attentively to her, letting her enjoy the moment. He was a bit shy–his voice was mild and words concise. He did not ramble. Walking shoulder to shoulder, she felt like he was huge–a good 2 meters tall. She had to look up to communicate at his level. Being a petite Asian girl didn't make her feel the least bit ashamed, though. However, from that day forward, whenever she went shopping for footwear she would always choose a style with a little bit of a heel. She would secretly make fun of herself, but there was no denying her method.

She would usually stay in the library until late at night. Her luck was always exceptional: without even needing to plan ahead, as the library was closing and the patrons were leaving, she would spot Gregory with a stack of materials pinned under his armpit. His tall, thin frame was easy to spot in a crowd. They would chat quietly, unintentionally falling behind the others. One time while they were preparing to go their separate ways, Gregory softly said, "The way you look up at me is charming. It is practically impossible to forget that smile."

His words weren't especially creative, but coming from his mouth, they were a blast of fire — in spite of his gentle tone.

Qian Xiuling was the first to ask him to go out for a walk in the small pine forest behind the university. Their first sweet and passionate kiss sent ripples through the small pine forest, as if the pine trees around them were reeling in the cool breeze.

Qian Xiuling told her brother Zhuoru about Gregory. She didn't feel like he was a foreigner at all — there was no obstacle in their emotional communication.

What she left unsaid was that it didn't matter to her whether he was Chinese or from her home province. What was important was their internal compatibility and passion — the collision and blending of two hearts.

This is how they came to walk hand-in-hand. There were no twists in this plot, no outside challengers daring to pursue her and

*Qian Xiuling and Gregory Perlinghi
walking in a pine forest*

make a clean break of their relationship. Zhuoru had a very good impression of Gregory as well. He only felt that he was a bit of an old soul and spoke too little. Xiuling said, "Hmm, I hadn't noticed. When it's just us two he talks all the time." The two siblings then brought up together the issue of whether they should tell their parents on the other side of the planet.

In actuality, her family knew about everything.

Wu Zizheng reported all the news to Qian Xixun. His son, Wu Hongyi, brought it up in one of his letters: Qian Xiuling had already found another companion, a foreigner. Wu Zizheng was so livid that he almost spit blood. He rushed over to the Qian home planning on raining a hailstorm of abuses on it, but found Qian Xixun bed-ridden. Such harsh words could not be taken back.

Qian Xixun propped himself up in bed and finally uttered for the first time in his life these three words: "I am sorry."

Saying those three words was like weeping blood. During his life, it was always other people letting Qian Xixun down. He had never been a burden to another. He sat there in front of his old friend holding back his tears. Their two houses had gone from an intimate relationship based on friendship and marriage to becoming irredeemable, mortal enemies. A mortal setback had led him to such a collapse that he was on the verge of departing this world.

In the documentary Tatiana directed, *Was My Grandma a Hero?*, there is a scene where Qian Xiuling recalls the time that Gregory Perlinghi and her met and then fell in love.

Their relationship lasted for 5 years. She finished her undergraduate degree, and enrolled as a PhD student, where she obtained her doctorate in Chemistry and another in Physics. In other words, their relationship in no way delayed her prefixed plan of study.

Gregory was always waiting for her. During that period, she also went back to France to visit Madame Curie's laboratory. Sadly, she was again not there. One of the staff said, "If you had been here yesterday, that would've been perfect. But early this morning, the Madame left for the United States." For Qian Xiuling, the regret she felt at this second brief miss was much worse than her first hastily arranged visit. In the realm of the spirits, it appeared that fate between her and her cherished idol was not to be. The Chinese like to blame stingy fate for things that don't come to pass. Later generations of the Qian family have another explanation: Madame Curie had already moved her laboratory to the United States at the time. The second time Xiuling visited her field of dreams, it was already completely deserted.

On July 4th, 1934, Madame Curie passed away in France. She had lived to the ripe age of 67. When she heard the news, Qian Xiuling cried herself hoarse. Madame Curie was buried in the Curie mausoleum in Sceaux, Paris. This small, obscure town instantly became sacred ground for the entire world. Xiuling and her classmates hurried to that tranquil little hamlet wreathed in flowers and found Madame Curie's resting place. They offered a bouquet of pure white calla lilies at her tomb, to demonstrate Xiuling's devout and saddened heart. For a very, very long time, Xiuling couldn't bring herself to leave. Only a spectacular spiritual prayer could pacify and alleviate a matter that had been on her mind for many years.

All of her original expectations had evaporated. Standing in front of Madame Curie's tomb, Xiuling suddenly came to a new recognition of the splendor of all of her success and achievement. It is true that life is a struggle, but the world is also vast. It's hard for anyone to guarantee they won't step onto a diverging path and lose their original way. It couldn't be that the world would ever have another Madame Curie, but we could all ardently labor and contribute our outmust, as she did.

CHAPTER 8

Dreaming of Guanshan

At the time she didn't really know just how big an effect Madame Curie's exit would have on the future direction of her life. Gradually, a number of issues began to arise within her mind, like whether to continue with her studies in Belgium or to return back to China. Madame Curie had left, shattering Xiuling's concrete goal. She had originally always wanted to draw closer to Madame Curie, but her workshop no longer existed. Moving in to replace that want was a deeply buried sense of nostalgia. It pulled slowly on the thread of her spiritual peace making her long to return to her native home and draw closer to her mother and father.

Gregory was a fine man. He would often listen to Xiuling tell him her China stories about the Wang Po Bridge in her hometown and riding those speedy sailboats along the river into town. He loved her so much that he found all of her descriptions of China mesmerizing. So, when she brought up returning to China to work after they married, he agreed without hesitation. As a descendant of Greeks and Russians, he was a firm believer in the Greek Orthodox Church. The vast majority of Chinese, however, were Buddhists. But this made no difference to him. He and Xiuling believed that the power of love was capable of melding everything — beliefs, ideas, traditions, etc. All the world's sects were incapable of repelling true love.

But there was one detail that couldn't be ignored. Qian Xiuling had decided to return, but the most important thing was that they would need Zhuolun's help. He and her exchanged letters during this period. Zhuolun approved of her desire to return to China and had already put her in contact with some solid work units: a cancer research institute in Shanghai underneath the Nationalist government. The unit seemed to be a welcome challenge to Gregory and her. And Xiuling had always deeply loved Shanghai. She felt like it was the perfect convergence of eastern sentiment and western civilization. Her depictions of the greater Shanghai area had been so enticing, vivacious and lively that they fully enchanted Gregory, that lad who had never left Europe.

According to the canon of the Greek Orthodox Church, Qian Xiuling and Gregory's marriage naturally needed to be conducted in a chapel. That was a place where Gregory's father had worked for decades. In the wedding photo preserved by Qian Xiuling, everything seemed to have gone perfectly. Her heart melted when she and Gregory exchanged rings. She liked the simplicity and gravity of the wedding ceremony. When Gregory kissed her, though, another scene unfolded in her mind of her father's face weighed down by a thousand worries and her mother covering her sobs with her hands. She stiffened for a moment, and then quickly softened underneath

Gregory's burning gaze fixed upon her.

After she was married, her advisor, Mr. Wilson, recommended she enter KU Leuven's chemistry laboratory as a technician. After a year in that position, she obtained the position of a teaching assistant. She got along very well with her colleagues and lived and ate mostly on campus. During that time, Gregory was completing his medical internship at a hospital in Leuven. He was extremely busy but would call her every day. From time to time he would take a buggy and go to see her. On the weekends, they would go and visit Gregory's parents. His family was rather expansive. Gregory's mother was a tall and heavy, outgoing Russian woman. Her roasted potatoes and beef cakes were delicious. Her father was a Greek immigrant and an organist who loved to drink. When he was young he went to Russia for work and joined an ensemble of musicians at a large church. You could sense the alcohol in his vocals through the endless cycle of wedding and funeral pieces. Later on, he came to know a tall and slender Russian girl. They fell for each other, got married, returned to Greece, and then settled down in Belgium.

His father still hung around the chapel more than any other place. For a cheery organist with a carefree disposition, drinking was still his primary love. The excessive alcohol had left its mark on his red nose, becoming an adorable little identifier. His body matched his oversized nose, putting on weight prematurely.

There wasn't much income for an organist. So, he had to find odd jobs from time to time — often ones that required a lot and paid very little. Gregory's university fees were paid in part by his older brother who was a teacher at a church school. This warm family was very harmonious and kind to each other. But Xiuling had noticed something: nobody was well off. She and Gregory definitely wanted to become independent, and that meant the possibility of having to

*Qian Xiuling and Gregory Perlinghi
on their wedding day*

subsidize some of the family's expenses. Their new abode was only 7 square meters — a room Gregory had rented in the suburbs. Though it was extremely small, they were still able to fit in an iron bed frame, two chairs, and a simple bathroom. There was also a south-facing patio and a garden one floor below them. At dusk on the weekends, Xiuling and Gregory would snuggle on the patio. The air was permeated with the fragrance of lavender and rose, making them feel like the world's happiest couple.

There were a few of those days when Xiuling's body felt off. At first it was abdominal discomfort — an inexplicable nausea. She originally thought she had caught a cold. Gregory's medical sensibilities led him to the early diagnosis that she was pregnant. So, they paid a visit to the hospital where Gregory worked. The test proved without a doubt that his diagnosis was correct. Gregory initially jumped for joy, wildly planting kisses on his beloved wife and thanking her for preparing to deliver a beautiful angel. Xiuling, however, felt a bit weird about it all. She was a little fearful — she was unprepared for this. She cried knowing that in its first moments this little baby would usher out the quiet passing of an era. It caused a rapid reaction of homesickness to rush back over her, stronger than the pregnancy itself. Since learning about her pregnancy, those two key words "going home" incessantly churned inside her brain. She sought support in her letters to her brother, Zhuolun, telling him about her situation and feelings. But Zhuolun never returned her letters.

She waited for a long time — probably two or three months. A letter from Zhuolun finally arrived. He congratulated her, naturally. But Xiuling unexpectedly sensed a bit of sadness behind his words. Zhuolun had always smiled philosophically in the face of difficulty. He was young and his career was off to a smooth start. Although he was always occupying some humble position, it was constantly at the highest centers of power. That meant that displays of aggression were unavoidable. The letter he had written her wasn't very long, but he still had some sad news to report: his position had been transferred. It was no longer within the lofty unit at the center of it all. He didn't say where he ended up, however. He asked her to temporarily hold off writing to him. When he had reached his new location he would reach out to her.

Xiuling's intuition was telling her that something had happened to her elder brother, Zhuolun.

She sent three letters in succession inquiring what had happened, but Zhuolun never responded. Xiuling obviously knew that he was no longer in his original unit, but she kept on sending her letters to his original address. She believed his colleagues would forward the letters to him.

Afterwards, Xiuling would discover that her brother had experienced a life-threatening tragedy.

CHAPTER 9

Heaven Spares a Life

It began like this, when Qian Zhuolun one day attended a highly classified, top-level military meeting.

According to a reliable source, the Nationalist army had laid out a meticulously arranged encirclement to annihilate the highest governing office of the Communist Party. The strategists believed that only divine intervention could now spare the Communists from utter destruction. There were only a handful of people attending the top-secret meeting. Zhuolun was present as General Jiang Jieshi's most trusted secretary, tasked with keeping detailed records from beginning to end. The meeting didn't last that long.

When Zhuolun returned to his home, two of his classmates whom he hadn't seen in years, were there waiting for him. The classmates were from his hometown. They were close friends back in the day. One of them was named Song Guozhong. They used to go swimming sometimes. One time, Zhuolun's calf cramped up in the water and he began to drown. Luckily, Song Guozhong was there and was a good swimmer, and he pulled him from the water. The other friend was Liu Shizhao. They knew each other very well too. When they were younger, they used to call him Liu Big Pants, as a nickname. Zhuolun was happy to see that both had come.

They drank the entire evening, recalling the good old days, from childhood events up to the current moment. What happiness remained, they chased down with more wine. Zhuolun's greatest weakness was that his gums always flapped when he had had too much to drink. Everything he was keeping hidden in his heart, he would remove and display for all to hear. Before long, two bottles of aged Luzhou wine were drained, and they were already calling someone else in the house to bring them some more. It was his second oldest son in the family, Qian Kexian, who brought them the wine. He, like his mother, usually made sure that Zhuolun didn't drink too much. But this time he acted differently — he unexpectedly carried in an entire box of wine and then closed the door behind him. The three old friends piled up a small hill of bottles, clinking their glasses, and cursing and talking freely without any discretion.

Among topics discussed was the war between the Nationalists and the Communists and the conflict and chaos it had caused. In confidence, Zhuolun publicized the Guomingdang's grand scheme, inadvertently leaking to them that the Communist Party would be toppled to the ground in a matter of days. His two companions seemed to be disinterested at first in that news. They both claimed to be wrapped up in business affairs, favoring the smell of the market to that of the political arena, which they only had a shallow and muddled grasp of. Zhuolun generously shared what he knew with them, anointing the minds of his two old classmates with privileged knowledge.

That night, he did much more than just drink too much — something he hadn't done in a good many years. He didn't know how much he drank, but with each cup he lost more control of his words until he lost all control of whatever he was revealing. In their daze, his two friends kept asking him questions about military affairs. Zhuolun didn't think anything of it — they were just being curious. It was like they were leading him along by the hand, toward a bottomless pit, stepping down into the dark. In the end, he didn't know what had happened.

The next morning, he was awakened by an urgent phone call. He was to rush to the office of the Commander-in-Chief. General Jiang Jieshi was livid, his roars audible from down the hallway. A coworker pulled Zhuolun to the side and whispered a few words in his ear. Zhuolun's face suddenly turned ghostly white. Somebody had leaked information. The Nationalists' flawless plan to annihilate the Communists had gone up in smoke.

Zhuolun suddenly remembered his two classmates from the night before. When he had woken up that morning, he asked about them. But the family said that they had left during the night.

It was like a massive punch to the gut. Qian Zhuolun stumbled down the expansive hall of the Commander-in-Chief. He suddenly remembered how his friends had kept on asking him sensitive military details while they drank together that night. At that very moment, he completely sobered up. He forgot what he had said, but just then every word came swimming back into his view from the depths of his brain.

Zhuolun felt an unforgivable sense of guilt in his heart. His entire body felt chilled and he broke into a cold sweat. Instantly, he felt terror picturing the faces of his two dear friends. They had actually been sent to carry out a very particular mission. That this was to cause immense repercussions for Zhuolun didn't concern them. It was going to make much more than a little difference in their own lives, since they were concerned with the survival of the Communist Party.

Zhuolun realized that he had unexpectedly fallen into the dangerous trap of a demon.

At first he pleaded with the Generalissimo for forgiveness, explaining in fine detail everything that had transpired the night before. General Jiang Jieshi calmed down and asked Zhuolun a few questions about his classmates. Then, he ordered him to cooperate with the guard at the command center to conduct a city-wide search.

Originally, he thought that in his fury the Generalissimo would command that he be executed on the spot. At the very least, he flig him onto death row.

The Generalissimo left him with a few words: "Qipei, you needn't worry. Your two classmates hadn't been caught and interrogated beforehand, so it doesn't count. I'm very pleased with your attitude."

Qipei was Zhuolun's stylized, official name. The Generalissimo always used the stylized names of the subordinates he valued — never their real names. It demonstrated a kind of intimacy between them and himself. For instance, the Generalissimo always called Daili "Yunong," and Chencheng "Cixiu."

From the looks of it, this tragedy hadn't spread as rapidly as he had thought. All the people around him had no idea about it. If he was lucky enough, he might be able to catch his two classmates in time and maybe even atone for his sins. But that thought was a fleeting spark that swiftly set blaze in his heart. He was already guilty of a capital crime. Those two classmates had walked right into his home, tied his life up, and then walked out as easily as if he were a belt.

The crux of the problem was this: after the initial state of alarm, Zhuolun didn't really feel like catching his two classmates in order to lighten the severity of his crime. Even if they were members of the Communist Party, it didn't change the fact that they had been good classmates — Song Guozhong had saved his life, after all!

In a man's life, loyalty was paramount. General Jiang thought highly of him. He had given him an exalted post and salary. He knew mercy and carried himself virtuously. But Zhuolun's integrity had a bottom line. He knew what he had to go and do.

He realized that he had made a grievous error. Life had gone too smoothly for him of late, and it was time to experience the winds and rains. If General Jiang found out about it, though, it meant the death of him. But he had to make this worst of calculations. There were children involved: the eldest, Keshun, had already enlisted in the army and was serving as a vice battalion commander in the Nationalist army; the second oldest, Kexian, was already steeped in studies, a paragon of intelligence and virtue; Suna and Yina, the two little girls, were lively and cute. If you wanted to point to something to be worried about, it was the two youngest boys, Xianhuang and Xiancong. They were just too young. But this was the nature of life: one thing makes and the other thing slips away. You gain one thing and then you covet the next. But when the time came to commit to what was right, Zhuolun always set his mind to do it and never turned back.

He prayed that his two classmates had already escaped danger. He remembered Song Guozhong when he was younger. He was particularly naughty. One time, he stuffed a water snake into the pen case of a private school teacher. And that Liu Big Pants had been a master at scaling tall walls and was unbeatable in wrestling. He would climb up onto people's roofs and clog their chimneys. Zhuolun deliberately delayed issuing the command for the city-wide secret manhunt until later that evening when he called the guard military command center. The Chief Investigator of the command center took his call. He told Qian Zhuolun that they had laid a dragnet across the whole city earlier that morning, but they hadn't received any information. In his estimation, the fugitives had already escaped their net. It was apparent that the Chief Investigator wasn't entirely clear on all of the details of the case, so Zhuolun kept his tone deferential.

His heart quaked — that was just like General Jiang Jieshi's style. With some simple sleight of hand, Zhuolun had fallen into a trap. His situation was now even more dangerous than earlier that morning. He returned to his office, but the office locks had already been changed. His key no longer opened the door. He was terrified. He looked for some paper in the printing room next door and hurriedly penned a confessional letter to the general, asking those present to deliver it to him.

He then requested to sit in the brig to await his final punishment.

That night, he was locked up in the army prison. He passed the night in a somewhat clean, private cell. After three consecutive days, still nobody had come in search of him. He knew that this was the procedure. In most cases, when there was conclusive evidence of treachery, the offender was executed on the spot — there was no room for dissent. As for those parties where evidence was unclear or doubtable, the punishment was always three months locked in a cell. With no one allowed to visit, you felt completely cut off from the rest of the world. They'd wait for you to have a mental breakdown and then come in to talk with you some more about the affair.

However, Zhuolun's luck was not that bad. After the fourth day of his incarceration, the guard came over and chatted with him. He had him wash his face and rinse mouth, and then let him out to meet with a guest.

He remembered that it was the day when he was supposed to accompany Song Meiling, Jiang Jieshi's wife, to her calligraphy class. Madame Jiang studied calligraphy and her real teacher was none other than the Generalissimo himself. He had inherited his style from the Tang calligrapher Liu Gongquan, his brush strokes vigorous and fresh. She began by writing characters with him, following his lead like a good wife. But she quickly made great strides forward.

General Jiang was too busy, though, and he never had enough time to dedicate to studying calligraphy with her. He enjoyed looking at Zhuolun's characters. They were culturally refined without being overly pedantic. One day, the General approached Zhuolun: "Qipei, I would like you to teach my wife to write characters." He knew that refusing would be impolite, so he piously consented. Madame Jiang was an understanding soul with uncommon wit, a kind of well-mannered nobility beyond what one could describe in pen and ink. He taught her to write *The Classic of Spiritual Flight* and the *Preface to Sagacious Teachings*. In general, when she would make the slightest improvements, he would heap praise upon her. Where there were errors to point out, he drew a circle around them. When she would paint a few forced or skewed characters, he would begin with encouragement and then tactfully slide into a correction. Madame Jiang found his teaching style beneficial and agreeable. She would always sing his praises to General Jiang. Later on, her reports were recorded in General Jiang's diary: "My wife's calligraphy is seeing remarkable improvement. I am quite pleased."

Originally he had supposed that Madame Jiang's study of calligraphy was little more than an elegant pass-time. He didn't think she would take it so seriously. Each time he would assign her homework, she would return having completed twice as much. Sometimes when foreign affairs delayed their lessons, she would have those at her side call him to ask for her to be excused from class. She always would make up the session.

He went to see Madame Jiang outside his cell. They greeted each other with affection. After taking their seats, they remained silent for a time. Madame Jiang had obviously already learned about his situation. She was protecting him. She mentioned how truly hurt her husband was. If he couldn't rely on his close confidante Qian Zhuolun, who could he really trust?

Zhuolun listened as the tears began to roll down his face. "I have failed the Generalissimo. And I have failed you. I deserve the harshest of punishments."

Madame Jiang stood up: "You shouldn't be saying things like that at this time. My husband won't do anything to you. I told him that you aren't a mole. If he came and openly confessed to you and you executed him, who would dare ever speak the truth to you, and who would ever loyally follow you?

"'Obviously,' I said to him, 'if you punish him, who will teach me to write calligraphy?'"

Her tone warmed when she uttered those words, though her mood remained distant and cool. She turned her face towards the opposite window. Zhuolun looked over her silhouette, the cold light sitting upon her high, protruding cheek bones.

Sweat and tears broke out at the same time. He felt like his life was on the line.

Madame Jiang mentioned how last night her husband recalled some of the events of the Northern Expedition.

"You were one of the men who followed him to hell and back

again. You slaved away night and day during the Northern Expedition, planning operations and schemes, and mixing with the enemy on the Longhai and Pinghan rail lines. The battle lines were vast and the bitter conflict lasted many months before finally settling down. These events in the past are something my husband will never forget."

Zhuolun bowed his head and said nothing for a long time. A single tear dropped onto the ink stone.

"One of the things I remember the most was when I tried to follow the Generalissimo to Xikou after he retired from the field. He wouldn't allow it, telling me that I needed to go home and care for my family and keep watch on 'stray dogs,' the hidden enemies He sent me with a photo as we parted. He had written an inscription in his own hand on the front of the photo: 'A Souvenir for Comrade Brother Qipei.' I still carry this photo on me to this very day."

Madame Jiang listened, using a silk handkerchief to dab the tears in the corners of her eyes.

He turned around and then grabbed a weasel-hair brush from off the table. He laid down a fresh sheet of paper and penned these two lines:

> Having seen the ocean, these waters are now meager
> Having seen the clouds on Mt. Wu, these skies appear so dull

Madame Jiang looked on the words and couldn't help from interjecting, "Mr. Qipei, these were the best lines you ever wrote. I will keep them."

At that moment, he knew that the calamity hanging over him had passed. He couldn't resist bowing to her. He then took the occasion to mention how he wasn't worthy to work alongside the

Generalissimo. Instead of struggling on at death's door, he might be assigned to become an instructor at a military school. He could live out his punishment alone there while also instructing the youth. With his combined war experience, he might apply his humble skills to the cultivation of the young and talented troops.

Madame Jiang looked at him, "My husband knows how to handle you."

Three months later, Zhuolun was formally released from prison. But there was no written assignment handed down to him. The temporary task handed down from on high was that he was to accompany a group of German military consultants to inspect the Nationalist forces across the country.

That is how Zhuolun ended up mingling with a lot of arrogant Germans, and getting to know a certain General Alexander von Falkenhausen. He was the head of the German military consultant group. To be frank, he was Jiang Jieshi's personal military advisor. The mission of the consultant group was to help the Chinese forces advance, reform, train, and to guide them. Falkenhausen was an expert on China. In 1900, he was only 22 when he appeared in the ranks of the Eight-Nation Alliance sent to attack China. He was officially a first lieutenant at the time. After 30 years, he returned to China at the rank of a three-star general. He honestly believed that his knowledge of China was superior to some of the Chinese generals who shared his same rank. Though Chinese males had since cut off their queues, their thinking had halted with the feudal era. Jiang Jieshi's military force was an outdated antique: discipline was lax, corruption was rampant, and their arms were less than ideal. How could such a force hope to win battles?

Falkenhausen was outspoken and straightforward — he said what was on his mind. His thought was sharp and his experience

Qian Zhuolun

Alexander von Falkenhausen

rich. Jiang Jieshi thought very highly of him. However, with regards to the particular case of military reform in a time of commotion and crisis, their thoughts didn't square up. A century-old house hosts generations inside of it — how can you just say it needs to be knocked down and then just knock it down? Reconstruction is never so simple. Daily improvements are the ordinary cycle of affairs. Falkenhausen understood all of this, but he wasn't convinced by the gradual approach. At that moment, the greatest danger concealed within Jiang Jieshi's mind was not the so-called "enemy without" but the ubiquitous "enemy within" — the Communist Party.

Falkenhausen liked to drink, and to hunt, and his western-style chess game wasn't too bad either. He passed his days quite contentedly in a beautiful courtyard in the Nanjing old city. Qian Zhuolun and he hit it off at first sight, as if they were destined to find one another. They both rose from within the ranks, and they both loved to drink. After his tragic incident, Zhoulun was determined to give up the bottle — he had sworn an oath to heaven. But now that he was accompanying Falkenhausen, drinking had once again become his daily habit. While on the road inspecting forces across the country, wine was never in short supply. All those personal preoccupations, misfortunes, and setbacks were just blended into that endless line of brimming cups. One time, in a drunken reverie, Falkenhausen staggered back and poured out his heart to Qian Zhuolun. He had discovered that General Jiang had been sending soldiers to keep an eye on him. He urged Zhuolun to be very, very cautious when speaking or making plans anywhere he was.

This wasn't unexpected. He was already very familiar with General Jiang's style. The General was afraid that he would never again gain the real trust of anyone. Being spared his own life was already a gift from God. But experiencing Falkenhausen's support and loyalty deeply moved him.

One day, in Shanxi, the warlord Yan Xishan dispatched his aide-de-camp to accompany Zhuolun and Falkenhausen on a climb up Mt. Wutai, one of the Four Sacred Mountains. When worshipping at the temples, it was always necessary to burn some incense. Falkenhausen couldn't help from bursting out in laughter when he saw Qian Zhuolun piously burning incense and prostrating himself. God and the Bodhisattva were ultimately quite similar. They both were the spiritual creations of the innermost heart. In the peaceful and karmic order of the spirit world, all things were in fact illusory. While coming down from Mt. Wutai, a telegram arrived for Zhuolun. He was to quickly return to the office, where he would take up the post as the Vice Provincial Head of the Military Affairs Committee's Office of the Civil Service.

This honorable assignment made him hesitate for a time. But then his entire body relaxed and he felt liberated from all his worries. The Office of Civil Service seemed like a department that dealt with personnel management, but it was in fact a bit of a hollow post. Within the jurisdiction of the Military Affairs Committee, the Office of Civil Service managed the screening and affairs of all personnel. In the 24th year of the Republic, after implementing the New Armies schema, all official ranks and ranks of position were strictly differentiated and governed by their own systems. Official military ranks were comprehensively considered by the Military Affairs Committee's Office of Civil Service based on job duties, experience, educational background, outstanding performance, and other factors. These were determined and formally vested by the Office of Civil Service and then awarded by a high-ranking official in the Nationalist government. Absent exceptional circumstances, such ranks were never stripped away, nor job duties casually changed.

At least the dispatch to occupy the role of the Vice Head of the office was an honorable position. It showed that General Jiang was still appointing those close to him to high positions. But anyone with a discerning eye knew that these so-called human affairs and personnel management offices were subject to General Jiang's word at any moment. The Office of Civil Service was essentially a rubber stamp organization, nowhere near the heart of where the military was conducting its battles. At best, it was a regulatory office. On the surface, the position looked decent, but it truly was a lonely appointment.

General Jiang had restored his honour, and that made Zhuolun feel worthy again. The horse is startled when the mule is kicked. Those keen to understand human affairs keep their eyes wide open. Putting himself in his boss' shoes, if a subordinate had committed the greatest crime under heaven, would he have acted so leniently and charitably?

He knew, however, that General Jiang's forgiveness was sometimes also a kind of penalty. He stayed on the alert, not by any means allowing himself to suppose that all this had come to an end. In fact, ever since that night of drunken revelry, his life had already taken a sharp turn down a dark and unknown path. It was a blessing and not a catastrophe for the time being. And if it was to eventually end in disaster, there would be no avoiding it.

That day, Falkenhausen opened up a bottle of his cherished brandy to congratulate Zhuolun. He offered him some meaningful words in the form of a German proverb; though his shadow would always follow him, it needn't darken the path that lay before him.

CHAPTER 10

A Jumble of Clouds Fly by — How are They so Calm?

She waited for a letter from her brother Zhuolun, but it never came. Instead, a calamitous telegram abruptly showed up: her father had succumbed to his illness.

That day had been full of ominous portents — not the kind that ordinary people have, like a twitching right eyelid, but more like bursts of inexplicable heart palpitations. She woke up that morning and was picking up her room when she accidentally smashed a Bohemian crystal vase given to her by a classmate at her wedding. She didn't know what would happen, but her imagination was inevitably running wild. She urged her husband Gregory repeatedly to be safe leaving the house. When the telegram arrived, the postman asked for her signature. She saw that it was from China and she knew instantly that it boded ill. Her heart beat suddenly gained speed — THUMP, THUMP, THUMP, THUMP! When the template characters, "Your father has succumbed to illness", entered her vision, a loud BOOM rumbled in her brain and she couldn't breathe or even cry. Something felt like it had become lodged inside her chest. She rushed out of the room and ran through the streets and alleys, coming to an empty plaza where she turned to the horizon layered with clouds and only then sobbed loudly.

A new kind of pain she had never felt before broke from her heart, shuttling downward and drilling into her bones and across her entire body. There was no cell inside her that could escape.

Her tears like rain in a thunderstorm released years of secret, pent-up grief. For Qian Xiuling, this was the longest, most painful episode of tearful grieving she had ever experienced.

Those things that had happened since she left China filled her with confusing feelings toward her father. It was more than just the interweaving of guilt and resentment, it was the persistent remorse of loss accompanying her memory. I suppose that it was her refusal to obey his commands that directly led her father's spirit and body to gradually crumble. His so-called failure to recover had taken off on the other side of the planet. In other words, the independence and freedom that Xiuling enjoyed at that time, in the end, required the exchange of her father's self-sacrifice. For this reason, she was guilty of being enormously unfilial. Even though she often thought of her tender feelings toward her father and mother, she hadn't in the slightest degree recompensed them for their tender graces toward her. Her offense was no less than the raging waters of the Yangtze River — enough to fill up all the books in the world.

She also despised the Wu family. That old, feudal Wu Zizheng — such an erudite gentleman. Yet when it came to the betrothal of children, he was bankrupt of flexibility and empathy. When he came face to face with the corpse of his old friend, how would he react?

Xiuling was still having trouble falling asleep after midnight. A voice kept speaking from deep inside her: our so-called parents, from rocking cradles to seeking marriages, aren't they just simply two irrelevant male and female people moving through life together, through victories and misfortunes. You can disregard that all as long as there are two families on earth obtaining the supposed perfection of honor, occasion, and sentiment. In her opinion, that shiny perfection was as deep as a bottomless gorge. If she pursued that fate, wouldn't she be crashing headlong into that bottomless pit?

She fasted for three days, and was in official mourning for three months. This was the old practice as she remembered it in Jiangnan village for blood relatives who passed away. On the early morning and evening of the 7th day following her father's passing, Xiuling burned some incense and prayed to him. Her Chinese-like ritual performance was of course difficult to do entirely right — it was nearly impossible to find anywhere with paper money and gold foil. Gregory located a pair of candles for her. Then he found a picture of the entire Qian household in Xiuling's scrapbook. He asked a technician in a photography studio to extract the image of her father from the photograph and then add a delicate frame to it to make a memorial image of the deceased. Then, he placed it just in time on the memorial altar Xiuling had improvised. During those days, no matter what Xiuling was doing, Gregory was always right there, quietly attending to her. He reminded her that she should send money back to her family. There were many sleepless nights when Xiuling wrote Zhuloun letters of anguish under candlelight, expressing her deep remorse and tortured thoughts for what she had done to her father. She asked Zhuolun to burn the letters in front of her father's tomb.

When Xiuling received another letter from Zhuolun, she had already brought her eldest son, Timothy, to full term. The emotional suspense surrounding this birthing event had finally ended.

Zhuolun didn't spill too much ink to describe his new circumstances, he just vaguely indicated that the danger had temporarily passed. He had only left the nerve center of the army to take up a position in the Military Affairs Civil Service Office. His main work was to manage the army's personnel and to examine its officers. The major responsibility at present, however, was to accompany and coordinate the work of a German military advisory team's efforts to reform and train the Nationalist troops. He also sent Xiuling a picture that a general had taken of him in uniform. In the picture, Zhuolun's face looked majestic, but there was no longer any light in his eyes. They concealed a thread of sadness and pity. Xiuling felt sorry for him, but she didn't know how to show him any consolation. Zhuolun made no mention of those painful, inner ordeals, but it was Xiuling who discerned from the white spaces in his letter that hidden anguish he found so hard to reveal.

In the bottom right corner of the photograph, were these words written in a clear and weighty neat regular script:

> Congratuations to
> Xiuling, My Dearest Sister, and
> Gregory Perlinghi, Brother-in-Law

Your Humble Brother, Qipei

Another picture was of Zhuolun and that general Falkenhausen in front of a temple on Mt. Wutai. She didn't know why he decided to send her that photo. Zhuolun humorously wrote in his letter that the Bodhisattva on Mt. Wutai was quite effective. Just as he had finished worshipping him, the telegram of his new position arrived. He mentioned in passing that the German general was a very upright professional soldier and a loyal friend.

At the end of the letter, Zhuolun urged Xiuling to pack up her things at once and return to China as soon as possible, then go to Shanghai to report to the cancer institute.

In fact, when she received Zhuolun's letter, she decided right then and there to set out on her journey home. Sadly, Gregory's father's heart problem flared up again and he almost lost his life. Even though Gregory's family had three brothers and sisters, he couldn't stand to be away from his father at such a critical time, never mind the fact that he was a doctor or that he was his son. And China was so far, far away.

Xiuling and Gregory stayed by his old father's side during those days. One day, his father unexpectedly turned to her and said, "Last night, I dreamt that the ship you and Gregory were on to go to China met with disaster in the Pacific Ocean. My Lord, I think that God sent me this dream. Please, it's best you do not go."

Xiuling and Gregory looked at each other in dismay. They really did want to go to China, almost as if it were an irreversible decision. She had for some time had her heart fixed on speeding home, and Gregory was determined to follow her. Fortunately, Gregory's father's nightmare didn't give Qian Xiuling any ill portent. Ever since she was very young, her father had told her; "Dreams are malleable." The day has its thoughts, and the night has its dreams. The old man just couldn't bear to let Xiuling and Gregory take his grandson away with them to China.

She said to Gregory, "Your father dreamt that our ship sank. In China, though, this is a good sign. It means, at the very least, that our journey will go smoothly."

Gregory cupped his face with both hands and said word for word, "My darling, how can you be so confident just by making reference to this is what they say in China?"

Qian Xiuling replied, "Because I believe in providence. It's the confidence my nation has given me. It is a kind of omnipresent power, a lot like how you believe in your God."

They began reserving their boat tickets, but then altered their departure date since Gregory had a few loose ends he had to tie up before leaving that kept on frustrating the precision of their plans. Were those ocean liners that sped toward China, the Sphinx, still in service? If so, Xiuling hoped that they could ride it back to her homeland. Gregory knew that these liners held a special symbolic significance to her.

The definitive news was that the Sphinx ocean liners had already retired and that the Viscount liners had taken their place. This was a new luxury liner. Its third-class ship was extremely comfortable. Qian Xiuling said, "It'll be the fourth class, then. We'll save some money that way." Gregory did not agree, "No, we'll take the third-class ship. We cannot go any lower. We'll earn back the money later."

At that time, the news of Japan's invasion of China was constantly circulating. They read the European newspapers every day. The situation was far from good. Overall, it felt like something big was about to happen. Qian Xiuling's dreamland reversal didn't seem to have any power in this instance, and certainly not any convincing power. Gregory became silent and a little bit fidgety too. As expected, on the morning of August 4th, he heard some astonishing news on the radio: "Japanese forces invaded Shanghai yesterday. The first shots of war have finally been fired."

The news kept on coming. The Chinese forces had resisted valiantly: Cai Tingjie, Xie Jinyuan, and the hundreds of brave heroes of the Sihang Warehouse. There was also a 15-year-old young lady, Yang Huimin, who faced down artillery fire to bring the Chinese flag to the warriors at Sihang. The eyes of the entire world were upon her. The Japanese army had launched an Airforce bombardment, turning the streets into a bloodbath and lighting up the skies with fire. Corpses floated down the Suzhou river. Shanghai had become a sea of flames.

There was also news being passed about her family members. Zhuoru had fled to Taiwan, where he was now working as an engineer for a coal mine machinery company. Their mother had fled with her family and relatives to the southern part of Yixing in Zhangzhu mountain. Zhuolun had taken on a role in the midst of the calamity. He was serving as the Chief of Staff of the Logistics Headquarters for the defense of Nanjing city. Shanghai had fallen and the capital was in crisis, and over 100,000 people were flocking to Xiaguan along a thin strip of riverbank. The army has commandeered all the available vessels for wartime emergency. 100,000 countrymen were left staring at the river, groaning. They had no way of crossing the river. As a result, a great number of them leapt into the water and committed suicide, so as not to suffer the bitter rain and snow, hunger and depravation. As the senior officer in the Logistics Headquarters, Zhuolun observed this devastation and it racked his heart. It was convenient that two funded ships, the Jianghan and Jiangyu, were controlled by the army's Logistics Headquarters in the event that the capital fell into enemy hands and they were forced to retreat. Zhuolun sought orders on high to use them, but he didn't receive any reply for a very long time. When the critical time arrived, a decisive command was needed; it was time to call the two ships on standby to save the lives of the refugees attempting to cross the river. The two military steamers ferried the people across the river around the clock, one round trip taking twenty minutes. The complications involved were too many to mention, but in the end they succeeded in taking 100,000 people to safety across the Yangtze River.

In hindsight, his commanders blamed Zhuolun for acting first and reporting on it later. They used martial law to convict him. Zhuolun made no strong defense of his actions, in fact, he wrote a letter of resignation, wishing to return to civilian life with his wife and children. Just when they were setting out on their journey, an even higher superior pronounced judgement, awarding Zhuolun a special commendation: a fourth-grade cloud banner medal of honor.

Xiuling broke out in a sweat for her brother. Her brother had a compassionate heart. He was an extraordinarily real man down to his very bones. When that critical moment came, he seized the task and left himself no way out of it. The members of the Qian family, whether in letters or martial arts, always possessed an ardent heart. Substituting Xiuling in his place, she definitely would have taken issue with it. But the gate and the mountain were far apart, and the seas and oceans were vast and boundless. She could only send letters and fret, and then secretly nurse her depression. But at that time, her heart had already flown off into China, thinking that if she were in Shanghai, she would have firmly determined not to hide like an ostrich inside the foreign concession, but to assign Gregory to the war hospital to become an emergency physician to those soldiers wounded on the front line. And Xiuling? Well, she would be good enough as a nurse bounding up the wounds of the injured.

Zhuoru arrived in Taiwan and also sent her a letter. Even though it was mostly filled with bland talk of everyday family life, each character felt amiable and precious. Her other brother Zhuochai, who was also in Shanghai looking for work, told her something, "The Japanese have found Zhuolun's father, that is their older uncle, and have asked him to take up the post of a puppet county commissioner. When Zhuolun heard this, he revealed his thoughts right on the spot, resolutely rejecting the notion to take up the false post, otherwise he would take to the newspapers and declare the severing of their relationship. In order to refuse the offer, his uncle first faked a sickness, and then with the help of some men who Zhuolun secretly sent to him, he escaped into the mountains, apparently dodging a bullet."

All of this, Xiuling didn't find that odd. It was the family tradition for the Qians to behave like that.

At that time, her child Timothy was already almost four months old. Because she was always thinking about returning to China, she selected a Chinese name for the boy: Hanchen. She promised Gregory that if they made it to China that her son would definitely use this name, his surname obviously remaining Qian. She also gave Gregory a Chinese sounding name: Ge Lixia. It was a kind of homophone for his French name Gregory. Gregory was rather indifferent about it. He believed that family names were really just symbols — as long as you loved another, you could live happily together until your days ran out.

Qian Xiuling said, "Alright, then. Regardless of whether I can return home or not, from this day on, you will be called Ge Lixia."

She then whispered a sarcastic remark into his ear, "And then when you're old, I'll just call you Old Ge."

Gregory also had some reservations about their long voyage to China. He didn't know if that vast country had a Greek Orthodox Chapel in which to worship, or if in Shanghai, a well-established city, there might be a bunch of inconveniences for a foreigner like him. In his bones, though, he was a bit of a traditional man — it was his duty to raise his family. His dear wife's words put him at ease. If you're living with someone you love, you can settle down anywhere. He hadn't deliberately turned into the world's most fair and reasonable husband. These were inborn traits of casualness and tolerance that made Xiuling always feel like she was the world's happiest woman.

Immediately following that news, Xiuling began to worry. Since November, every scheduled route to Shanghai had been cancelled. They were predicting that their tickets for the 18th of November would turn out to be worthless.

"This is the Will of Heaven."

Ge Lixia's father leapt up from his sickbed. He was not at all depressed about the fact that his son and daughter-in-law's plans to go to China had fallen flat — quite the opposite. The news had brought his heart quickly back to health. Though his doctor warned him not to drink anymore, during his happiest moments, he would place an empty bottle with a strong scent of alcohol under his nose and smell it. That was a pleasant enough experience for him. Gregory's mother of Russian descent, like a hard-working hen, had been swimming in a sea of delight with her grandson. Her grandson's clothes and cloth diapers were all meticulously prepared by her. Gregory's underwear and outer garments from his childhood were all freshly cleaned and pressed and put on the new boy, emotionally transporting the woman back in time. Timothy's arrival picked up the spirits of the entire Perlinghi family. News of the cancellation of the scheduled route to Shanghai only occasionally was brought up at the Perlinghi dinner table. The father believed that the war had been cursed. He really did not want his own son and daughter-in-law, especially his little gurgling grandson, to head to a distant foreign land enveloped in flames, even if it was his daughter-in-law's motherland. What was the point of that? Weren't there thousands of people still dying every day?

Furthermore, China, in the Perlinghi family's understanding, was as backward as the Middle Ages, even though it was a nation filled with wonder. Apparently, men still wore long queues, and women still bound their feet (despite the fact that their daughter-in-law denied this, saying it was a tradition of past centuries). Europe's mainstream media had never covered up the irreverent and loathsome characterization of China as the "Sick Man of Asia." Clearly this had had an effect on the Perlinghis. Although Qian Xiuling's sweet-tempered character and learning made everyone like and trust her, the nation behind her was engulfed in flames, naturally labelled now with the sign "Unfit Dwelling."

In this low valley of her life, Qian Xiuling's sense of loss and hopelessness unconsciously evolved into a raging torrent. At times it only trickled by her feet, but at other times it seemed like it would inundate and drown her. At the Perlinghi dinner table, China only occupied a very small corner of conversation. Ever since they had found out she could not return to China, her appetite had changed. Those memories of Jiangnan homecooking buried in the depths of her stomach — light and fresh tripe soup, shrimp and seed chili bean paste, roasted scallion carp, fried egg rolls with fine grain red bean filling, chestnut-filled mini wontons, and those kind of noisy, chewy luck dishes they ate over New Year's celebrations that burst forth — dragging her along by her taste buds. When she was single, she would go into the kitchen during happy times to treat herself a little. The scents pervading the air in Gregory's dining room were either borsch or potatoes or bread. She could adapt to this all, but her Chinese guts at this time were regularly alerting her to make some delicious food or they would abandon her.

She couldn't teach her newborn son Chinese, because they weren't in the appropriate linguistic context. The powerful grandmother of Russian descent wanted her grandson to be raised a Greek Orthodox Christian when he was only a few months old. To her surprise, Gregory did not resist. She kept quiet. A woman followed her husband — best to go with the flow, but inside she was sighing. Her son was bound not to become a proper Han gentleman. He would only be known by the name Timothy.

To say this was just simple homesickness didn't explain it all away. It was, actually, depression, a kind of persistent grief that couldn't be blocked from spreading, turning into a stinging pain of acute hopelessness.

When the war broke out, it was hard to predict what might happen. Happy days had all fallen away like pearls cast to the ground. However hard you tried, you couldn't pick them all up. Zhuolun was on the front line, and nobody knew how he was. And he had just passed through the deep sorrow of loss for his frail mother. He was hiding out at the time along the borders of Suzhou, Zhejiang, and Anhui in a small mountain gorge. The family was burning their lamps through the dark and light of the day. He couldn't make an offering at her mother's side. Even just the ability to offer her some water or ask her how she was would have consoled his heart. Thinking of this only reopened the secret wound inside him.

Gregory perceived this different aspect to her: his sweet-tempered, agreeable "Asian Belle" would suddenly transform from a cheerful, limpid brook into a perilous wave from a Caribbean hurricane. That kind of near despair and helpless look unexpectedly arose from an unforeseen stubbornness. She didn't eat or drink for days, which made Gregory very worried.

In the end, the rhythms of ordinary life made her gradually settle down a bit.

Xiuling's personal temperament would always reach a kind of equilibrium under such an oscillating grind, as if her natural disposition was to be as sleek as satin. Actually, it was something she had to face early on in life: she had travelled to the ends of the earth as a young woman, and that was her fate. Youthful will is never swayed. Although there was no longer any sign of Madame Curie's soul, she still had Gregory by her side. Wherever her most beloved was located, that's where her final destination would be.

The most important thing was that she couldn't make things difficult for her children. She didn't have the right to take an almost four-month-old infant into a land teeming with soldiers, forcing him to spend his childhood hiding in air-raid shelters and fleeing war atrocities. "That was the way it had to be." Out of all the words that spewed from Gregory's father's mouth, these were the only ones she remembered.

One day, a big-bellied, old man came to the house. He was the friend of Mr. Perlinghi, Father Stefan. He was from a remote hamlet on the French border called Herbeumont. In the wordy way he described it, after a long and strenuous ordeal, he had staggered in from a village 200 plus kilometers away from Brussels, a folksy and simple, peaceful and tranquil town called Herbeumont.

"If you went to Herbeumont, you would be the instant celebrities of the entire village. You would receive a royal treatment, second only to the emperor. Certainly, your wife would be treated the same, though every woman in the village would be jealous of her fine complexion. Believe me, there really is no bad person in Herbeumont."

Father Stefan's silvery tongue was infectious, but Gregory brought up something he hadn't thought of in advance: "I hear that all the inhabitants of Herbeumont village are Catholics. But we're Greek Orthodox Christians. Wouldn't these differences in belief arouse some ill will between us?"

Father Stefan drew a cross on his chest and said, "All religions present in Herbeumont are thoroughly respected. What's more, there were no meddlers in the hamlet. Everyone is extremely friendly and appreciative."

As a result, Herbeumont became the next stop on Gregory and Qian Xiuling's matrimonial resume.

"Why are you afraid of those people's Catholic beliefs?" Qian Xiuling asked her husband.

"My darling, Ling. A long, long time ago, the Catholic Church, the Protestant Church, and the Eastern Orthodox Church were all a single church. They all believed in Jesus Christ. But later on, some differences crept up among the sects in their administrative organizations and statutes, turning them into irreconcilable enemies."

Gregory then told her the story of the Crusades, the war launched by Pope Urban II that lasted two hundred years, from start to finish. "Pope Urban II called a meeting in Clermont, France, summoning everyone to come with a weapon and march off to battle to take back from the grip of the infidels the 'Tomb of Our Lord.' He then proclaimed that all those who participated in the Crusade would be absolved of their sins, sending the spirits of those who died in battle straight into paradise. The main target of the Crusades was the Islamic faith. Their next target were other non-Catholic Christian sects. The Eastern Orthodox Church was one of these targets."

"In China, we have Buddhism and Daoism, but they've always

lived side-by-side in harmony. In high school, our teacher explained that Buddhism is used to train the heart, Daoism is used to train the body, and Confucianism is used to train the world. When I was very young, I read an odd Chinese classic, *A Dream of Red Mansions*. I still remember to this day how that book was always talking about a Buddhist monk and a Daoist priest working together. They never had any disagreements."

"Huh ... *A Dream of Red Mansions* — that's a pretty name. Is it that book you often have beside your pillow?"

"It is. When I'm not sleeping well, I'll grab it and read a few pages. The characters in it are my friends."

Xiuling told him that in Chinese philosophy particular attention was paid to "different paths working together, not against one another." On one mountain, you would have some Buddhist temples and some Daoist halls, and they would all coexist.

They hoped to leave early for Herbeumont. They didn't think it was in the least bit far off or remote. In general, people in love have a kind of self-confidence that wherever they are, their love carries with it its own beautiful landscape. Wherever they went was like a freshly cut mango dripping honey just waiting for them.

At the time, Qian Xiuling was intensifying her desire to act as a nurse. A woman with both a Chemistry and a Physics PhD would probably have little problem with a few well-known medicinal terms. She also didn't think serving as her husband's clinical nurse was demeaning to her in any way. A good Jack makes a good Jill. She and Gregory had a kind of tacitly shared value system. When you're with your loved one, using your two hands to support your family, no matter where you are and no matter what you are doing, it is all splendid.

CHAPTER 11

A Messenger Sent from God

Our translator Mr. Peng Fei's phone rang. It was on a bright and clear morning three days after we had departed Ecaussinnes. It was a call from Mr. Raymond. During the call, a great, big, chrysanthemum smile bloomed across Mr. Pei Feng's face:

"Mr. Maurice got his memory back. He can't stop talking about Madame Qian Xiuling today."

This sudden news flash made everyone euphoric. Speeding back on the road to Ecaussinnes, I unknowingly lifted my head and looked at the tall, vast horizon. The smile of Qian Xiuling seemed to penetrate the clouds and shine its affectionate warmth upon us.

"Are you from Qian Xiuling's hometown? That is incredible. I can't believe it. So much time has passed. You still remember her. Right, I mean, all of us who were there at the time have moved on, including Madame Qian. This absurd world has sent so many good people away, leaving me alone."

Maurice's prologue was a bit wordy and vague. But his stable manner made me hopeful. He had already pulled out the key to open the door of rebirth.

> Heaven knows that you came here from the other side of the world. What do you hope to gain from it? Nurse Basta repeatedly asked me how Nurse Qian saved so many of us.
> Actually, at first we didn't really know that there was anyone like her behind this. It wasn't until we were freed that people told me how an angel from heaven had helped us all. I was one of those people in that famous photo of the 96 freed hostages. Have you seen it? I'm the fifth person in the fourth row, pressed up against that tall Mr. Mitchell. That's me.
> More precisely, there were only 91 survivors. There were 5 others who perished in the concentration camps. It was Nurse Qian who saved us. She was familiar with the commander of the Gestapo — an incredible thing to imagine. I regret that I wasn't a member of the resistance. That wasn't because I was a coward, though, you know. Back in those days, it wasn't that easy to be an upright citizen. Why at one time would we have 96 people captured? It was because 4 members of the German Waffen SS had discovered the transmitting station of the resistance visiting a residence in town. In that very household that night, they interrogated all those they arrested.
> Afterward, resistance forces surrounded the home. It was a nerve-wracking gun fight. Four of the Waffen SS members were shot. Three died and one, by some fluke, escaped.

Then, a large German force arrived from Brussels, encircling the city of Ecaussinnes. That frantic night, the German soldiers went up and down every street and alley arresting people. They first shot four of them dead, and then seized 96 others. The media often only reported the last 96 that were captured, without mentioning the innocent ones who were first killed. That's the part you must write about. The next morning, in front of the plaza of the city hall, they made an announcement that if the citizens didn't hand over members of the resistance they would kill five people with the passing of every six hours.

I still remember that German Waffen SS officer standing in the plaza telling everyone this in such a refined tone. He said that he hoped to see the resistance put on a real military uniform and fight a proper battle — tank vs. tank, cannon vs. cannon, instead of this secretive, sneaky, cowardly style of fighting, conducted like a thief in the night. He said, "You all pretend to blend in with the people and think you'll avoid capture that way? Alright, then. Alright! In that case, that makes every one of you one of our enemies. Our words may sound extreme, but I promise you there will be no leniency when your sentence is finally handed down. But don't worry so much about that. Of course, if you wish to hand over those extremists, we can still end on friendly terms. We all know that Ecaussinnes is an agreeable and endearing city. The sky here is so blue and the lasses are especially passionate and romantic. There must be gin houses here too — they say they are splendid."

Just as you all know, the underground resistance retreated, but they didn't distance themselves too far. The lives of those 96 prisoners had stirred their hearts. Our Benevolent Lord incessantly reminded them of it, and they immediately went in search of this Ms. Qian. She was the only one with the power to rescue the prisoners.

Did you know about this? Ms. Qian had already saved people in the past. But we didn't find out about that until later. At the time, her husband lived about 160 kilometers away from Ecaussinnes, in the hamlet of Herbeumont. Only Heaven knows why she had gone to that desolate, little place. If you walked straight, you would run right into France. Oh, I remember now, her husband had gone there to open up a clinic.

Maurice's memories were at times crystal clear, but at other times quite fuzzy. Occasionally, his words flew straight and sharp as an arrowhead, and then at other times they toppled out sluggish and backward — repetitive, like a lonely old boat bobbing on the surface of a fog-covered sea that might lose its direction or capsize at any moment.

Nurse Basta came over and checked his blood pressure, then gave him a dose of valium. The old man complied like a young child, and then smiled at us apologetically. Nurse Basta told us that all the excitement had probably elevated his blood pressure, might we let him rest for a bit?

He suddenly grew a little nervous. I could hear his heart pounding. Nurse Basta said it was nothing to be worried about, he'll have settled down in just a little bit.

I took advantage of Maurice's break to take a stroll down to the end of the hallway and stop by a window to smooth out my thoughts. There were a few questions like tree branches that were extending

Group photo of the hostages saved by Qian Xiuling

in new directions. Their trajectories were obscure and overlapping. How would I choose one path to approach them and return to the historical moment of the event? I would have to rely on luck, and certainly a healthy dose of patience. The gloomy tunnel of the past was already under our feet. Despite the fact that it appeared the real history was already widespread and well known, I felt more convinced by the narration of a 103-year-old man. Though much of the detail was duplicated, his words contained the emotional force of a first-hand account.

> It's better to begin from Herbeumont, where if there had been no first rescue, the people of Ecaussinnes would never have been so fortunate ...

Mr. Maurice's tone grew calm and steady. He was no longer agitated. His gaze was firm and forceful. The perilous nature of the passing moment had already been left behind, but he was no show-off or grandstander, calmly and coolly controlling the narrative. In his somewhat melancholy account, Herbeumont once more raised the dusty veil from his mind.

There's no accurate way to vividly describe the complexion of Herbeumont 80 years ago, unless you were somebody who actually lived there. One cannot fabricate history, but there is a kind of inherent tolerance involved in retelling it — from a single kernel truth, one is permitted to splay the wings of their imagination.

From a motley sampling of old photos, we stumbled upon a simply-built, three-story home, which they say had never really assumed the stunning presence of its stature among lesser edifices at the time. Its unassuming and warm quality mostly derived from a couple who inhabited the home after 1937. To be more precise, it was actually a tender family of three. Ever since the smell of traditional medicine and alcohol permeated the air, the entire structure discharged a kind of freshness and warmth. Dr. Gregory always had a stethoscope hanging in front of his chest, which matched his beard well. His youthful yet sage-like demeanor seemed to be just the thing to set his patients at ease during their visits. And then there was his beautiful and refined nurse wife, who never delivered a painful shot — a laudable skill. As she stooped down to stick in the needle, you could sense the meditative concentration of her breath. The gentle tone of her words was its own kind of remedy, a focused skill that educated Asian women seemed often to possess.

"I didn't quite catch that term you just used. That's just normal for me, though. Yes, the existence of the act of smiling itself, I never really recognized it before. However, it never costs a cent — so why shouldn't I smile?"

The smiling Ling: this is what the inhabitants of the village called his wife, and Dr. Gregory was glad about it. Along the way to earning a KU Leuven dual PhD in Chemistry and Physics, she had become the village clinic's nurse in Herbeumont without the least bit of drama or difficulty. She was always so cheerful, and whatever book it was or object, or even class of person she met, she had the gift of a clear understanding of their basic nature. But she would very rarely display that knowledge openly. The mouth of a woman is easy to break. When she would pass by a gaggle of gossiping housewives, she would politely greet them one-by-one, but she wouldn't stop to talk with them. The view of her back was not something to be decoded by others, but it did harbor an implicit charm. It reserved a kind of easily ignored beauty. Gregory would fix it on her body at times. He vowed that he would have five children with her in this little hamlet nigh to heaven.

You could never say that Herbeumont didn't have beautiful scenery. From Tatiana's documentary *Was My Grandma a Hero?*, we see a series of gorgeous shots of the village: gently sloping hills, tiny streams twisting and turning. The landscape, actually, wasn't all that different from Xiuling's hometown around Wang Po Bridge. There were groves, shrubs, lawns, and fields upon fields of grapes that all seemed to blend into each other so harmoniously. And there were lavender and irises swaying with their individual charm inside the bounds of Tatiana's lens.

Sure enough, when Timothy turned two, his little brother Coetzee was born. His own father was there to deliver him. When that new tiny life emitted its first cry, filling Gregory's small home with its wailing, droves of villagers ran over to offer their congratulations. Their next-door neighbor, Mrs. Abatha, was a Dutch woman with a warm heart and a hefty waist. She brought Xiuling a pure woolen New Zealand blanket. Because Mrs. Abatha suffered from asthma, when she fell ill, Xiuling would visit her home and give her injections. Her family was considered an influential household in the small hamlet. Her husband was the head of the local train station, and her son Roger was a lean young lad who loved to fight. That night when Xiuling gave birth, Mrs. Abatha stayed by her side the entire time. There was something she didn't understand that Xiuling mumbled in her delirium, though: "Little Wonton, add more bone broth, put in the onions and coriander." Her husband didn't understand those words either. But this is how he explained it to Mrs. Abatha, "During every momentous occasion, Xiuling's dreamscape always involved her hometown. It would be a sin to wake her from her dream."

In Gregory's experience, whenever Xiuling was talking in her sleep words that he didn't understand, she was definitely back in her hometown. She was overwhelmed with the presence of relatives and friends and her own homesickness. She let out an unrestrained laugh and then wept copious tears. Gregory lightly wiped the droplets from the corners of her eyes and then sighed, thinking to himself what a mysterious place she must be in in her mind. It deeply concerned him, actually.

One day, Timothy returned like a muddy monkey. He was always playing with the other little boys in the village. Sometimes he would come home with a black eye. Gregory and Qian Xiuling were never distressed, though — boys will be boys. You need to be able to take a licking, they said. But this time, Timothy had a gloomy look on his face. He told his mother, "They made fun of me. They called me 'Chinaman'!"

Who were they? In such a simple and honest village, how could somebody say such a malicious thing? Qian Xiuling held her boy that day and cried with him. Gregory paced anxiously back and forth inside the house. Later, he heard the sound of his wife softly speaking to their son, "That's right. Mother is from China. But your mother is very proud of China because it is an incredible place! There are loads of people there just like your Mom. You would love them. Do you know where China is? When you get a little older, I'll take you there. There are towering mountain ranges, and then there's the Yangtze and the Yellow rivers, and so many delicious things to eat! Mom's hometown is in Jiangnan, a place even more lovely than Venice."

Gregory looked into his wife's eyes to see the sparkle of happy tears. After tucking her child into bed, Xiuling stood up, quietly walked over to the window and sighed. She stayed there for a while staring at the empty night outside. She didn't move one muscle until Gregory embraced her from behind. She rested her head upon his chest, but said nothing.

In this practically forgotten corner of the planet, Xiuling kept her ties to the outside world alive, keeping a stream of letters flowing between East and West. Zhuoru had moved to Taiwan, where he had settled down and started a new career, making quite a name for himself. Recently, he was promoted to the position of Coal Mining Deputy Chief Engineer. Brother Zhuolun's achievements were also outstanding: his rank had been upgraded to Provincial Head of the Human Resource Office of the Military Affairs Committee. One time, Jiang Jieshi paid a visit to the Human Resource Office for an inspection. He casually picked up an officer roster and asked about the status of a few generals and ranked officers. Zhuolun was ready with the answers. If that wasn't impressive enough, he had the names, background, promotional history, behavior, and performance of every Nationalist Army active duty member over the rank of colonel riveted in his head. It was as if he knew the intimate details of each one of them, without any error. General Jiang nodded his head approvingly, then departed shortly thereafter.

In a letter to Xiuling, he mentioned how General Falkenhausen was leaving China on account of the alliance formed between Italy, Germany, and Japan. They had signed the "Tripartite Pact," and according to its articles and stipulations, Adolf Hitler was requiring that Falkenhausen's inspection team return to Germany with all haste to shift into the new role of aiding the Japanese troops. Zhuolun also explained that General Jiang thought very highly of Falkenhausen, and when they met to bid farewell, he gifted him a painting by the famous European-trained artist Xu Beihong called "The Cat and Rock." He also gave him something he personally adored: the painting "The Weeping Willow" by late Qing painter Chen Ziqing. General Falkenhausen was extremely pleased with these momentos.

Of course, there was something that Xiuling couldn't know, an extremely important detail and Zhuolun intentionally held back from her. The last night before he left, Zhuolun and Falkenhausen drank together. This time, they didn't get drunk, though they did drink enough to be giddy. Falkenhausen announced, "General Qian, I have no gift for you. But I do have a story to share for reference's sake."

The story, in fact, contained only one sentence, but every word was indispensable: that so-called highly classified Military Affairs Committee's activity long ago, the military campaign to assault the Communist Party's highest governing body — that was all a ruse. The Generalissimo simply used it to try the loyalties of those closest to him.

Qian Zhuolun's first reaction was to tremble. Then he remained still for a long time. Until that point, he had preferred to believe that everything related to this "story" was no more than the tip of the iceberg. The things that General Jiang excelled at were also his own Achilles heel. Regardless, Zhuolun could only swallow this revelation and accept it.

"There are some problems with how he treats people. He's going to run into some big trouble in the future. He doesn't generally like people that are truly talented. And those with their own thoughts, are dangerous in his eyes. He prefers flunkies and pushovers."

Those were Falkenhausen's words. That night, they kept on drinking. Zhuolun didn't end up saying very much, but his forehead was sweating profusely. Falkenhausen knew that human life in the chaos of war was impermanent — tonight could always be the time you say goodbye to all. But he didn't have any regrets at all, just the pleasant memories of good friendships.

Qian Zhuolun took in Falkenhausen's words. He felt that this gift Falkenhausen had given him was much more valuable than the painting he had received from the General — much more valuable.

Qian Xiuling read through Zhuolun's letter and then suddenly began to worry: if Falkenhausen was now going to be serving the Japanese Army, how would he not leak all of the military secrets he learned about the Chinese forces?

She immediately wrote him a response letter, expressing her concerns.

Zhuolun replied with the following: No need to worry, little sister. He wouldn't do that. You must know that General Falkenhausen is a true gentleman. That kind of lofty mountain, flowing water, sage-like character isn't confined to Chinese culture. Believe me that even within the Nazi forces, there will be those who still preserve their unique concern and compassion for others.

Is there truly a utopia on earth? For example, although the war is occuring far from us, the smoldering consciousness of it is still everywhere, travelling through the spaces between us and influencing all of our daily lives. Dr. Gregory's family transistor radio played not only the beloved classical music of its female hostess, but it was also endlessly booming forth the male host's breaking international news and internal circumstances and developments every day and night.

> Under the German attack of its dive bombers and the immense pressure of a tank assault, Rotterdam in the Netherlands had already surrendered, an attempt to save the city from utter destruction.

On May 15th, 1940, at dawn, the German Berlin Broadcasting Station transmitted a special announcement from the office of the Netherlands highest ranking commander. Rotterdam had surrendered, followed by the surrender of all the armed forces of Netherlands. Queen Wilhelmina and members of her government had boarded naval destroyers headed for London.

Father Stefan heard that bit of news and rushed over to Dr. Gregory's clinic. When his blood sugar levels were unusually high, his knee would swell and hurt. He found Gregory tending to other patients. He liked to listen to his analyses of current political situations. Gregory is usually quite introverted and taciturn, especially if it concerned other people's business. But, if you wanted to discuss international news with him and have a real quality back-and-forth, he would involuntarily switch personas and turn into a current affairs commentator.

He predicted that Belgium would quickly surrender as well. Netherlands had already done so, so Belgium, France, and England's military fates were now set too. Although the Allied Forces had fought pretty well since the beginning of the war, the majority of France's elite first, seventh and ninth legions, and the nine divisions under the command of England's William Gott, had, according to predictions, already met up with Belgian forces and were following along the Dyle River to set up a firm line of defense. From Antwerp through Leuven to Fafuar, along just 60 miles of battlefront, the number of Allied forces had, in fact, already surpassed those of the invading German army. However, one military campaign after another demonstrated in succession that they were not fit rivals for the Germans. The Germans used their consistent, meticulous methods to launch singular attacks of massive scope. Their tank forces were unprecedented in their use of numbers, concentration, flexibility, and striking power.

From the German border via the Ardennes forest, their forces headed out. The leaders of their troops, though divided into three columns and extended over a hundred miles behind the Rhine River, speedily pushed the Allied Forces in Belgium up against the English Channel. The Belgians were dumbfounded. It was a terrifyingly tremendous display of power. One line of bad news followed another.

In a matter of just a few days, the monarch of Belgium, King Leopold III, announced surrender on the morning of May 28th. Dr. Gregory heard the news from his radio. He sat down on his sofa and didn't budge an inch, as if he had frozen into an ice sculpture. He wasn't a warlike visionary, but he had the kernel of a patriotic heart. His surgical instrument could never transform into a weapon, but he felt dejected by the decision of his king. This obstinate, young ruler had once already made his country retreat from the British-Franco Alliance to adopt a foolish position of neutrality, and when he learned of Germany's preparations to cross their border and launch an attack, he refused to restore that original alliance. Only after Adolf Hitler had launched the attack did he finally, at the very last minute, appeal to the British for aid. Now, once again, in a moment of despair, he was tossing England and France aside and opening up the front gate of his country, letting the German army waltz right into the heart of their nation. That's right, and on the first day that the founder of the German forces' blitzkrieg, General Heinz Guderian, and his tank division were charging through Belgium's sovereign territory, the Belgian Air Force, in a matter of a few hours, was reduced from 171 to 91 planes. My God! It would have been harder to kill sparrows that quickly!

Things had turned dangerous — the radio was blasting it, and the newspapers were confirming it. Gregory was quite troubled. Herbeumont was very close to the French border. Father Stefan was sick at heart when he ran in to tell him the news, "The French on our borders are worried and ready to rush into Belgium to fight against the Germans. They're already halfway here. They have their flags and trumpets with them. Our army must resist the invaders!"

I wasn't actually worried about this. Dr. Gregory still harbored some disdain for the French.

Father Stefan uneasily asked when the Germans would enter Herbeumont. Would they kill them or rape their women? "Oh, God! Have mercy upon us, Lord!"

Dr. Gregory's conclusion was that really anything was possible.

"Are we really about to become the slaves of a foreign power?" His Asian belle's face grew stern, her look harboring resentment.

He knew what her underlying meaning was: if they were to be slaves to a foreign power in Europe, they might as well return to China!

Dr. Gregory was adaptable by nature. He understood his wife's perspective. Every time his Asian belle brought up a suggestion of great importance, his body would bend to listen more closely. He had the habit of opening up his two hands as if to say: I see your point. Let's do as you say, then.

However, every time returning home was truly considered, Xiuling felt that the actual possibility of doing it was practically nil. Every shipping route had been dismantled. You could never know when those extremely rare passenger ships would set sail, and all replies to inquiries were met with the uniform hum of uncertainty. France, England, Netherlands, and all other neighboring countries, were caught in the whirlwinds of war and couldn't extricate themselves. Who was to say that there was a safe Pure Land outside of theirs anyway? That former cancer research institute in Shanghai had lost communication with Xiuling because of the War of Resistance. People were all living separate lives now, and when misfortune suddenly occurred, you could only quietly pray for consolation. The war muddled the borders between territories, muddled the times when simple home meals were eaten. This indeed was everybody's life now.

In 1943, in the hamlet of Herbeumont, Belgium, the conflagrations of war finally arrived. It was predicted that this would occur in that year, a horrible event that felt like a karmic arrangement. When four Waffen SS members entered the village with loaded weapons, the tranquil Herbeumont village did not immediately succumb. Located on the border of France, the village had always seen its share of soldiers carrying guns. But one day, Father Stefan appeared in Dr. Gregory's clinic, extremely agitated. Not only were his sugar levels sky high, but he hadn't recently been able to sleep and was experiencing dizziness. Dr. Gregory prescribed him some medicine. But it was like before when he would give him all his thoughts on the war. Father Stefan took the medicine, but didn't depart right away. He wasn't waiting on another prescription, but wished to chat with Gregory about events. Gregory's tone was grave and he told him that he no longer had any desire to listen to the news because it had all become like a dirty, used handkerchief. Every day it was the same old lines. Father Stefan drew a cross with his hand over his chest and leaned toward his ear, "Have there been any people from the underground resistance visiting the clinic to get medicine or receive treatment?" He later brought up to the doctor that the reason the Germans dispatched the Waffen SS to the village was that one of their rail lines close by was blown up.

The resistance movement functioned a lot like an owl in the night. It came out into Herbeumont in the dark corners of the night. Gregory returned the Father's inquiry with silence. He was in low spirits lately. People were dying every day in the war. Talking around it didn't change that reality. This certainly influenced his emotions. He cursed the war and hated the Germans for it. However, he didn't want this to directly link to his family life, so he practiced a policy of keeping his mouth shut. His understanding wife came over and started up a conversation with the Father, thanking him for bringing the news to their attention. She said that her husband would pose no problem to anyone and that the clinic would only be involved in medical matters.

As Father Stefan was leaving, he inadvertently dropped that day's *Southern Post*. When Xiuling was tidying up the room, she discovered it. She would usually have discarded such an item, but for some reason she opened it up without a thought. On the first page in bold print she recognized a familiar name: General Falkenhausen. He unexpectedly had become Germany's Viceroy in residence over Belgium. His photo in the newspaper wasn't very clear, but she recognized him. She took out the photo Zhuolun had sent her of them together and compared it to the one in the paper. Falkenhausen's picture in the paper looked comparatively cold and detached. The downturned corners of his mouth revealed a great many bitter, lived experiences. In that moment, her heart dropped as she thought of how her brother's friend had actually just become their invading ruler — the number one most wanted enemy on every Belgian's list. And that was no exaggeration. War always has the power to change the impossible into the possible. However, during those turbulent times, twists and turns are hard to fathom, and even rulers who seem to be controlling it all, might at any point suddenly fall and become a prisoner themselves.

Mrs. Abatha cheerfully came in search of Xiuling. Her son Roger was about to be married, and her new daughter-in-law was coincidentally the daughter of Father Stefan. This fairy-tale couple had decided to hold the wedding ceremony in spring. It would be a magnificent gathering of the entire village. She wanted to get Xiuling's opinion on how to arrange her son's new room and what to give her new daughter-in-law as an exciting gift. From her point of view, this refined woman from Asia had always given off an enchanting impression.

God had been a bit partial: this Chinese woman who had given birth to two children was still as thin as could be. She still looked stunning in her qipao dress. It made everyone quite jealous, but it didn't give rise to any ill will because she was a good person with a good heart that was eager to help others. Sure enough, Xiuling did give her a bunch of suggestions, and she even took out a satin blanket to give them as a gift. It was as green as spring grass. If you put it out in the sun, its countless threads formed harmonious lines that sketched the outlines of limpid ripples and greenish blue lotus leaves. A pair of mandarin ducks flew through those elegantly-stitched plants. Mrs. Abatha was stunned!

"This is the Lord's handiwork! My goodness!"

Xiuling told her the blanket was a product of her hometown, from a village in Jiangnan, China. There were lush green mulberry gardens there as far as the eye could see. And they raised silkworms that toiled night and day. Diligent weavers would take the thousands of silk threads and weave them into dazzling satin. In the Chinese context, a pair of mandarin ducks was the symbol of an affectionate, loyal couple, growing old together.

However, before too much time passed, Father Stefan came running back over again in a panic. Something had happened to his daughter's betrothed, Roger. The German Waffen SS had captured some people attempting to destroy the railroad during a small patrol on a dark night. Surprisingly, it was the son of the head of the train station. The entire village was waiting to offer him their congratulations on his new marriage. The villagers were left speechless when they read the announcement signed by Falkenhausen that the accused, Roger, had been sentenced to death by hanging. He had been involved a number of times carrying out orders for the resistance movement. As the dexterous son of a train station chief, it was rather easy for him to sabotage his own railroad track and cause a train loaded fully with military supplies to rush along and then burst into flames!

Dr. Gregory's first reaction to this was to be cool-headed beyond all expectations. The night before this happened to Roger, a German lieutenant had paid a visit to his clinic. His name was Keitel. Something was awry with his neck. Dr. Gregory took less than twenty minutes to lance an infected mole. The lieutenant was very pleased with his skill, but he had no money to pay him. Dr. Gregory politely turned down the German pack of cigarettes he offered him. He waved him off and told him he could leave without paying. The affair was that simple. In his view, everyone seeking treatment was a patient, even if he were a devilish murderer.

Dr. Gregory's opinion on it all was that since Roger chose his line of work, he should have known that the day would come when he would have to pay the piper. He admired the courage of the seemingly haphazard youngster. But he also regretted it, since the hopes of two households would be accompanying him to the hanging post.

Qian Xiuling's reaction, on the other hand, was intense. Such a young man, whose life had barely begun, and yet he put it all on the line to dangerously perform such a deed. It was in essence an act of principle over life. Underneath his apparent immature exterior, he had taken on a truly heroic responsibility.

Every word on the announcement felt chilling — even Falkenhausen's signature at the bottom! Xiuling looked at his name and her heart thumped hard.

Her feelings at that moment were surprisingly completely

different than the first time she saw his name on the front of the newspaper. She wanted to believe now more than ever that this viceroy was Zhuolun's friend.

She remembered what he had written to her in the letter, "He is an upright gentleman."

Following this moment, we enter a period of history repeatedly written about and narrated: the first person rescued by Qian Xiuling.

If we adopt a kind of duplicating style to repeat the story, it might be better to just ask the reader to ignore the rest of the chapter.

However, I believe, as the heroine was deciding to save others, billowing waves of emotion in her heart exhibited multiple dimensions, compelling her to once more analytically sort and seek out.

The first dimension of those emotional waves wasn't necessarily that she had any kind of hesitation toward saving people, but was more about not knowing Zhuolun's former friend, the viceroy. Was he really still a good person at that point?

She had no real way of being sure. However, she felt that if she could save Roger and didn't, she'd never be able to sleep again. It was like standing on the side of a street just watching a child who had just slipped cry loudly. Would you be able to ignore the child and walk right past it? So it was that she didn't hesitate between saving or not saving him.

At the beginning, she said nothing of it to anyone. In fact, she didn't even discuss it with Gregory at first. She just quietly went to the village post office on her own, filled out a telegram, carefully weighing her words. She wanted Zhuolun to get in touch with Falkenhausen as quickly as possible to lay aside the hangman's noose.

She almost believed that her request wouldn't be turned away. In other words, whatever Zhuolun was able to do, she wasn't in the least bit worried he could carry it out. She had made up her mind that she would personally seek an audience with the occupying general. She was determined to save Roger.

Past accounts of the story overlooked how the aire postale assistance from General Qian Zhuolun was blocked. On his way back from accompanying his superiors on an inspection of the embattled front lines, Zhuolun suddenly received a telegram from his younger cousin. Then, with all the nimbleness and resoluteness of a general, he expeditiously sent an urgent letter to his friend General Falkenhausen back in Belgium.

He fired off the letter without thinking about it. In fact, after sending it off, he completely forgot all about it. It didn't seem like a big deal to him at the time.

Xiuling knew nothing about what he had done, initially. Correspondence in wartime can pass through all kinds of unimaginable detours. We have no way of determining why Qian Xiuling wasn't able to receive Zhuolun's response telegram. Her heart hit rock bottom. However, this didn't become a reason for her to stop progress on the path to rescuing another. She felt that whatever the case, she had to keep on trying, futile or not. Time was of the essence; only a dozen or so hours remained before Roger's sentence to be hanged was carried out.

The second dimension was how to convince her husband, Gregory. Originally, this shouldn't have been a problem. Gregory had a righteous heart, but he did have a rather conservative disposition. In Chinese terms, we would say he had principles, but also self interest. His reaction to Roger's capture was rather indifferent — he wasn't rocked by it in the least. It was almost as if he had known it was going to occur. Xiuling felt that he had changed — become a bit more cowardly and timid. So, at first, she had him look over the draft telegram that she sent to Zhuolun. Then she fished out the picture of Zhuolun with Falkenhausen and his letters, reading them to Gregory sentence by sentence. While she read those aloud, she kept her emotions in check and her expression firm and tranquil.

She thought that Gregory would at least kindly oppose her. He would definitely say something like; "But your brother never returned your telegram. So, how can you be certain that he petitioned the German general, or that the general would even acknowledge him?"

But, after hearing the declarations, Gregory met her gaze and said — "My dear, if you have already decided to do this, then don't turn back. What can I do to help?"

The stalwart part of Gregory's character was his consistent value system. But, if his wife was resolving to do something, he could convince himself to act otherwise. Sometimes, this only took a moment after looking into the expectant eyes of his Asian belle.

Gregory's attitude at the time was extremely important to Qian Xiuling. She decided to take her eldest son, Timothy, on the road with her, leaving their youngest, Coetzee with Gregory. In the western context, a mother carrying a child will normally attract all kinds of care and interest, making the situation safer for her.

She walked over to Roger's house. Mrs. Abatha was crying when she arrived. German soldiers had taken her husband in for questioning. When Qian Xiuling revealed her plan to her, Mrs. Abatha looked like a drowning victim that had just been thrown a lifebuoy. The astonishment in her ashen, foggy eyes, suddenly turned into clear teardrops of gratitude.

Father Stefan came over later. He was in a hurry and sweating. Roger had less than three days left. He had no other means in this desperate situation than to use the old "petition" method to try and save his future son-in-law. He filled his time urgently going from house to house pleading for signatures.

When he found out about Qian Xiuling's rescue plan, it struck him like a moving story from the Holy Bible. He believed it was a display of God's power. After that moment, he insisted on placing a Holy Bible within Qian Xiuling's luggage. He knew that this seemingly delicate Asian woman was no disciple of Christ, but the firm path she was on was making the Lord rub his eyes and take notice.

It was March 12th, 1943, and it was Qian Xiuling's birthday.

Dr. Gregory accompanied his wife to the train station. It wasn't unheard of back then that he might want to purchase a bouquet of purplish-red roses for her, but they were carrying children in their arms, so their romanticism had to give way to a hurried goodbye as they moved along. Luckily, it was breakfast time, so they were at least able to share a slice of cake together. Qian Xiuling raised her hands in a prayer gesture and made a wish as her three candles flickered.

In reality, as Qian Xiuling hurried on her way towards Brussels, Zhuolun's telegram had finally reached the Herbeumont post office. Though she knew nothing of its arrival, her faith in Zhuolun hadn't weakened. At times her nervous emotions would seize her, which is why she left so quickly to go and see General Falkenhausen. Her hastily packed luggage contained the following items:

1. A signed photograph of Zhoulun for her and Gregory.

2. A letter written by Zhuolun regarding his comments on Falkenhausen.

3. A picture of Zhuolun and Falkenhausen in front of a temple on Mt. Wutai.

4. Father Stefan's letter begging for Roger's release, with the signed petition of more than 300 people from Herbeumont.

5. An entreaty from Roger's father and mother, signed by the

mayor.

As for that secretly inserted Holy Bible Father Stefan had snuck in, Qian Xiuling actually opened it up and read a few pages. It was actually a pretty good read. The literary style was fairly graceful and the stories were moving. But as she was reading it, she couldn't help remembering Mr. Gao from her youth, teaching her how to read *Tao Te Ching* in the Qian Family Ancestral Hall. When an older person is going on and on in your ear about the truth, at least you can meditate and hold your breath. The pitch black landscape flitted by outside the car windows of the train, stretching her thoughts out to the horizon.

Below, I discuss a little regarding the meeting between Qian Xiuling and Falkenhausen. Originally, this was a challenging thing to do. According to ordinary procedure, she first had to transit through the Chinese Embassy in Belgium, then post an application with the German Viceroy in residence in Belgium. Stuck inside a tall pile of official requests, who knew when she would actually be granted an audience. The crucial moment was when General Qian Zhuolun's name was brought up. In the documentary "My Grandma was a Hero?," Xiuling gave an account of it for the cameras:

> Originally, the general wished to meet with me that weekend, since he had many other things to attend to ahead of time. However, time wouldn't permit the delay, since Roger's life was at stake. I asked his secretary to send my request again to him, saying that the little sister of General Qiang Zhuolun had a most pressing matter to discuss with him. It was then that the general remembered Zhuolun's urgent telegram to him. So, he moved the appointment

up two days to Wednesday afternoon at Schaefer Castle, outside of Brussels.

Schaefer Castle was situated dozens of kilometers outside of Brussels in the suburbs along a birch tree forest. Nearby was a peaceful river valley with a mountain slope covered in lush vegetation. In the early morning and evening, mountain mists would curl out of the river valley. In the vast spaces next to the birch forest stood the elegant residence of a Jewish banker. Why it bore the name Schaefer Castle probably had something to do with the name of its owner. After the war broke out, the residence was converted into one of the central offices of the German Viceroy.

Xiuling repressed her emotions. Walking those 100 meters to Falkenhausen's office door, Qian Xiuling began to panic a little. Repeated questioning by sentries along the way didn't help her mood. The air in the building was permeated by a smell that made it hard to breathe. On the verge of finally meeting him, Xiuling did her utmost to regulate her emotions: she was here to just see the friend of her brother, she told herself.

She then entered the office of General Falkenhausen. All the furniture was surprisingly underwhelming. The only thing that left a deep impression on her was a colossal military map hanging on the wall. On the shelf next to it were two highly polished, antique shotguns.

He was on the phone at the time. His back was straight. His thick military uniform outlined his slim figure.

He finally turned around and politely acknowledged her with a nod.

He had a nice complexion, though a bit wizened. Deep wrinkles at the corners of his mouth made him appear old.

She told this kind but stern-looking, unflinching and imposing general in fluent French that she was Zhuolun's younger cousin, Xiuling.

She waited for his reaction, holding her breath, striving hard to calm her nervous heart.

Falkenhausen walked up to her and looked her up and down. She wore an old blue cotton coat with a thick cape draped over her shoulders — a winter outfit. Her hair was cropped short. Just one look and he knew that this was an Asian woman par excellence.

Xiuling received his gaze, the look of her senior. The atmosphere felt warm. His breathing was hoarse and his chin roughly shaven. Because he was so close to her, Xiuling could practically smell the oil on the skin of his neck.

"You look a lot alike. General Zhuolun and you look very similar. Greetings from him are extremely hard to come by, you know. God knows that we will never forget each other. Hmph, you probably don't know this, but I was happiest when I was with him — we drank so much together."

He casually grabbed one of his business cards and gave it to her. Xiuling gently thanked him. They moved to the sofa and sat down. He poured her a cup of tea prepared by his secretary. She noticed that the tea cup was European style enamelware, with gold flourishes and iris branches and leaves draped over the lip of the cup. If a Chinese master had painted the cup, it would've held immense significance.

She pursed her lips. The liquid was a British black tea, a bit bitter, but still fragrant.

It was like a casual conversation with an older neighbor.

When she laid out the materials asking for Roger's release in front of General Falkenhausen, she saw an expression of amazement flit across his eyes. He picked out one of the photos and looked at it closely, sighing:

"My forever lost days in China"

Then he asked her a question: why did she choose to live in Belgium? Qian Xiuling could only reply with one phrase: "It was fate upon destiny." Then she hurriedly changed the subject to the main topic at hand. She stated the case concisely after drawing up who knows how many mental drafts. When she mentioned that Roger was about to become a young groom, Falkenhausen interrupted her. He asked her how many children she had.

"Two. Both are boys. I'm very sorry, general, but my eldest son has come with me. He's with a classmate right now. He is very sensible and knows that his mother will return quickly."

Falkenhausen seemed to grow more interested.

"Do you have a picture of him with you?"

Qian Xiuling hesitated for a moment, and then she took out a jade pendant with gold inlay from her chest. On the back of the pendant was a miniature picture of their entire family.

Falkenhausen put on his glasses, making him appear even more like a grandfather. He studied it very closely. Then he remarked that Timothy resembled his father a bit more, but Coetzee's eyes were a lot like his mother's.

"You Qian's are instantly recognizable. You know why?"

Qian Xiuling smiled and shook her head.

"Your and your brother's eyes can talk."

He told her that his greatest reward from being in China was meeting such a friend as General Qian Zhuolun.

But Qian Xiuling soon felt like he was wandering off topic again. She wanted a number of times to drag the conversation back, but, after all was said and done, Falkenhausen was still chattering on about his impressions of China.

Time ticked by slowly. The secretary occasionally came in to whisper something in his ear, putting a telegram she had just received into his hands or urging him to rapidly sign some document. He would dispatch with the paperwork at lighting speed, giving Qian Xiuling the impression that he had completely forgotten that he was hosting somebody.

Ultimately, he would lift up his head, facing the unconcealable worry in Xiuling's gaze. He whispered to her in a low voice:

"Go home and wait for the news. I shall do my best."

Xiuling swallowed back a sentence surging up her throat. She wanted to remind him that time was of the essence and that Roger's execution date was quickly arriving.

She stole a look at Falkenhausen's work desk, at the thickly layered pile of endlessly amassing messages and reports. And which one of them was not urgently pressing? He impatiently picked up the phone that wouldn't stop ringing.

She left the Schaefer Castle in a state of bewilderment for a time. The entire village of Herbeumont was waiting for news from her. Falkenhausen's "I'll try my best" was no irreversible promise. That day was Roger's last day before his appointed execution. Heaven knew his life was hanging by a thread and what kind of luck he required. If he wasn't able to dodge this calamity, then today would become a day of great suffering for everyone in the village.

At one o'clock in the afternoon, she appeared at the entrance to the village, travel-worn and covered in dust, carrying Timothy with her. She didn't see any pressing, angry or frenetic crowd as she entered. The scenery didn't look any different. The sun was shining down on everything and a gentle breeze was moving the tops of the trees. In fact, the plaza regularly used to make grand announcements was standing empty. There were only a few sparrows sprinkled across the withered sod.

She had a kind of intuition that Roger had been spared.

The actual situation was that Roger's originally planned execution was set for that afternoon at noon. At ten o'clock in the morning, the plaza filled up with people. However, time passed, and that imagined German prisoner vehicle never appeared, and no official word arrived to explain why. They say that Father Stefan was so moved that his face turned red, and he prophesied that no news was actually good news in this case. Afterward, he wandered about trying to dig up more information on the matter.

Gregory returned and the news spread rapidly across the entire village. At that moment, the heart of the city was no longer the plaza where people congregated, but was Dr. Gregory's tiny clinic. People began showing up and gathering on the first floor of his clinic. They hoped to hear from Qian Xiuling's own mouth the story about Roger's rescue. Mrs. Abatha, her face stained with tears, and her dispirited husband, the train station chief, were holding each other up by the arm, casting glances at Xiuling with their eager but haggard faces. Their unstable state of mind made her feel for them. She consoled the couple saying that maybe the news would arrive soon. Sure enough, the news did arrive. Who knows where Father Stefan burrowed in from, but they heard him loudly shout out, "Roger has been saved! His execution has been commuted to hard labor!"

Mrs. Abatha hugged Xiuling tightly. A life had had a close brush with Death, but was snatched from him at the last second. The crowd that had gathered in the clinic cheered. At that happy moment, Xiuling couldn't hold back her emotion and tears. She felt for a brief moment the feeling of victory. Then she remembered Zhuolun. She had in her hand the late-arrived telegram from China. She told everyone there that his savior had actually been her older cousin, she was just acting as his messenger. Father Stefan drew a cross in front of his chest, "You are our angel! If it weren't for your courage and efforts, the merciful arm of the Lord would not have been able to reach us."

From that day forward, Dr. Gregory's clinic became a special place of interest far and wide. A great many people from far away would stop into the little building. They weren't seeking medical attention but only wanting to see with their own eyes that rumored elegant Goddess of the East. Some would even arrive weeping, looking for Qian Xiuling, saying that a loved one had just been captured by the German military. Their lives were hanging in the balance, waiting for her to save them.

Dr. Gregory privately grew worried about his wife's widely proclaimed fame. There was always someone being captured by the German military every day in this country. Furthermore, every day the military would execute a bunch of people as well. You couldn't go out and rescue every soul from the clutches of the enemy.

In fact, he came to feel that Herbeumont was no longer a suitable place for them to live, even though they had received the affections of everyone living there in no small measure.

Qian Xiuling had also become unsettled by it all. That singular act of deliberately saving a life had truly changed her entire life. She wasn't used to that many admirers, discussion, and attention. And the fame they were heaping upon her head was perverting the original intentions of her act. Because of her success, her peaceful home life had been turned upside-down, and she was feeling uneasy and guilty. She would often look like she had committed some kind of error in front of her husband. She knew that being on edge and worrying did not conform to his kind of reserved character. She consoled him by saying that it would all soon pass.

But before too long, there was another case that fell into her lap from the sky. One of the four Waffen SS members left as sentries in Herbeumont had suddenly gone missing. The German military dispatched forces to surround the entire village. That Lieutenant Keitel, whose infected mole had been treated by Ge Lixia in under twenty minutes that one time, stood in the town plaza and demanded that the townspeople hand over the assassin with all speed, otherwise, they would be drawing lots as to who was to be punished, selecting one of them to be killed every 6 hours.

This meant that even though it was Dr. Gregory's entire household, they also might not narrowly escape this lethal drawing of lots. Herbeumont had come face to face with an unprecedented catastrophe.

Naturally, everyone turned to Qian Xiuling.

When she and Gregory first found out about the news, they were greatly terrified. Qian Xiuling grabbed her handbag and dug deep inside to find Falkenhausen's business card. At the time, she didn't even notice the general's German signature on it.

When Dr. Gregory saw the business card, his reaction was stronger than a crashing wave. Maybe this card could help Herbeumont pass through this calamity unscathed? However, this would cause his wife to be pushed onto an even bigger stage. Behind the scenes there might be a correspondingly large hidden danger. She had already become a public figure — good Lord — a famous wartime figure, in fact! This wasn't the result anybody wanted. Gregory didn't like attention, living openly under the public eye. But, if his wife didn't take a stand and help out, how would they avoid this catastrophe?

He didn't pay it much attention.

This time around, Dr. Gregory accompanied his wife to go and find his former patient, Lieutenant Keitel. He brought with him some extra ointment and a roll of gauze. He assumed the role of the visiting physician, checking up on the wound on the lieutenant's neck. It was a little infected, but it was nothing serious. Dr. Gregory didn't request the lieutenant's opinion, but directly spread some anti-bacterial cream and alcohol on his neck, followed by a layer of ointment. A slightly bitter but fresh mint scent quickly permeated the room. However, receiving the simple treatment didn't remove the lieutenant's ill will toward the doctor and his wife. He said that drawing lots to execute the villagers was an old game with ancient origins — and he thought it was a pretty amusing game to play.

Of course, what he was really hoping was that Dr. Gregory was bringing him news of the assassin, not the misfortune of being selected. He never noticed the small woman standing behind the doctor. She had the look of an Asian woman. When she reached her hand into her handbag, the lieutenant only imagined she was grabbing a tube of lipstick. Instead, she surprisingly pulled out a business card. The lieutenant looked it over. He was somewhat mystified. Good heavens! General Falkenhausen, Brussels' supreme Viceroy's business card, signed the card in his own hand. How did this possibly fall into the hands of a tiny wife tucked away in this remote village? Her calm and elegant manner seemed to indicate to him that she was the purposeful holder of the card and that she wouldn't be revealing the true power of it to him. An interesting dialogue followed:

"Lieutenant. That phone on your desk should be a direct line to Brussels, am I right?"

"Oh, that one ...? Madame, I'm not at liberty to say at the moment."

"Huh, you shouldn't waste this opportunity in front of you. You're not interested in hearing General Falkenhausen's own voice?"

"Well, you might as well tell me, Madam. What is the general's relationship to you?"

"I'm afraid that is beyond your scope of authority, lieutenant, my apologies. If you do not wish to assist me, I will seek help somewhere else."

Dr. Gregory, who had kept quiet this entire time, finally spoke out humorously, "Who knows, maybe the general will invite you to Brussels for a turkey dinner."

As the couple turned to leave, the lieutenant told them both to halt.

He very painfully explained that, indeed, the phone line was a direct line to Brussels, but that his rank wasn't high enough to use it — at least not high enough to make the phone on General Falkenhausen's desk directlyring. That being said, with a few transfer calls, they might be able to reach it."

"Only God knows. Let's try our luck and see."

The lieutenant started to dial the phone. He cleared his throat as he tapped the receiver. A while later, the call finally went through. However, it wasn't General Falkenhausen who picked up the phone — not even his secretary, at best some shift officer at the Schaefer Castle Viceroy switchboard.

"I guess you can reach anyone at the Viceroy's office!"

The line was then cut off.

The lieutenant was delighted in the misfortune, shrugging his shoulders and laughing, "You can't say I didn't try to help out. The only way you're getting to the general is by taking the train and eating his turkey dinner with him in Brussels. Give him my best, but our little game of drawing lots isn't going to wait for you."

He looked at his pocket watch for a moment, and then blinked his blue eyes, "We've got a few hours left until it all begins. I'm imagining the beginning is going to be extremely exciting ... Unless of course, God grants you the gift of sprouting a pair of wings to fly directly over to the Schaefer Castle."

They had to try and call the castle again.

She asked the lieutenant if they could try once more, and this time she would make the call. He unconsciously rubbed his neck and looked at the couple. He really didn't understand why this husband and wife wanted so much to give the highest official in the army a call. In just a few seconds, he made a wise decision. Though he had never before personally seen the Viceroy, he had seen on every single one of his announcements the man's confident and imposing signature. He asked to see the general's business card again in Xiuling's hand. They both were truly one and the same signature. At that point, he knew that he couldn't neglect the request of the viceroy's distinguished friend.

Nobody could quite explain it clearly, but when the receiver was in Qian Xiuling's hand, the call went right through, loud and clear. It only took a few minutes and that rough and melancholy voice of the switchboard operator at the Schaefer Castle answered on the other end of the line. Qian Xiuling skillfully and gently greeted the operator in French and said that she was one of General Falkenhausen's friends. She had meant to reach him at this number as this was what he had written in his own hand on the business card he had given to her. She went on to say that the general had mentioned that the viceroy's operator was the world's most astute and diligent person. Since things were quite urgent, she asked that she connected him directly to the general's office.

"Thank you, Madame. That is the kindest greeting I have heard since arriving in Brussels. Your voice is truly beautiful. I wish you the best of luck."

There were some "doo-doo" sounds that followed, and then General Falkenhausne's personal office phone began to ring.

Unfortunately, nobody picked up.

It kept on ringing. Qiang Xiuling felt her heart beat accelerate.

The switchboard operator's voice returned to tell her that nobody was picking up in the general's office.

"But, but, Sir. I have a very, VERY pressing matter to speak to the general about. It needs his attention at this exact moment."

She could sense the agitation in her own voice.

The switchboard operator cut the line.

"Your fortunes are like the weather." Lieutenant Keitel shrugged his shoulders. The weather had been pleasant earlier, but it had suddenly begun to rain.

Qian Xiuling wasn't about to give up, though. She picked the phone up and dialed again.

"Madame, it is you again." The operator's voice sounded a bit impatient.

"If the general knew just how anxiously I was in seeking him, he would be more nervous than me."

There was silence on the other end of the line. Time seemed to stretch out unbearably. Qian Xiuling's palms began to sweat. Her husband's eyes were staring at her.

Suddenly a cough was heard in the receiver, then some words in German, "Since the Lyceum has already made its decision, what do they want me to do?"

She grew excited. That was General Falkenhausen's voice! He was obviously speaking with somebody else in his office.

She tightly gripped the receiver, like it would slip from her hand. She quietly introduced herself with her name, fearing he would have already forgotten her, adding a sentence to her introduction, "The little sister of your Chinese friend, General Qian Zhuolun."

The general's breathing was heavy — it sounded like he must

have caught a cold. He seemed a bit astonished to hear from her and asked, "Why are you contacting me like this?" Qian Xiulin heard in this question that using the switchboard operator was not a safe method. The trailing tone in his speech seemed to contain a hint of complaint.

She explained that time was extremely short and that she had no other recourse but to risk a phone call to him. Then she explained that the loss of one of their soldiers was being answered upon the heads of their entire village — over 1,000 inhabitants! No matter what, the retribution was absurd. There are too many games in this world. but to take one man's life and dignity and turn it into a pawn for a game of murder was both cruel and devious!

The general calmly listened. He coughed every now and then, and then asked her where Herbeumont was located. She didn't quite know how to answer at first, since her knowledge of geography was quite limited. But she knew it bordered France.

In the anxiety of the moment, she handed the phone to Lieutenant Keitel.

The lieutenant did not want to take the call at first, but Qian Xiuling told him that the general had asked where they were located.

Lieutenant Keitel trembled as he took the phone. He straightened up to attention and his face turned red as he began speaking German. Qian Xiuling understood a few words here and there, "carry out" and "follow orders" were among them.

Lieutenant Keitel's face was sweating profusely as he forced a smile, trying to win over the general. He walked Gregory and his wife to the door, telling them that everything had been decided and that they would be carrying out the Viceroy's orders.

Dr. Gregory hadn't forgotten to let down his internal heat a bit, "Lieutenant, we would like to invite you to a turkey dinner at our very own clinic. I believe that you will find my wife's cooking to be up to your standards."

The lieutenant cracked a knuckle, "At first, it was my neck that thanked you, and now it appears it will be my mouth. A splendid turkey must first be in the company of the great Viceroy, and I'm not sure he would ever personally be able to come to your clinic. I hope you will be able to keep on feeding that turkey for a while to fatten up, doctor."

They exchanged pleasantries like longtime friends. However, in the lieutenant's eyes, Qian Xiuling was still a bit dismayed.

That evening, in the middle of the Herbeumont village plaza, hundreds gathered around a bonfire. On the night before what was to be an explosive tragedy, the people were cutting loose, dancing gleefully to the accompaniment of accordions. Father Stefan went in search of the Perlinghis. The front door to their clinic was locked up tight, all their lights were turned off. Their neighbor, Mrs. Abatha said that a buggy from a neighboring village had arrived to pick them up, as a pregnant woman there had suddenly gone into labor and she was at death's door. Mrs. Abatha had gathered their two children and promised to keep an eye on them, "It is so hard to find good people. They truly are angels sent from heaven," she remarked.

CHAPTER 12

Hostage Street: Maurice Passes the Memory Baton to Raymond

Truth be told, Maurice's memory was a staggeringly shocking thing. Recounting the story of how Qian Xiuling saved Herbeumont made us feel like Maurice was taking us personally with him through every peril and danger. As a stubborn narrator, he often would fall into the marsh of his own memories, unable to extricate himself. At times, he looked pained, his two dim eyes flickering with the look of someone unable to carry on. He was one of the famed 96 rescued hostages. He lived through being suddenly captured and nearly killed to surviving imprisonment in a German concentration camp, forced to perform hard labor and every kind of torment.

Hygienic factors were vile to the extreme. In Kelamai Platz, there was only one toilet for every 1,200 people. It was originally meant to service a dozen children. During the winter, nobody had any coats or shoes. When it snowed, everyone had to go to work barefoot. Because the living quarters were so bad, and the food was so coarse, we could never eat to satisfaction. With hard labor and insufficient rest, those with weakness began to drop like houseflies.

He first heard about Qian Xiuling while being shipped off to the German concentration camp to perform hard labor. Without her help, they would have resigned themselves to death on that cursed evening. Fortunately, Mrs. Qian saved them all. At the time, he thought, "Oh, Ms. Qian, what kind of goddess are you?"

When the war ended, Maurice and 90 other survivors returned to their homelands. The other 5 perished from disease and other incidents inside the concentration camp. The first thing they did after returning home was to decide when they were going to go and meet Ms. Qian Xiuling. She was really quite young at the time — still so charming and beautiful.

Afterward, "Hostage Street" became a term, repeatedly appearing in Maurice's subsequent accounts of events.

But what did Hostage Street mean? Where was it located?

Maurice mumbled a name: "Raymond Maucq."

He said, "Raymond will take you to Hostage Street. The rest of the story should be told by him. His father was one of the leaders of the resistance at the time. It was he who drove his busted up car 160 kilometers through the night to find Ms. Qian Xiuling in Herbeumont.

Originally, Ms. Qian had no connections to Ecaussinnes. Nobody knew who she was there either. But how she rescued those lives in Herbeumont blew across the landscape like a prairie wind where it reached Ecaussinnes and the ears of its desperate souls.

We followed Maurice's directions and went in search of Mr. Raymond. There weren't many people walking the simple streets of the small city of Ecaussinnes. Mr. Raymond's home was on the corner of an unassuming side street. The gate to the courtyard was wide open. The moment we entered, we saw Mr. Raymond dressed in a western suit and leather shoes headed towards us. From the looks of it, it seemed that he was ready to go out to the town. He told us that an old man had just passed away and that he had to go to the chapel to preside over the funeral. He looked at his wristwatch and said it would take about half an hour. Despite all that, he retraced his steps and took us to see his collection of World War II weapons.

The collection filled three small rooms. Conventional weapons used by the different warring nations covered all the walls and floors: machine guns, rifles, pistols, helmets, bullets, artillery shells, grenades, landmines, bayonets, daggers. canteens, all kinds of transmitters, telephones, cloaks, ponchos, bugles, insignia, epaulets, etc. On a dusty windowsill, the model of a soldier in uniform stood helplessly with dead eyes. He had more than 3,000 real guns and munitions — how could the government allow such a collection?! Raymond smiled: Belgium was not a nation that prevented the possession of arms. The museum was free and open to the public, handed down to him by his father. His father had spent most of his life's savings and earnings purchasing this collection of World War II weapons. His eyes and footprints had been all over every country that participated in the war, from Europe to Asia.

My father's original intent was to collect and display the

items to his grandchildren and their posterity so that they would never forget the disaster that the war had brought upon humanity. After his passing, I picked up where he left off. Now, my daughter and her husband are here to help me.

He confirmed that his father, Raymond Keit, was one of the leaders of the resistance during the war. He led us in front of a fuzzy, black and white photo: "This is a picture of my father alongside Qian Xiuling."

A tall, somewhat heavy middle-aged man was talking to a casually clothed Qian Xiuling. From the Chinese style padded coat she was wearing, you could still feel the dense Asian air about her. But the two peoples' expressions in the photograph were a bit heavy. Within that heaviness was a kind of deep mutual understanding, or perhaps they were both feeling regret about the same thing. Of all the pictures we saw of Qian Xiuling, this might have been the only one where she wasn't smiling. Raymond's explanation for this was that this photo wasn't planned. They probably were really in the middle of discussing a serious matter.

Afterward, he took us to a buggy shed on the left side of the courtyard. We walked around some collapsing war vehicles and artillery guns. He gestured toward a dilapidated army jeep: "Look, this was Marshal Rommel's noble steed. There were only five of these made in the world under that brand." Then he tore open an immense military canvas flap to reveal a shabby, rusted out Chevrolet.

> At the time, my father drove this with one of his war pals to Herbeumont to look for Ms. Qian Xiuling.

When our expressions promptly froze in their stupefied state, a

Maucq Raymond Museum of Weapons

casual sense of success swept across Raymond's face. Then, he looked at his watch. He seemed like a chaplain praying, as if to say to us, "The bell is about to toll for a funeral service about to begin in the Ecaussinnes chapel."

Though Raymond's tale wasn't to be revealed from behind a deceitful curtain for two more days, from the time we were inside the World War II museum, a kind of cruel, belligerent atmosphere and a pressing desire to listen closely seized us tightly in its fist. There was no suspense to the tale. Publicly published books and widely circulated articles had all already repeated many times Qian Xiuling's night journeys over hundreds of kilometers to save others at the risk to her own life. However, that fading scene and the sheen of its popular feeling and impact were still tugging at my heart.

Hostage Street: this key term was a bit fuzzy and unclear before it surfaced at midnight on May 15th, 1943. For convenience sake, allow me to temporarily switch over to the perspective of Raymond's father, whom I will refer to affectionately as Old Raymond. Acting as a leader of the underground resistance, on that night, he brushed shoulders with the god of death a number of times. Bullets had already whizzed by his ears but failed to harm a single hair on his head. This made him feel that his luck had come too cheaply.

There was one even more thrilling time when a member of the German Waffen SS opened fire on him from behind, but only a couple of seconds before a war friend sent a hail of bullets flying into the German soldier's chest from a machine gun. On the battlefield, this type of thing wouldn't catch anybody's eye. The god of death is truly quite wretched, only with sufficient courage can you send him fleeing. But when four members of the Waffen SS attacked a home for the underground resistance with a transmitter, a usually quiet street suddenly shuddered violently.

The German soldier who seized the transmitter carried out a series of nightly interrogations on the homeowner. When Old Raymond found out about this, he disguised himself as a shepherd and made his way to the location. If the transmitter had truly been seized by the German army, that would sound the death knell to the resistance movement. As a result, he ordered an "encircle and annihilate" command for the resistance. They were to double and triple their manpower and arms and mow down the German soldiers inside the residence. Just as Old Maurice recalled it, three of the German Waffen SS members were killed, but one, a second lieutenant, luckily slipped away. He changed his clothes and climbed aboard a night train headed for Brussels. Early the next day, he led a large troop of German soldiers back. They encircled Ecaussinnes and conducted forced searches of every home on every street and alley. By that time, those working under Old Raymond had all escaped to safety, but the news of 96 innocent, young men being seized was circulating. Old Raymond interpreted this as a failure. If they wanted to remedy the situation, they needed to save all of these boys, or pay the price.

The term Hostage Street was born from that moment, embodying the palpable sense of life in calamity. The tedious old games of the German army were beginning to recur: if after so many hours the resistance didn't hand over their assassins, then the Germans would execute so many people every so many hours. There was a story published in the French paper, *The Beacon*, that was widely used by the German soldiers across Belgium. It read like this:

> October 20th, British and Russian forces hired a gutless assassin to kill one of our commanding officers on the battlefield in Nantes. The assassin has yet to be apprehended. I have given the order to execute 50 hostages

as a recompense for this crime ... If the assassin is not brought to justice before October 23rd, another 50 hostages will also be executed.

These types of announcements usually appeared in the streets and alleyways of cities across Belgium, including remote villages. The Germans' fixing of this "price" just kept on rising as the result of the tenacity of the resistance movement, to the point that if only a single German soldier was killed, then a hundred hostages were sought as a reprisal. Adolf Hitler wrote the following in a secret internal document:

> Our enemies will under no circumstances enjoy the protections of the Geneva Convention. If after a needed interrogation we must temporarily leave our enemies in good health, immediately after we must execute them.
> (William L. Shirer, *The Rise and Fall of the Third Reich*, Volume 2)

With time limitations and innocent lives at stake, the knot had been tightened. The butcher in this manner was exercising no real imagination. But that was war.

Old Raymond for a time grew rather fretful and impatient since they had no comprehensive rescue plan. At the time, there were some folks who planted the seed of Qian Xiuling's name in his ear. He summarily refused it, since the distance between Ecaussinnes and Herbeumont was 160 kilometers in a straight line. The situation on the roads was bad and the mountain roads were riddled with holes — it was a dangerous proposition. The most crucial aspect was that there was no gas. It must be borne in mind that underneath the rulership of the German army, all the gas in Belgium's villages was placed under strict surveillance. But somebody spoke up and said that he knew a way to get some gas, at least fifty liters of it too. Another quieter man said that he could arrange to procure 20 liters.

Old Raymond's eye's slowly began to light up. He flicked a cigarette butt and decided to collect in the fastest way possible at least 100 liters of gas, even if it cost them a life. Later, he and a few war friends like conjurors pushed out a beaten-up Chevrolet from a forgotten nook. They found the gas, but it was nowhere near 100 liters. Old Raymond jumped into the driver's seat and his two war buddies squished into the back. The loud crank of the engine shattered the peace of the night sky. After rushing out of the little city, the car bounded through the pitch dark roads of the open country like a crazed machine. After flying to Herbeumont at an ungodly speed, they arrived at the first floor of Dr. Gregory's clinic. Old Raymond looked briefly at his pocket watch. It was exactly midnight on the dot.

He knocked softly on the front door of the clinic, but it was unusually quiet inside. Dr. Gregory and his wife had just fallen asleep and he thought someone with an urgent condition must have shown up. He hurriedly threw some clothes on and went downstairs. However, the three men who entered his clinic looked stern and cold. Though they were carrying no weapons, their entire bodies emitted an energy of death. He knew with one look that the men across from him had come in from the battlefield. They were the posterboys of resistance fighters: strange expressions, messy appearances, nervously looking around, and so close to you that you could hear their guts gurgling.

Dr. Gregory had a virtue of taking things calmly however they came. Everyone who had come into his clinic before that point had been sick, or were related to the sick. He instinctively asked, "Who needs to see a doctor? Where are they injured? Or, what medication do they need? Whatever it is, I can assist you."

However, the head of the operation, Old Raymond, didn't say the kindest thing to him next, "Excuse me, doctor. We aren't here for any type of treatment. We would like to speak to your wife."

This somewhat upset Dr. Gregory.

"Well, I'm sorry about that sir, but my wife is asleep. I invite you to come back later. Good night."

He made a polite gesture for them to leave.

Old Raymond apologized. He realized that maybe he had been too impolite. The explanation that followed was more cordial and sincere: they had rushed there from far away Ecaussinnes. The Germans had captured 96 hostages — all innocent civilians, most of whom were in the prime of their lives. In ten or so hours, they would be executed by firing squad, one by one.

Dr. Gregory interrupted him. "Hearing this does make me sympathize, but how do you think my wife is always going to have a way to save you?" That's right, she had saved people in the past, and on more than one occasion. Whenever somebody out on the periphery got grabbed by the Germans, their family ran over in search of Qian Xiuling. And then she went in search of the German general. They say that she saved a few more, including a doctor, teacher, and a railroad worker.

In fact, just a few days earlier, she had saved someone from China, Lu Zengxiang. He was a chaplain in a church in Bruges. He had a gifted writing style and liked to send pieces for publication in newspapers and magazines. However, his writings had recently become more heated and heavy, scolding the Germans and making a bad name for himself. He would pay a price for it, as the Germans arrested him and sentenced him to death by firing squad. His wife

Mrs. Lu didn't know where she heard about Qian Xiuling, but one evening, she arrived in Herbeumont village travel-worn and looking for help. That night, Qian Xiuling accompanied her on the last train to Brussels. Surprisingly, she was able to save Mr. Lu that day. They say that she arrived with barely ten hours to spare before her husband was executed.

That was all amazing. But rescuing others was only a past duty, not an enduring, never-ending job — certainly not her sole responsibility or obligation. Moreover, she was already five and a half months pregnant … On that moonless night, travelling so far, he almost couldn't see any kind of possibility for them. He couldn't bear to wake his wife in the middle of her slumber. It was both impractical and unkind!

Dr. Greogry explained this all emotionally, as his visitors' faces fell. Suddenly, a spark of pity flashed in his eyes, and he sighed, "May God keep you all. I feel awful that there is no way to help you."

He turned around and saw his wife already standing in the opening of the stairwell. Greogry's face showed his sudden astonishment. Obviously, she knew everything that was going on. She softly moved down the stairs, slowly placing one foot below the other, like she was carrying a heavy burden. She walked in front of Old Raymond and said,

"Alright. I'll go with you."

Old Raymond stared blankly for a moment, standing firmly in his original spot. He looked over this young married woman of slight stature, her bulging belly and sallow complexion. But there was a special glint in her eyes that he could feel. And it wasn't the pedestrian kind of sympathy or friendliness, but a compassion that sprung from deep inside her heart, as if somebody among the hostages was one of her own family.

Qian Xiuling and Raymond Keit, the then leader of the Ecaussinnes resistance

Old Raymond and his two companions exited the clinic and quietly waited outside. Whether for the couple or for them, this was a crucial moment.

Inside the house, Qian Xiuling turned to look at her husband. Her voice was very quiet, but in the air of that tranquil night, her words sounded crisp.

"I know that you are worried about me, but I will be fine. You get some rest and take care of the children. I'll go and return shortly."

Dr. Greogry began to cry like a child. He embraced his wife, "You can't. You can't. You know that I'm a doctor. If you were just any old pregnant woman, I couldn't allow you to take such a risk — God! 200 kilometers over rugged mountain roads! God won't be able to assist you out there!"

Qian Xiuling snuggled up to his chest, raised her head and looked up at him, "My dear, you know what my favorite words are that you've said in the past?"

"Hurry! Go call two buggies!" She imitated his shout on the side of the street trying to save that man years ago at KU Leuven. She explained how that was the first time she had admired a heroic person. Heaven knows that she had never adored any hero before that point, but from that day forward she knew in her heart that she possessed a hero complex.

"If I don't do what I know I can, I won't be at peace, you know. I cannot ignore and violate my own heart."

He said nothing in reply. They hugged and kissed, and then Perlinghi climbed up the stairs and grabbed a first aid bag and handed it to his wife. He carefully warned her that if for any reason they ran into any kind of emergency that she would use the medicine inside the bag.

He walked his wife out the door and into the Chevrolet, then turned back around and grabbed a blanket for her. He and Old Raymond locked eyes for a moment. Old Raymond then gave him a hug, "Don't worry. I will safely return your wife to you."

In later interviews it was said that when Qian Xiuling set off on this trip, she told her husband, "If something happens, at worst it will happen to just the two of us: our child and me. But if you add up those whom we will save, that's 96 lives."

In her later years, Qian Xiuling put the record straight in her granddaughter Tatiana's documentary *Was My Grandma a Hero?*:

> That's not how I think. At that time, I didn't really think that deeply about things, I just thought that if I could do something, then I should go and do it. Rescuing another is an urgent affair, you can't waste thought on fear — don't think. You can't be meticulous about your calculations either. People's lives are precious.

There is a designated time for everyone to have a fearful heart, but wartime was a ruthless tutor that taught you how to fling fears aside. Exploding catastrophes can stimulate a person's heart, causing the sprouts of conscience, kindness, and courage to emerge. However, even when a colossal legend is produced, its starting point is never gorgeous or stunning — it all appears mediocre at the beginning stages.

Old Raymond had to resolve his concerns about gas at the midpoint of their journey in a small inn. In a cellar room, they surprisingly found 200 liters of hidden gas. The owner of the inn was the head of a resistance contact station. Old Raymond noticed Ms. Qian's extreme calm in the pitch darkness of their night journey. She had her eyes closed the entire way, looking as if she was sleeping for a time through big jolts on the road. What made him feel odd about her was that she seemed so unperturbed during such an unsettling moment. He obviously couldn't have known that Qian Xiuling was in fact dreaming. She was dreaming that she was travelling with her father on a sail boat being pulled into the city. She stuck her head out of the cabin on the little boat and saw a group of white egrets hugging the edges of the river reed. They sped past her face, flying toward the heart of the lake, when a gunshot abruptly rang out. The wings of a white egret flinched. The scene pricked her heart. She yelled and then woke up. Old Raymond was sitting next to her, propping her up. He said softly, "Madame, Madame, everything is fine. Please rest some more."

The depressing thing about that dilapidated Chevrolet was that even though it had drunk its fill of gas, the rough roads were actively tearing it apart. Old Raymond's two war buddies that had come along happened to be car mechanics. They would turn on their flashlights and make some quick repairs underneath the vehicle. One time, the car wouldn't budge at all. They pushed the car for a stretch until they reached a downhill slope, where the Chevrolet finally coughed and bucked into forward motion.

The most vivid sensation Qian Xiuling felt during that endless night trial were the first rhythmic movements of her unborn child. Despite the fact that this was her third child, this was the first time she felt it during her pregnancy. This was accompanied by nervous excitement — some worry that she couldn't shake. She grabbed the blanket her husband had given her and covered her belly. Each time the baby moved, he was talking to his mother. And she listened. Xiuling suddenly felt guilty, tears started streaming from her eyes. She used both hands to rub her tummy and soothe the baby, "My precious little one, Mamma is here to protect you. Thank you for going with me on this journey. When you're older, I'll tell you all about it. You're going to think it was all so very exciting!" She quietly mouthed the words. All of a sudden, she felt weak and ill and began sweating profusely. The palms of her hands were already soaking wet. She unconsciously gripped the first aid bag that Perlinghi had sent with her. But she didn't open it. She held her tummy with both hands and softly asked Old Raymond, "How much road is left?"

In the descriptions of many readily available accounts, Qian Xiuling arrived in Ecaussinnes early the next morning. The news of her arrival travelled fast and citizens from every corner pressed into the streets to welcome and pay their respects to her. The mayor of Ecaussinnes also formally received her.

However, the way Raymond Maucq recounted it, a different situation played out on their arrival.

> This couldn't be happening. The situation was critical, and Ecaussinnes was under the control of the German army, which meant that the resistance movement couldn't afford to have news that Madame Qian Xiuling had arrived to rescue the people leaking out and setting up a hero's welcome spectacle. Madame Qian couldn't be seen in public before the deed was done. People who understood the situation were waiting in the wings, acting as if nothing was happening.

There were about 20 kilometers separating Ecaussinnes from the Schaefer Castle. It was approaching four in the morning when they arrived. The further they went, the thicker the morning fog became, making the mood feel ever more ominous. Armored cars and tanks filed past them on the road, one after the other, as they crossed layer upon layer of sentry posts and checkpoints. At that juncture, it was only Old Raymond and Qian Xiuling. This was at Xiuling's request. As for how to deal with the incessant interrogations at the sentry posts, they spent some time rehearsing their lines. The business card from General Falkenhausen Qian Xiuling held in her hand had been used so much it was already crumpling. However, the sentries along the way recognized it. At about two kilometers' distance from the Schaefer Castle, Old Raymond's vehicle was halted for an inspection by the military police. They had him park the Chevrolet in a designated area. Old Raymond watched as Qian Xiuling climbed into a German's vehicle. The captain who whisked her away was expressionless. Old Raymond recognized that even the chauffeur was well armed. As the jeep slowly pulled away from him, Old Raymond's heart began to tighten. He later described the scene to his son Raymond in the following words:

> She seemed rather calm to begin with. In fact, she was quite humorous dialoguing with the military police during their interrogations. Her words garnered the respect of her interrogators. Indeed, she had already been this way a number of times. Some people actually recognized her as General Falkenhausen's friend, but she didn't abuse that privilege. The innate qualities she possessed didn't require her to use rhetoric to decorate her image.

However, the situation was much more complicated than Old Raymond supposed at the time. Even Qian Xiuling was surprised by the turn of events: General Falkenhausen almost wasn't able to see her.

Of course, that wasn't because he was too busy, or because it wasn't a convenient time for him, but because he had met with an extremely big problem.

With regards to General Falkenhausen, generally people only knew him as a German general, and the senior commanding officer of the German army in German-occupied Belgium and northern France. Chinese female author, Zhang Yawen, while writing her book *Gambling with the Devil* visited Falkenhausen's hometown, Nassau, for an interview. The lot of precious materials she obtained there gave great force and support to her writing project. Launching off of Zhang Yawen's book, I attempted to sort out the skein of psychological networks related to General Falkenhausen:

He actually was an anti-war figure. He ardently loved peace, and cherished every single innocent life. He esteemed charity and freedom. This psychological center ran through his handling of all affairs during World War II. He wouldn't accept that Germany was the slaughterer of the world's peoples. Adolf Hitler once said that even the lowliest German worker, from a biological point of view, was worth 1,000 times more than the loftiest Jewish and Slavic aristocrat. Falkenhausen opposed this concept. He recognized every nationality and race in the entire world as being equal. He was severely disillusioned by his comrades' massacre and looting of the peoples whose territory they occupied. One time during a meeting of high-ranking military officers, Adolf Hitler said, "When we find something that Germany is in need of, you must command your soldiers like attack dogs to pursue it and to seize it, and then deliver it back to Germany."

He scolded that remark to himself, "You shameless rogue!"

In actuality, he very early on participated in the anti-Hitler secret society. He and the Chief of Staff of the German ground forces General Ludwig Becker were the heads of the anti-Hitler conspiratorial bloc. These German generals with a moral compass recognized right away that Adolf Hitler was a blood-thirsty war hawk. The eruption of this war was completely the result of Adolf Hitler's ambitions to become the hegemon of the world, not at all the wish of the German people. Because of this, during his four-year tenure as Viceroy of Belgium, General Falkenhausen did not carry out any of the executions commanded by Adolf Hitler, but instead implemented a quite humanitarian administrative regime, hoping to preserve to the greatest extent possible the interests of the Belgian people.

(Zhang Yawen, *Gambling with the Devil*)

This was how we finally realized that Falkenhausen's willingness to help Qian Xiuling was not merely the consequence of private ties, but grew out of an inner sense of righteousness and morality. At a particular point, he must have felt extremely sorrowful, but destiny always finds a way to bind kindred hearts together in friendship even across thousands of miles of mountains and seas. That brother-sister bond of Qian Zhuolun must have stirred his heart, making him aware of the ubiquity of righteousness and goodness.

Then there was the marvel of the little sister of the Qian family, whose silhouette from behind had its distinctive charm. Her elegant manner demonstrated her fine upbringing, tied to her gentle and cultured family background. In her eyes was a kind of resolute firmness and sullen compassion for all of mankind that glinted with humane beauty. For Falkenhausen, this was the world's most fascinating landscape. He admired Qian Zhuolun for having such a sister. Taking measure of her with his older eyes made him feel that he was a part of a world that had suddenly blossomed with beauty.

Her coming to him a number of times to plead for others' lives, in his view, was an actual boon to him. It let him know that there were more innocent victims out there suffering injustices. Though he faced immense pressure when sending down such commands, inside he felt a sense of accomplishment. However, in order to protect Madame Qian, he couldn't reveal his true feelings, but rather maintain a necessary distance from her, otherwise the Gestapo would set on her and she would never escape them. If by chance a tragecy were to occur, how would he be able to face his good friend General Qian Zhuolun?

Naturally, much of Falkenhausen's anti-war record raised the dissatisfaction of Adolf Hitler — even Goering and Goebels criticized him on a number of occasions, claiming that he was incompetent, disloyal to the head of the state, and suspected of betraying the Third Reich.

From this, at least a couple of secret agents were planted by his side to monitor him. They were commonly known as the Gestapo, in German they were called the Geheime Staatspolizei — Gestap for short. They all possessed elevated ranks and positions, but on the surface listened to and carried out General Falkenhausen's orders. In fact, every single one of his actions and movements were under their watchful eye and recorded in their secret reports. Every day a stream of telegrams would promptly fly to the desk of Adolf Hitler.

In the meantime, the Allied Forces' invasion of Normandy Beach had been a success, and the European battlefront had suddenly experienced a fundamental reversal: Germany was now on the eve of its defeat. On more than one occasion, Adolf Hitler had to dodge assisination attempts on his life from anti-war figures inside his own country. This made him intensify his control of his highest-ranking officers. Falkenhausen had been called to Berlin, where he suffered the harsh criticisms and final threats from the mouth of Hitler. It was very clear at that moment that his days were numbered. The Gestapo could at any moment issue a hand-written command from the Fuhrer, drag him to Berlin and hand him over to the military court for trial and sentencing.

Against that background, Qian Xiuling was approaching Falkenhausen once more and seeking to liberate a lot more hostages — not unlike the 1,001 Arabian Nights.

However, that stubborn part of Qian Xiuling's character inflated at that particular moment. Though Falkenhausen's secretary had already refused her request to see him with a kind smile, she sat down on the sofa in his waiting room and wouldn't move a muscle. She insisted that she had an extremely urgent matter that the General absolutely had to attend to, otherwise she wasn't going to budge an inch, unless they decided to move her dead corpse. She was nigh to profanely swearing, though every word she spoke was delivered with the sweet-temperament of her Asian femininity. The secretary finally consented, telling her that the general had agreed to see her, but not at that moment. The earliest she could meet with him would be in twenty-four hours. She resolutely shook her head and said, "You can't put a price on human life! At most we have only one hour before many innocent lives that are cruelly snuffed out." Her eyes widened as she clearly enunciated every word, "Whatever the consequences, I must immediately see the general, even if it means I drop dead on the spot!"

Death in those extreme times was almost the easiest of things to accept. If it were an irrelevant, mutually forced death, it would be derisively laughable to others. But the secretary was moved to pity by the force of the aura exuding from her entire body. He knew that the general thought highly of this Asian woman, so he turned around and entered a secret conference room. There was an extremely pressing and secretive meeting being conducted at the time. A few anti-war generals were facing the threat of immediate arrest and extradition to Germany. They weren't there to discuss how to dispel the imminent danger they faced, though, but rather to try, to the greatest extent possible, to eliminate Adolf Hitler. This was their best and last effort to save Germany.

The secretary very cautiously and solemnly whispered to General Falkenhuasen the report of how Qian Xiuling was here to see him once again and that she was threatening to die, if need be. He was stunned. As a result of a succession of defeats, the German army had become abnormally frantic. The Waffen SS had commandeered the entire security force of the Schaefer Castle. That dangerous morning was concealing too many perils. He thought that were it not for an especially urgent matter that Xiuling, with her refined education, would never have threatened her own life to come and see him.

He involuntarily stood up, and a minute later reappeared in his office. He looked at Qian Xiuling's pale face as the secretary walked her in. Her complexion was not healthy. The vigor that her skin usually glowed had given way to a ghostly pale white. Her eyes were full of worry and exhaustion.

He couldn't help himself from walking over and blurting, "My child! Why have you come at this hour?"

Qian Xiuling explained the situation in the simplest terms possible, "96 innocent lives are at stake and will come to an end in just one half an hour. A massacre is about to begin. These people are all real citizens. They are utterly innocent, General, whatever you have to do, you must save them!"

Falkenhausen muttered to himself for a moment. It felt fairly long to Qian Xiuling. She sensed that he was in a tough spot, something he had never before experienced. He had obviously aged, the muscles at the corners of his mouth had slackened, and his grizzled beard had been left to grow. He looked around, making Qian Xiuling feel that something peculiar was in the air. She didn't know that the Gestapo were right next door, maybe even eavesdropping on them or discussing whether or not to seize General Falkenhausen earlier than anticipated.

"Alright. I shall do my utmost to help."

She sensed that those words were very hard for him to speak at the time.

As she passed the list of the 96 hostage's names, she saw a heaviness fall over his eyes.

He softened his voice and told her that he was in a desperate situation. The Gestapo were right next to him and he had completely lost their trust. Regardless, he was going to do his best to help.

Then he urged her to leave the castle immediately and not to come looking for him again. He spoke emotionally what felt like his parting words:

"I don't think I'll be here much longer, probably no more than 48 hours."

He pondered for a moment, and then added:

"When you see your brother again, please give General Zhuolun my best."

He then waved her off, "Leave."

Qian Xiuling suddenly burst into tears. She stood there, not moving.

"Leave!" he repeated.

She made a deep, respectful bow, then turned around somewhat clumsily. Falkenhausen noticed her awkward movement and told her to stop.

She was too embarrassed to tell him that she was pregnant with her third child and that she was already five and a half months along.

Falkenhausen's dim eyes suddenly brightened. He excitedly walked up to her and opened up his two hands in an unfathomable gesture, then his expression turned grim once more, "How could you dare ... threaten your own life to see me? Who gave you the right to make that unborn child in your womb suffer and follow you into death?!"

He was agitated, the dark corners of his mouth trembling.

"I apologize, General. I was worried to death and truly had no other option. If I hadn't said that, your subordinates would never have allowed me to see you."

Tears gushed out of Falkenhausen's eyes. He fumbled his words as he urged her that she must lead a fine life and take good care of and raise well that child in her womb. He wished that all those kindhearted people would continue to live good lives as well. He walked her to the door of his office and said one last thing that she would remember for decades to come, "Live well!"

She knew that this might actually be their last goodbye. The tears welled up in her eyes again and spilled out. She perceived that that castle had suddenly become a stifling tomb for the General. She lamented that Falkenhausen was about to be swallowed up by his stone grave. Decades later in the documentary, *Was My Grandma a Hero?*, she recalled that event in these words:

> At the time, I had no idea how extremely challenging the General's situation was. At any moment, the Gestapo at his

side could arrest him and ship him off to Adolf Hitler in Berlin and claim their credit. The General was hanging by a thread over a dangerous precipice. His last great effort was to commute the execution sentence of the 96 hostages to hard labor.

Falkenhausen's prediction of his personal fate was sufficiently clear and accurate. After a few days, on June 14th, 1944, a letter signed by Adolf Hitler issuing the command removing him of all duties landed on his desk. All honors had been stripped from him.

Not only was there no departing ceremony for him, but the General was removed from the Schaefer Castle in a fully armored vehicle under the surveillance of the Gestapo. But his inner state wasn't as conflicted as most people would think, since it was the conclusion he had long foreseen. His only hope was in someone named Claus von Stauffenberg, a lieutenant commander in the German army, who was assigned to place a custom-made brief-case bomb inside Adolf Hitler's office. Inside the office stood a six-foot long oak desk. Adolf Hitler often conducted his most important meetings there. If the bomb were placed underneath his seat and went off, well, then history would have changed course and all the cards would have been reshuffled. Regrettably, when the bomb exploded, Hitler was not among the dead. Instead it was a colonel named Brandt, who had inadvertently placed the briefcase next to his own seat.

CHAPTER 13

That Street

The recording of Maurice's interview was intermittent, but the harvest was rich.

The first time he saw Qian Xiuling, it wasn't like with other fellow sufferers at a welcome home party after being released from a German concentration camp and repatriated to their homeland. Instead, he met her at the celebration ceremony of the christening of "Qian Xiuling Street" in Ecaussinnes. During his time in the German concentration camp, Maurice and his fellow sufferers often brought up the goddess who had saved their lives. They talked about what kind of person she must be. One among them was a painter named Katja. Many times, he grabbed a pencil and some discarded paper and imagined her image in its blank spaces. He drew a tall and slim, blond-haired young maiden with big eyes, who could ride a horse, shoot a gun, while at the same time being refined and intelligent.

Undoubtedly, the image of that free goddess resided in the hearts of every single one of the hostages. This became a psychological prop for them in their cruel and inhumane condition. That day when the small Asian woman with her bashful smile appeared before them all, Maurice and the other freed sufferers couldn't help but run towards her, shouting and showering her with flowers and hugs one by one. For a while, her eyes held back the tears. If she had been a man, she certainly would have been tossed into the air by the congratulatory party.

Maurice had forgotten whether Madame Qian had shared any of her thoughts on the occasion. But he didn't think that detail was important. What was important to him was that the Ecaussinnes government had decided for the first time in its history to unite the name of a street with a foreign woman. In other words, by entering the annals of history, Qian Xiuling Street was actually tying the woman to the city, to the nation, and to a peace-loving world.

Maurice was easily embarrassed. He clearly remembered that on that day he gave a bouquet of carnations to Madame Qian. She cheerfully received them and then deeply inhaled their fragrance, offering her thanks. Then she said, "You have suffered hardship, but the crisis is past. Your future is as beautiful as these flowers you have given me."

When he and his companions discovered that she was a dual PhD in chemistry and physics but that she was currently known only for being the nurse in her husband's clinic, they clicked their tongues and shook their heads, feeling an even greater veneration for her.

Maurice also remembered that the Belgian king and queen at the time sent her a congratulatory telegram. The Belgian government had awarded her the title of "National Hero", with its accompanying precious and elegant ribbon and medal. Officials and celebrities took part in the festivities, along with hundreds of citizens from all around. The impression he had of Madame Qian was of her always trying to evade media interviews, her tall husband playing the role of her personal bodyguard.

Fortunately, Raymond Maucq's World War II Weapons Museum also preserved a precious film, memorializing that winning smile of Qian Xiuling at her own celebration. She looked healthy, hair in a high bun, looking very feminine. The cameraman clearly was attracted to her smile as he held his breath for a solid minute shooting the scene: at first she only grinned, but slowly she turned that shapely body to the side, holding up her flowers and sending her regards to those cheering for her. There was a little boy strenuously trying to push his way through the crowd to lay more flowers at her feet, but he was knocked down by the surging throng of people. He began to cry. Dr. Gregory, who was standing at her side, burst through the crowd and pulled the boy out, holding him close to his chest. Qian Xiuling let out a laugh. This nearly perfectly scripted scene documented the deep dimples on both of Qian Xiuling's cheeks. Later, that happy and carefree smile stayed on her face for quite some time, displaying the varied aspects of her beauty and charm.

That day, the mayor shared these opening remarks:

> We are gathered here together today in the name of the Belgian government and the citizens of Ecaussinnes to demonstrate our reverence and commemoration of Dr. Gregory Perlinghi and Madame Qian Xiuling by naming this street after Madame Qian. She exercised extraordinary courage in saving the lives of 110 of us resistance fighters as well as innocent bystanders. Her incredible character can never be replaced in this city. At this time, at this very

moment, our usually abundant French expressions suddenly fall short and flat. Indeed, we cannot find the accurate terms to express to her, Madame Qian Perlinghi, the highest esteem in which we hold her.

(July 21st, 1945, *Ecaussinnes Weekly*)

The *Ecaussinnes Weekly* was a high-circulating newspaper at the time. The front page had this advertisement: "More than two out of three Ecaussinnes households subscribe to the Weekly, loyal to its facts. No lies, no matter the times or the events." The Ecaussinnes City Museum has well preserved her speech from that time, also delivered on July 21st, 1945. You can imagine that her and the Mayor's addresses were delivered during the same gathering. After that celebration, her words were published in the 2008 winter edition (Page 158) of a literature and history magazine remembering the passing of Qian Xiuling:

> Ladies and Gentlemen,
> Hello!
> Your words have been filled with praise for me. I warmly thank you for your kind reception and for blessing me with such fine memories. They truly move me. I will strive to express here my deepest gratitude.
> Today, I return to Ecaussinnes to pay tribute to this city's hostages and sacrificial victims. I am filled with relief to remember that a little over a year ago, when I first saw them, my heart was so heavy. I count it an extreme privilege to offer my respects to the good people of this city, especially those who endured the savage treatment of the German army. Together with you, I salute the heroes that fell for the

independence and freedom of our nation.

When I was fortunate to stand before the head of the occupying state to plead on behalf of these innocent hostages, I realized that I was there to resist on behalf of those whose lives were ready to be snatched away from the cruelest of dictators. I completed this great responsibility. If you were to say that these precious lives were saved because of this, then I have already received my reward: Though I had no such expectation, I truly feel, in no small part, a great, warm satisfaction, for I have carried out my sacred obligation. Since first stepping foot onto Belgian soil, I have always appreciated and admired your beautiful qualities: your cordiality and your sincerity, which have made me feel like I unconsciously am one of you.

The war caused me to see the patriotism and fearless courage of the Belgian people. I sincerely admire the heroes who fearlessly struggled for this nation's freedom.

The people of Ecaussinnes have chosen July 21st this year as a day worthy to remember and to give thanks. This is a testimony to the patriotic feeling of the city government and all citizens. For this, I deeply express my approval.

In my view, your warm invitation is also a testimony to the friendship of the Belgian people. I love this nation and count it as my second home.

This short piece was filled with profound emotion. Unfortunately, the valuable document was hidden by time for more than 70 years. Although the Belgian government had conferred upon her the title of "National Hero," Qian Xiuling still considered herself to be Chinese. The Belgium she admired would always be a "second home" for her.

A number of years later, Maurice would serve as the Mayor of Ecaussinnes. During his almost 20-year tenure in office, "Qian Xiuling Street" was enlarged and lengthened at least three times. He was at heart a great storyteller. At the right moment, he would once more return to that iconic photograph to set the scene of the era. His oft repeated story always inadvertently grew longer and longer. The photo of the famous 96 hostages made almost everybody who saw it experience a common regret, which was that Madame Qian Xiuling should've been in the photo alongside them. For without her, they wouldn't be alive.

Maurice's career as the mayor was full of regrets. Among them was not being able to purchase the home that led to the hostage situation in order to convert it into a lasting memorial hall. That sounds a bit unimaginable, but after coming across many other such places in Ecaussinnes, we felt better about it.

We walked up and down Qian Xiuling Street three times. It wasn't far, but it was nothing like the national Chinese media say, sitting at the center of Ecaussinnes. It's not quite located in the city's distant suburbs but if there were no street sign for it, you wouldn't be able to differentiate it from any of the other streets around it. The road isn't long — one or two kilometers. A smattering of common homes flank its sides. They seem a bit sparsely spaced from one another. You might say that it is a quiet place, at least there's no heavy traffic. There aren't any particularly famous trees planted along the road, either. It doesn't look like they're done anything special to spruce up the road, apart from the occasional repairs, but those are generally standard. There's not really anything special about it — but maybe that's just a judgement coming from the limits of our own value system in China.

Walking along Qian Xiuling Street there is still a real sense of emotion. If you say that westerners believe eulogizing somebody turns them into objects of worship, why then in every city you go to, whether it's a plaza or a park, are there so many statues of historical figures towering over you, making you crane your neck to look up at them? It is incredible to think that Qian Xiuling's accomplishments have been relegated to the global background of history. If she had been a Belgian, her influence would still persist to some degree — at the very least she'd enjoy a bit more recognition than she currently does, right? It's impossible for me to get rid of that kind of faint sense of deficiency in all of this.

Mr. Raymond was too busy. Besides being a dedicated undertaker for the small town, he was also a social celebrity. Since he couldn't remove himself from this, he introduced us to a small town historical and cultural researcher, a Latin instructor named Mavournee and her Taiwanese husband Xue Jiaren to show us around.

On a late autumn afternoon, as the sun shone down upon the empty streets of Ecaussinnes, Mavournee and her husband guided my wife and I through a number of simple, small alleys until we came to that street that Maurice and Raymond would never stop talking about: Hostage Street. This was quite obviously an ordinary road. It wasn't very wide. If there hadn't been a sign in French on the corner, I really wouldn't have known it was a special place at all. Its memory had been completely preserved by the connection between the 96 rescued hostages.

My first question to them was: "Can a government actually not purchase a house?"

Mavournee gave us an account of the particulars. During the ceremony that year, the Ecaussinnes government named the "Mrs. Perlinghi Qian Xiuling Street," and the mayor of the city also gave Xiuling a gift: an interesting, ancient copper Chinese incense burner.

They say that it was an antique from the Southern and Northern of China dynasties. On top were fine engravings that looked exquisite and delicate. There is a saying that the gift from the mayor came out of his own pocket. There is another rumor that another wealthy citizen, moved by Madame Qian's achievements, purchased this ancient incense burner said to have originated in the Southern and Northern of China, which they then gave to the city government to present to her. Whatever its origin, the government hadn't gotten any help with the bill. It was not on the government's budget, thus it couldn't be done and wouldn't be reimbursed.

Mavournee's explanation was that in the eyes of Belgians, the government didn't possess all of the power. The government was just the instrument used to carry out taxpayers' wishes. The taxpayers were the ones who gave their leaders their jobs. The government had no right to go against the taxpayers, using their money on something else — like buying a house. Frankly speaking, the government didn't have that much money, and even if it did, if the owner didn't want to sell it, the government was out of luck. Furthermore, even if the owner agreed to sell it, there was no item line in the budget for the purchase of a home to turn into a memorial hall. Government was under the eye of both the national parliament and their own voters. So, in the end, the government was required to look to its people. In the end, the government hoped to nail a sign to the wall of the house, explaining what had transpired there. But the descendants of the owners felt like a sign hanging on their house would become a nuisance, so they disagreed. As a result, the government hung the sign in an alley not too far from the original home.

The second question I had was, how many people did Qian Xiuling save in total?

The answer to this was clear and definite. It was carved into a black granite memorial in front of the entrance to the Ecaussinnes City Museum. Two groupings of numbers told the tale:

Group 1: 300 (the total number of deaths in Ecaussinnes during the World War II).

Group 2: 110 (the total number of hostages whose lives Madame Qian Xiuling saved).

There were no descriptions, only numbers.

Mavournee said that in the minds of the locals, pure numbers conveyed a more proper sense of things. When history just provided numbers, it wasn't forcing anyone to believe in this or disagree with that interpretation.

I told Mavournee that literature was nothing like this. It solely concerned itself with the spiritual encounters and matters of the people behind the numbers — hunting down the incident and aesthetic sense behind the material.

Mavournee smiled forgivingly. She believed that any non-fiction book always carried the flavor of something fictional, because its writer was always inclined to select some things and to disregard others.

Mavournee tried to show that her perspective was objective and fair by purposefully leading us to the Ecaussinnes City Museum. As luck would have it, though, the museum was in the midst of a relocation, its exhibits scattered all about. The front manager was a rather sturdy old seventy-year old man named Ruell. He was happy to hear that two Chinese people from Madame Qian's hometown had come inquiring about her. He made an exception by allowing us to break open a couple of sealed boxes. In one of them was a copy of the 1945 Belgium *Southern Daily*. Two issues were entirely dedicated to reporting on the rescue of the 96 hostages, one of them described Qian Xiuling:

The stone stele in front of the Ecaussinne City Museum, recording Qian Xiuling's deed of saving the hostages

Looking at her, she seems quite ordinary. She has the small stature of an Asian person, and she clothes herself in typical Asian colors. She almost avoids watering down her Chinese concepts while at the same time remaining quite subdued. Even without her already eight year-old boy, people wouldn't connect her to the rank of a national hero. When she climbed onto the stage to receive Belgium's highest national honor, she revealed her shyness with a somewhat nervous expression, which only won her greater applause. So many people crowded around her, certain that she was the only bright-eyed goddess in attendance at the assembly.

My third question was: After all the fame and noise following the war, when did she actually leave Herbeumont? Did she live in Ecaussinnes?

Mavournee used an utterly certain tone of voice to say that Madame Qian never lived in Ecaussinnes, notwithstanding the close ties she maintained with the city in the second part of her life. As for her fame, she didn't believe that it was a bother to Qian Xiuling. People with a strong sense of inner self, facing life with their own solid sense of values and judgements, have their own way of handling things. Certainly, the remote village of Herbeumont was not a place Madame Qian stayed for very long.

This fulfilled my one-time, on-site investigative experience. The first day we arrived in Brussels, I was thrilled to go to a bookstore in the city center. I wanted to go there to buy one of Qian Xiuling's biographies, or at least a book that recorded her achievements, even if it took up just a fragment of a page. The female shop assistant searched the database for a good while before apologizing that they didn't have any books on the subject. I didn't give up, though. I wanted her to keep looking. So, the shop assistant called over an older, more experienced worker — a manager or something. The result was the same, just as before, they didn't have any. I asked them if they happened to know the name Qian Xiuling. The older man nodded his head with certainty, "She was the recipient of the royal hero's medal of honor. But that was a very long time ago." From his expression, it looked like he was attempting to drag out some distant memory. The younger female shop assistant was still standing there with a blank expression.

In other words, even though she was decorated a National Hero, she didn't enjoy the privilege of having a biography written about her; or, to put it another way, no author had taken up the pen to make more widely known one of Belgium's national heroes.

I don't know how, but my mind suddenly flashed back to those towering historical statues in the public squares and parks. A question that I had been holding back this whole time: were those statues of famous historical figures in the plazas and parks a part of a personality cult, or not? What was the basis for erecting these sculptures?

CHAPTER 14

The Gate to Heaven is Narrow

So, where did Qian Xiuling go after leaving Herbeumont village?

I asked Mavournee this question as we were leaving Ecaussinnes. She hesitated as she answered, then chose a very general response, "Anyway, she didn't return to China, but stayed in Belgium. That is for certain."

Mavournee modestly admitted that she had never been to China, and hadn't the minimal understanding of that ancient Asian nation. However, according to what she did know, Madame Qian Xiuling never did return to China. She had her reasons.

When we collected all of our materials and news, we discovered that Qian Xiuling didn't have many moving options at hand.

They could have obviously returned to Brussels. It was the nation's capital and was home to its finest hospitals. Dr. Gregory was still quite young. He must have known that those days of quiet living in the village clinic would ultimately waste his skills. One of his close older classmates was currently managing a surgery unit in a prestigious hospital in Brussels. If he could become an important doctor in that hospital, his future prospects would certainly be great. Worrying about the family's clothes and food were secondary to Dr. Gregory. What he yearned for was the mastery of knowledge.

In Qian Xiuling's view, she wanted first and foremost to return to China. The background for this must have been 1946 as the War of Resistance had come to an end, but internal fighting was still going on. The Communists and the Nationalists were locked in a battle to the death that hadn't yet reached its final conclusion. She secretly returned to China, where she attended a family reunion in Shanghai with her mother. Then she went to Nanjing to visit her paternal cousin, Qian Zhuolun. She wanted to get his opinion on something. Zhuolun's mood had deteriorated a great deal since earlier times. In fact, he had become a bit pessimistic. Though he had not given her a clear-cut judgement, Xiuling could tell from his state of mind that fighting was not going in the Nationalists' favor.

At the time, Qian Zhuolun had already become the Head Provincial Governor of the Ministry of Defense, still responsible for personnel management. However, his rank was now that of lieutenant general. His classmates from the military academy Gu Zhutong and Chen Cheng had already become generals. Qian Xiuling of course had no idea what the crux of the matter was. Facing Xiuling's questions, Qian Zhuolun muttered to himself for a while, not yet giving her a direct answer. Instead, he wrote down some Chinese characters in response, a poem by Emperor Taizong of China Tang dynasty, Li Shimin, "Passing My Old Residence":

The carriage stops at my old residence, sound of reeds preparing the way.
The yard is empty, a pathway cleared, moss climbing up the pathway.
The old pond still fed by the spring, the old tree fresh blossoms grown.
When I left for war before, I believed all the world was home.

She suddenly understood Zhuolun's meaning. The world had been thrown into chaos by a king's game. Though it was too close to call, Zhuolun already felt the signs of dynastic destruction, he just couldn't say it directly. She returned to Shanghai, where she met up again with her brothers and sisters to talk about the nation. One of her elder brothers recalled their discussions some decades later:

> She asked us who in the end was going to occupy the seat of power, the Nationalists or the Communists? I said, "Think about it: are there more poor or well-off people in the world?" She responded that of course there were more poor people. I told her, "Well, then you understand it. The Communists speak for the poor, and the poor follow the Communists. The majority of the people support the Communists, so that should make it clear who is going to end up on the throne."

In Shanghai, she heard a relative say that the Communist Party would seize power and not treat the landlords and capitalist classes kindly — this was called "class struggle."

She asked, "But what if you only own a little land? Are you still considered a landlord?" Nobody knew the answer to that. But there was one point on which they were utterly clear: the term "landlord" wasn't meant to simply be shorthand for owners of land, but rather possessed another kind of meaning that definitely meant the enemies of the poverty-stricken masses.

In the end, she had been away from her homeland for too long. She no longer really understood the internal political situation. Too many questions and too few answers. On her return to Belgium, Qian Xiuling made a heart-wrenching decision: she would, for the time being, remain in Belgium. After all, the country was recovering quickly from the aftermath of World War II, and life was already improving. And from the king down to the pauper, everybody knew who she was. Honor and dignity aren't by any means a luxury good, but form the sufficiently trusting atmosphere of an ordinary life. She had already become the mother of four children. That lively home was calling for her every hour of the day.

"When I left for war before, I believed all the world was home."

Reading those lines of poetry truly grieved her heart.

You can't overlook the awakening she experienced from that original dream rooted deep inside her heart: returning to KU Leuven, becoming a professor, conducting research, working closely on the path of Madame Curie. Those extravagant hopes of her youth cooled into frozen homages. Granted, if it were possible, she would still have given it a go.

The final result was that their family moved to Brussels. She went to KU Leuven to work as an instructor. Working in the clinic in Herbeumont village hadn't left them with much savings. During the war years, they couldn't rightly ask the destitute sick for payment. Gregory was no orator, but he had a merciful heart, and it often came out in his attitude towards his patients. They had left such a mark on the community, that when they left, their reputation quietly transformed into reluctant tears.

Father Stefan wanted to hold a grand parting ceremony for them, but they declined. A buggy took them to the train station, carrying their simple luggage. When they came to Herbeumont, they brought with them only one child, now they had grown into a little herd of people. They shipped a few medical tools and furniture ahead of them to Brussels.

Mrs. Abatha cried for days. In her life, Dr. Gregory's clinic had become a landmark piece of architecture. The savior of her son Roger, Madame Qian, also happened to be a close friend she could share anything with. Not long ago, Roger had returned home from the German concentration camp, and immediately an extravagant wedding ceremony was hosted and attended by everyone in the village. Gregory and his wife were honored to serve as witnesses to their matrimony. As Qian Xiuling left Herbeumont that day, everybody — including Roger and his new bride — went to the train station to bid them farewell. Father Stefan, of course, led the procession. However, he was feeling a bit depressed that day, mumbling incessantly to himself. Nobody could understand him. As the train began to pull away, his eyes like fountains began to stream tears. He covered his face and turned his back away.

It was all pretty simple: their arrival and their departure was both done pretty quietly. A few people who caught word of it rushed to the crude train platform where villagers were gathered to try and wave goodbye to them as well.

Dr. Gregory went to the bank to take out a large loan to buy a home in a Brussel's urban district. It wasn't a bad second-hand home. He also hired a nanny of Dutch descent for his children. Everyday, Qian Xiuling took the light rail to KU Leuven to teach her classes.

Sometimes she wouldn't return home until late at night when the children were already asleep. It always seemed like Dr. Gregory had a lot of night shifts. Without him, it felt like the home was lacking vitality. Working hard never really bothered Qian Xiuling. She actually quite liked to bustle about. If this insipid and orderly life never changed, she would never become picky about life's banality and trifles. The rich textures of life were dependent upon the awareness of people's rich interiors. This was all until one day when an important announcement hit the papers, exploding her past peace. She suddenly felt another large door slam shut in her face.

> The German war criminal, General Falkenhausen, had been extradited from abroad to face judgement in Belgium.

This news headline pounded her heart for days.

Previously, she had brought up a number of times the sudden disappearance of the German general in front of Gregory. Every time the media inquired about her rescue of the hostages, she mentioned, without the slightest hesitation, the name of General Falkenhausen. War always creates too many concerns created by separation. For her, Falkenhausen was, first and foremost, an elder she deeply revered. Their face-to-face meetings during those critical moments were engraved deeply upon the tables of her heart, so much so that his conduct and demeanor had secretly transformed her own character. If it weren't for him, there would have been no rescue to speak of.

Finally, news of Falkenhausen slowly began to leak out from secret places, piling up and beckoning for her attention. Without noticing it, she became a garrulous commentator on the topic. On every possible occasion she felt necessary, she repeatedly talked about General Falkenhausen's key role in her rescue operations.

She frequently moved in and out of these bureaus such as the Ministry of Justice, the highest court, the Taiwanese "Embassy" in Belgium, and the St. Renard's Gerand Prison, which she ordinarily had nothing at all to do with. Her line of questioning always made people feel strange. But she was Qian Xiuling, and everyone knew her as a National Hero. There was nobody who wouldn't see her. As a result, Falkenhausen's fate after 1944, like the vague and fragmented pieces of a puzzle, carrying with them their own pains and grievances, slowly began to come together for Qian Xiuling.

On July 30th, 1944, the 66-year-old General Falkenhausen was locked up inside a remote concentration camp in Germany. Though he was well prepared for it, he was finally placed inside a cramped prison that stunk to high heaven. With interminable attacks from black swarms of bedbugs, fleas, and cockroaches, he felt pushed to the limits of his resistance. He starved all day and all night for almost half a year and was never spoken to. The goal of this psychological abuse was to choke him with silence, at least to make him breakdown.

On May 30th, 1945, Adolf Hitler committed suicide and history turned over a new leaf.

In the meantime, General Falkenhausen had already been transferred to an Italian prison in South Tyrol. He actually couldn't remember clearly how many prisons he had passed through during that time. The artillery blasts of the allied forces resounded all around him, making even this professional soldier a bit alarmed. General Falkenhausen knew his life was quickly coming to an end, since those who escaped early slaughter became the losers' easy pickings. The SS locking them up in the prison would assure no "survivor" might be around to provide proof of subsequent crimes. However, the speed of the allied forces' attack surprised everyone:

On May 4th, 1945, South Tyrol, a group of people were freed by American soldiers. At the time, the secret guards watching over them were preparing to exterminate all of them. Alexander von Falkenhausen was apprehended by Belgium to be interrogated as a war criminal. He awaits trial from prison, where he will be locked up for the next four years.

(William L. Shirer, *The Rise and Fall of The Third Reich*, Volume 2)

And so it was by some fluke that Falkenhausen and other imprisoned personnel survived.

In *The Rise and Fall of the Third Reich*, the author also provides this detail: when the American soldiers began, they didn't have any clue that these illustrious, high-ranking leaders of the Third Reich were all anti-Hitler. Luckily, there was a German anti-war officer named Randolf who was also standing trial. He had previously participated in an assassination attempt on Hitler, but he failed. At that very moment, an American artillery shell exploded inside the German court allowing him to escape with his life. He identified for the Americans those figures in prison who were high-ranking, anti-Hitler officers. Among them was Falkenhausen.

People like Falkenhausen certainly had a different acquaintance with death than the average person. Surveying his decades-long career as a professional soldier, from his participation in the Eight-Nation Alliance's invasion of China, to assisting the Nationalists fight against the Communists, to providing assistance to the Japanese in their Asian expansion, to finally serving as the viceroy of German-occupied Belgium, killing or nearly being killed, rivers of blood and carcasses scattered about were his daily vistas. They say that one of his nerves must've always been numbed, but that is perhaps a bit partial, because his humanity was never extinguished — his conscience was still quite alive. Fairness and righteousness, freedom and fraternity, these unbreakable convictions still flowed through his body like blood.

He had a great many regrets throughout his life. In his personal life, he had been robbed once and his house had burned down. Fortunately, he had a loving wife, but he had no children with her. He wanted children, but God would not grant him that gift. His wife, Paula von Wedderkop, saw very little of him. While they were separated during the war, she suffered a sickness that led to amputation. In the end, her ailments led to her death in a subpar hospital in a foreign land.

> On March 21st, 1948, after being imprisoned for three years and eight months, tossed about between Germany, England, France, Netherlands and a number of other prisons, Falkenhausen, Enemy #1, was brought to Brussels, the capital of Belgium. He was locked up inside the high security St. Renard's Grand Prison to await trial in front of Belgium's military court.
> ... All the grief, hatred and pain suffered because of the loss of loved ones falls directly upon the head of this 'viceroy,' whose crimes during the Nazi occupation of Belgium are monstruous. Their cries for his execution crash like waves, each louder than the other."
> (Zhang Yawen, *Gambling with the Devil*)

At this particular time for Qian Xiuling, relying on her strength alone to overturn the punishment of Germany's number one war criminal would've been harder than climbing her way up into heaven.

It seemed like there was some inertia from the world of spirits behind her actions. She wrote her brother Zhuolun a letter again. At the time, he was already following the retreating Nationalist forces into Taiwan. But the central offices of Jiang Jieshi's government had nobody named Qian Zhuolun working there anymore. A nominal, hollow position on the surface had prematurely given Zhuolun the first taste of marginalization, something widely known at the time. With respect to Qian Zhuolun himself, he had already psychologically prepared himself for this and had made peace with his lot. Qian Xiuling only found out about it all later. Zhuolun became more sullen than he ever was. There was no solution for this kind of intuition; Qian Xiuling was left to just pray for him in her heart.

She told Zhuolun in the letter all about Falkenhausen's situation, pouring her heart out on paper. Zhuolun immediately replied. He felt shocked and helpless, hoping she would do her utmost to help this German general behind bars. He passed the news onto Jiang Jieshi. They say that Jiang Jieshi sent a hundred thousand dollars to Falkenhausen through the Taiwanese "Embassy" in Belgium. Heaven knows if he ever received it.

Afterward, she decided to go to the prison. She knew that this would be difficult. However, her will was firm. Dr. Gregory didn't offer his opinion on any of this. He knew that once his Asian belle set her mind to something, nobody could get in the way. Regardless, he didn't think that the Belgian government would ever let Falkenhausen out alive. Fortunately, he and his wife had a tacit agreement: when one of them decided to do something, the other didn't get in the way, even if silence was their only response, it still counted as a sign of support.

She steeled her will and marched down to the Jiang Jieshi regime's diplomatic mission in Belgium. To begin with, she received no active response. But she kept on coming back, persuading one of the embassy's key staff, who knew Qian Xiuling's true identity, to agree to mediate her case, but he needed some time. After all, the embassy was just a visitor in the host country and in no position to make demands, only requests. A week passed, and there was still no news. Qian Xiuling didn't think she could wait passively like that any longer. She calmed down and thought deeply about it. She also had her own problems — her energy had its limits too. She still had to go to work every day, laboring at her work desk often until the dark of night. And she had children at home too. She remembered something her father often used to say to her, "You can't burn a candle at both ends." The most pressing need at the time was to defend Falkenhausen. And time was running out. The cold and sinister hangman's noose was already beckoning for Falkenhausen's neck.

Her posting as a teacher at KU Leuven suited her perfectly at first. She loved the intellectual atmosphere at her alma mater, and it was where she first fell in love too. However, as time went on, she faintly began to detect a fatal dilemma: there was an omnipresent, yet hidden and difficult to define, anti-foreign sentiment there.

She was an assistant professor at KU Leuven. She had finished a dissertation and the fruits of experimentation. But she couldn't seem to get promoted. The most important academic activities were not presented as opportunities for her. She was included in the most significant research projects, which meant she wasn't permitted to apply for those associated funds. The honor conferred upon her by the nation almost didn't seem to matter to this independent university. They couldn't seem to let go of her Chinese identity. Despite the fact that the kingdom of Belgium had proclaimed itself perpetually neutral since 1839 in the famous Treaty of London, the nation's ideological form couldn't extricate itself from the mainstream European capitalist tendencies of the time. A woman from China being granted a professorship at KU Leuven, a Top 10 European university, was as fantastical as a tale from *The Arabian Nights*.

Dr. Wilson, her advisor, had already retired, and had already tactfully expressed his heartfelt regret — he had no way of helping her. Either she could continue on as an outsider in the system, or decide to move on. But where would she go? Nobody could tell her which direction to go.

She had unconsciously reached a fork in the road in her life. She was bound to have to let go of something and cling to what she wanted most, or she would succumb to exhaustion.

At that moment, she became exceptionally clear-headed. She needed a great deal of energy to petition Falkenhausen. But this was nothing like that time she handed over a list of hostages to plead for his help. This task was much more difficult. She was at a loss with regards to KU Leuven. Though she loved it dearly, a phrase slowly began to rise from her heart: Adieu. When she had finished handling the pressing things she needed to attend to why couldn't she return. A centuries-old institution of such high repute was worth a lifetime of her admiration. Even though there were some lingering, unpresentable prejudices and haughtiness that hadn't been reformed, she could still search for that one in a million chance to set them right.

Deep down inside, this was her personal philosophy. And so her resignation letter was gentle and her tone was agreeable — to the point of seeming a bit humorous. In fact, there wasn't a trace of regret or blame in it.

Just like that, she pushed KU Leuven into the back of her mind. She never again used that early morning and night train to rush to and from campus for work. She made an all-out effort to prepare to see Falkenhausen. In the end, she received her approval. She sorted out her thoughts and then headed to that ancient prison in full confidence.

The prison authorities had arranged for a temporary room to be set up for her to meet with Falkenhausen, but Qian Xiuling refused the plan. She recommended that she meet with him inside of his own prison cell. She wanted to know his actual living conditions. She was also worried about wire-tapping or interruptions. In her view, the safety arrangements should be higher in the prison cell.

The prison agreed. After the event, Qian Xiuling discovered that because of Qian Zhuolun's efforts, the Taiwanese "Embassy" in Belgium had informed the Belgian government once more of the need to treat him well. The prison didn't get this message in time, though.

Despite the fact that she had grossly miscalculated Falkenhausen's treatment, when she actually saw him, she was stunned by his disheartening appearance. Indeed, you cannot expect that a prisoner who has been locked up for a long time would be in good spirits. Instead, he seemed like one of the walking dead, curled up in the corner of a busted cell, staring back at her in a daze from two sunken, lifeless eyes, like dark holes with no spirit left. This man used to be so physically imposing.

Qian Xiuling instantly clutched her abdomen. She couldn't breathe.

Indeed, at that time, Falkenhausen was little more than a breathing corpse.

Who was this young woman sitting in front of him? She had entered with a bright aura, casting out the gloom from every inch of his cell. His turbid chest had seemingly been irrigated by clear waters. The hazy wretchedness of the air was suddenly dispersed. His numbed spirits began to awaken somewhat. He finally saw clearly that the woman across from him was Madame Qian!

He struggled to stand up from a heaped up rotten carpet.

"Why are you here, Madame Qian?" he asked, surprised.

"General, I've come to see you!"

She stooped low to lend him an arm for support. His arm was an ice-cold bone. The bony joints in his jagged, emaciated hand popped out like horns through his thin skin. Cafe-colored patches of skin covered the freckled back of his hand.

Tears streamed down her cheeks.

She helped him over to a seat that a prison guard brought in for her. She stood across from him, "General, you have suffered so much!"

Her mind went blank following a simple greeting. She could no longer recall the words she had carefully prepared. Her heart was too sorrowful. This was a situation she had never experienced before.

She opened up the fruit and snacks she had been permitted to bring in with her. The sweet fragrance from the fruit permeated the room. Falkenhausen sneezed over and over.

"General, please believe me when I say that your efforts to save Belgian hostages will never be erased. You must let this uplift you. I will come back often to visit you."

Falkenhausen could hardly believe his own ears, "Madame Qian, thank you. I am somebody who has already died a hundred times — it's too late for me now. I know how things work in prison. I thank you, but you shouldn't be here ever again."

His voice was frail, like a leaky bellows. But Qian Xiuling's words made his deep black eyes slowly illuminate.

"No, General. You must stay alive. You have the right to continue to live. You worked to encourage me at the time — you have to stay alive too! All those people you saved are all alive and well. They want to see you. They want you to be rescued just like them and see the light of freedom once more. You did your best to contribute to the peace of this world."

Tears dripped one by one from the dry wells of his eye sockets. He choked with sobs, turning his back toward her.

Qian Xiuling shared greetings from Zhuolun, and told him that his old friend, Jiang Jieshi, who once ruled Taiwan and had now retreated to the island of Taiwan, was also thinking of him. She brought up the matter of the 100,000 US dollars sent to him. Falkenhausen just blankly stared back at her for a while. Then his breathing suddenly quickened, his withered chest rising up and down like a kayak about to be swallowed up by a surging wave.

The predetermined time alloted for this visit quickly ran out. Then, he seemed to have been given a shot of morphine, Falkenhausen's spirits came alive in the blink of an eye. He stood up and accompanied her to the door.

While he was waving at her, that old general-like dignity and grace suddenly returned. His crooked back straightened up like a rod. The spectacle deeply moved Qian Xiuling. When she returned home, she told Gregory all about what she saw inside the prison. Gregory abruptly mumbled in response, "You're too prone to miracles."

What was that supposed to mean? Qian Xiuling was a bit upset. Don't tell me you think that a good person like Falkenhausen didn't deserve fairness and justice?

Dr. Gregory kneaded his hands. His silence was not ugly at all. Maybe conceptually, he and his Asian belle really didn't differ all that much. He knew that Falkenhausen was a good man. But, as a man, he also hoped his wife wouldn't expend so much energy on another man, even if he were old enough to be her father. Eliminating that unspeakable reasoning, there was nobody that would take pity on Enemy #1 — the risk was just too great. And public opinion would only repel it.

For him, that so-called hope gripped tightly by his Asian belle, was not only remote but downright dangerous. Her poor luck at KU Leuven didn't really surprise him, perhaps because in his unconscious mind, the ceiling for advancement for women was always a bit lower than men's. Since there was no hope for her promotion, maybe she would assume the more traditional roles of womanhood, maybe she would raise another child. After all, they had agreed that they would have five children.

In their husband-wife relationship, Qian Xiuling ordinarily relied on him. But on larger matters of principle, she was obviously much more intense and decisive. When those moments came, Perlinghi was used to retreating and compromising, not because he wished to passively observe from the sidelines, but because he needed silence to seek the understanding that he lacked.

Qian Xiuling wrote out a plan for herself:

(1) To convene a press meeting, where she would narrate to the media how Falkenhausen contributed to the rescue of hostages;

(2) To go to Ecaussinnes and Herbeumont to find the hostages that Falkenhausen saved and have them sign a petition;

(3) To write an article that expounded her point of view in support of Falkenhausen, and to publish it in Belgium's most influential outlet, *The Final One O'Clock Times*.

(4) To hire a lawyer who would defend Falkenhausen at crucial moments;

Besides all of this, she would need a lot of money.

They didn't have a lot of money saved. There were a lot of expenses with her four children too. And every month Gregory needed to put away a lot of money for his aging parents. Qian Xiuling knew about her own family's holdings, but when she brought up finances with Gregory, he would just answer, "No, no. You don't need to worry about financial issues."

He'd joke around with her, "Besides, 'money' is your last name! So, why worry about not having enough?"

Qian Xiuling went back to the prison again to pay General Falkenhausen a visit. She listened to him talk about his participation in the secret anti-Hitler organization in Germany. They had on more than one occasion tried to carry out assassinations. He told her that since 1933 he had begun to oppose Adolf Hitler. At the time there wasn't, strictly speaking, any organization in place. However, a few upright soldiers would gather in secret to discuss how to deal with the devil pushing Germany to the verge of the abyss.

It was like travelling down a dark tunnel with him. Inside there were all kinds of sinister beasts, torrents, whirlpools, and shoals that massive waves crashed upon and threatened to capsize your boat. Time was always too short. Every visit, it seemed like he had only just begun to tell his story when time would run out.

The result of this unfulfilled storytelling was that it forced the draft of an article that seemed difficult to publish. Commuting back and forth only made her feel uneasy. But there was a powerful voice inside of her — almost as if it didn't come from within her own heart, but from the borders of heaven — telling her to plead for Falkenhausen. The voice was honest, persistent, booming, resonant, and unrelenting in its persistence. Every word and sentence boomed like a drum, reverberating inside of her heart. She feared she couldn't contain the voice. She would hurry home and lock herself up inside of her study. She became the transcriber of that voice, recognizing that it came from the hall of heavenly justice. She didn't believe in God, but at that moment she knew for certain that there was a kind of righteous energy in the universe that could cut down the wicked in a stunning fashion.

She didn't know how many days she had been writing, but

she had produced a stack of papers for a draft. Qian Xiuling had completely lost herself in this work. After a thorough edit, she had reduced the article to 3000 or so Chinese characters. The newspaper editor, Mr. Staff, reminded her that the article shouldn't be very long. He explained with a prime example, "When you bring up the origin of clothing, you don't need to start from the planting of cotton."

The article was on the cusp of being published in *The Final One O'clock Times* under the title of "A True Anti-War Combattant — General Falkenhausen Saves Hostages."

She had determined to go for broke for General Falkenhausen. She handed the article over to the newspaper and then made the worst estimation for her own situation — end up in prison or maybe just be rebuffed by public opinion. The public unified in their opposition, satirizing, even slandering her. But she was prepared for that.

She and Gregory had a heartfelt conversation about it. She asked him, "What is the worst thing that can happen if I defend Falkenhausen?"

Gregory responded with a rhetorical question, "Is that what you've finally decided? Have you given yourself a path for retreat? Or, do you really have no doubts or hesitations?"

Qian Xiuling instantly fired back, "There is no turning back."

Gregory grabbed one of her hands, "At the very worst, we'll just move back to Herbeumont and open up a clinic."

Those two kind-hearted, greyish-brown eyes were suffused with warm light. They made Qian Xiuling feel like she was always a woman that could be counted on.

The newspaper finally published her article. The thing that annoyed her, though, was that a few essential points and details, such as her historical relationship to General Falkenhausen and his participation in the secret anti-Hitler organization, had been deleted.

She called up the editor, Mr. Staff, to express her displeasure. He had also graduated from KU Leuven the same year she did, from the Communications Department. They had met each other at a school party.

Mr. Staff felt hurt; he had already done everything he could. If it weren't for his editing, perhaps the article would've been compressed even further or would have never even made it to the printer.

The underlying meaning of what he was saying was that the newspaper's chief editor really did not agree with some of the views put forth in the piece. As an objective and neutral paper, they fundamentally should not have deleted the ideas of its author, but since this one involved Belgium's Enemy #1, the newspaper's authorities couldn't not consider the perceptions of their larger readership.

Later, he hemmed and hawed as he explained that soon after its publication, the editing office had received calls from its readers. Some were absolutely livid, some were coldly satirical. Some even said they'd like to meet this Madame Qian and give her a piece of their mind.

None of this was unexpected for Qian Xiuling. She said, "Alright ... I'm not afraid that there are those who do not agree. I'm only worried that there would be nobody interested at all."

Gregory returned home from work, not saying a word. This wasn't his usual demeanor. Qian Xiuling immediately perceived that something was on his mind. He wasn't very good at hiding things — good or bad, it was all written on his face. Qian Xiuling guessed that his mood had something to do with the article she had published. But she ignored it, acting like nothing had happened. One of Gregory's particular traits was that when he wanted to talk with you, he couldn't hold back; and when he didn't want to talk with you, he would die before pronouncing a single word.

But, in the evening, wrapped in his blanket, Qian Xiuling turned over to turn off the light and Gregory couldn't restrain himself any longer. He tugged on his Asian belle's arm, "Ling, we need to go back to Herbeumont village!"

She nuzzled up to his broad chest, and softly replied, "My dear, is the pressure of public opinion getting to be too much?"

Gregory didn't directly respond to her. He just said that he missed their old life back in Herbeumont.

Qian Xiuling would later find out about the head of the hospital where Gregory worked, a man named Cohen Nellis, who was a thoracic surgeon. Gregory adored the man. During World War II, four people in his family died in a single Nazi bomb attack. When he found out that that absurd article published in the paper was written by the hand of Gregory's wife, he unexpectedly called Gregory over for an exchange of words. Cohen was worked up and lost control of his emotions, naturally saying some unkind things. Gregory's silence from start to finish made him feel embarrassed. Finally, Gregory left him with this thought:

"Esteemed head of hospital, what can I do for you, then? Shall I call my wife over to debate the issue with you? I can tell you that it is not a sure thing that you would win."

He bowed courteously — something he rarely ever did — and then left. When he returned to his office, he grabbed a pen and paper and wrote his resignation. The hastily written resignation letter quickly arrived on the desk of the head of hospital.

The secretary of the head of hospital, a young man with red hair and a face full of freckles, nervously found Gregory and stated on behalf of the head of hospital that their confrontation was limited to their topic of discussion and had nothing to do with Dr. Gregory's remarkable work and perfect service day in and day out. Cohen Nellis was deeply pleased with his work and wouldn't sign his letter of resignation.

This one was of those occasional instances where the cautious and staid Dr. Gregory showed his irritability. For shrewd people like him, you can only decipher this as an upright act. But Qian Xiuling's viewpoint on it was that Brussels was the frontline in her battle. She couldn't leave. She could only give him a satisfactory response for what he'd done. She told him that she couldn't overexert herself, or antagonize the enemy too much.

In fact, that head of hospital didn't actually have a divergence of opinion with them. It was only because there had been too much cover-up regarding people like Falkenhausen. China had an old expression, "Even if you jump into the Yellow River, you could never wash yourself clean." Letting an innocent man serve as the sacrificial lamb for an era was one of the oldest tricks in history. Wasn't it wrong to concentrate all the hatred for the Nazis upon the head of one war criminal? Qian Xiuling felt no fear about the expected explosive controversy on her doorstep. Quite the contrary, she seemed invigorated by the potential conflict.

An unexpected guest paid her a visit. At first, Qian Xiuling didn't take the forty-something-year-old woman very seriously. At that time, there were always people getting easily excited and coming to visit her, mostly to debate with her. Sometimes it was actually quite hilarious, they were all utterly sincere, but also mostly neurotic, saying they had trouble sleeping. They were easily angered and didn't agree that an old German should be forgiven and let off the hook, as if she were the one to swing the gavel and pass judgement as his grand judge. Then when they noticed just how long they'd be ranting, they would walk away in a cloud of curses.

But this visit was nothing like those times. You couldn't say that she wasn't pleasant to look at, but you couldn't tell from her manners whether she was well-to-do or not. She wore normal clothing, and when she smiled, the signs of having passed through trials climbed up into her cheeks and around the rims of her eyes. She was gentle and sophisticated. The rhythm of her words and movements were all a bit measured and slow.

> She was tall and slim and introduced herself as she passed through the door. Her name was Cecile Vent, born in 1906, married in May 1926, later divorced. Due to her anti-Nazi work during World War II, she was honored with Belgium's National Hero medal of honor. She and her entire family despised the Nazis to the core. However, after reading Qian Xiuling's article, she was deeply moved by the type of supranational and supraethnic justice sensibility possessed by General Falkenhausen. She had been arrested by the Gestapo, and a friend had found General Falkenhausen to plead for her release.
>
> (Zhang Yawen, *Gambling with the Devil*)

To Cecile's surprise, there were other people in the game too, and deeply at that. The only way she found out about it, however, was by unexpectedly reading Qian Xiuling's article. Qian Xiuling was dumbfounded for a moment. She had underestimated the power of her words — no wonder all those Humanists walk around so proud and arrogant.

Cecile Vent got right to the point and said that she had fallen in love with Falkenhausen. This middle-aged woman, while meeting a total stranger for the first time, confessed to falling in love with a German war criminal. She feared no taboos, obviously, and surprisingly she didn't make her counterpart feel like she was being rude. Whether it was the power of love or experiencing life and death scenarios, it was all worthless stuff to her; honor, fame and the like held little importance for her. She even said that if he was let out of prison, she would go with him, even to the ends of the earth. No, in actuality, when she finished Qian Xiuling's article, she had already melded with him spiritually.

Qian Xiuling cherished her visit. That one exchange instantly reduced the distance between them. As Cecile recounted her story, Xiuling realized how many of the world's most marvelous things begin at the root of the heart.

That's exactly right! Ms. Cecile Vent had been deeply struck by General Falkenhausen. She put down the paper that had changed her destiny and felt the compulsion to go visit the general in prison surge within her. Sadly, she didn't have the kind of status or accomplishments of Qian Xiuling. Her first attempt at visiting the prison quickly ended in failure. The prison guards outside of the gate simply brushed her off. Sitting there at the prison, Cecile knew that that place was no walk in the park, where a simple ticket could let you freely walk out. But she saw no other way to go about it. She was eager, and the wonderfully prepared foods she brought with her were sent back with her over and over.

The second and third times she risked a visit ended no differently. Later on, a guard who felt sorry for her secretly gave her a hand. He allowed her to leave some of that delicious, mouth-watering food. Of course, barely a tenth of it made it into the hands of Falkenhausen. Nobody told him who it was that had shown him the kindness. This happened over and over, increasing Falkenhausen's bewilderment. For the life of him he couldn't believe that a Belgian woman whom he had never met before was outside the high walls of the prison pacing back and forth. You might say it was his "luck with ladies," but it is better described as a bit of sunshine thrown down on him from a regretful God.

"Do you have any idea how old General Falkenhausen is?"

Qian Xiuling asked her subtly. Cecile Vent immediately shot back.

"I know what you're getting at. My former husband was just two years older than me. But his views were stuck in the Middle Ages."

Her expression communicated to Qian Xiuling that age was not a problem for her.

"Does your family agree with this?" Qian Xiuling unconsciously grew a bit worried for her.

"Not a single one approves. However, that's not a problem at all. I'm the kind of person whom death bothers. Truly, if it weren't for General Falkenhausen's rescue efforts, I would've already left this world in 1943."

She spoke very frankly — not a single oblique comment. When she looked at you, her gaze was fixed and sharp. What seemed unimaginable, though, was that somebody with her experience could still discover love, and in such a passionate, irresistible way. Maybe it was a form of unrequited longing — who knows. It filled Qian Xiuling with new emotion.

In the end, she placed a fat envelope into Qian Xiuling's hand.

"I trust you. You can open it and read it, if you like."

Her expression was calm and confident as she handed the letter to Qian Xiuling. It made her feel like this person had been waiting around the corner for Falkenhausen to appear, and would never leave until he did.

"Don't worry. I'll deliver it untouched to the General, and

speedily at that."

Xiuling placed it on her chest. She was sincerely moved.

However, Qian Xiuling was struck by the fact that Falkenhausen coldly reacted to the news at first. He said to Qian Xiuling that he had recently been receiving a number of things coming into the prison — food, and even underwear (the weird thing was that it actually fit him!). When Qian Xiuling explained things to him, he suddenly struggled to stand up, and blurted, "I don't wish to see this person. Tell her that she must stop!"

His expression was cold, like a frozen, weathered statue. Qian Xiuling understood his meaning. He was on death row. Longing for him was wasted effort. This made Qian Xiuling think that the most sorrowful darkness was nothing compared to that which adapts to the darkness, and the most frightening darkness was the detachment and abandonment of the light in the darkness.

She didn't respond to his comments. After a short while, she removed the letter she had hidden in a pocket against her chest and handed it to him.

Falkenhausen hesitated for a moment as he took the letter, almost as if what he was taking was an answer to a fathomless riddle.

It took him great effort to open the letter. It looked quite long, containing a lot of pages with characters written in a handsome script. He read it slowly, stopping at times to take a breath.

"No more than a fantasy." He mumbled with his eyes closed.

He seemed like somebody who had spent far too long in the darkness. When light suddenly floods in, they can't even open their eyes.

"She is very sincere. She's just like you — she's been through the trials of life of death as well."

Qian Xiuling tactfully urged him on, "It would be nice for more than one person to support you, right?"

"I owe too much to women in this life. I can't bear to think of bringing harm to one more woman on my deathbed!"

His voice no longer sounded so feeble, his breath taking on a great deal more weight and substance. Though his complexion was still dark and gloomy, a forceful ray of light shone through his eyes. Qian Xiuling decoded his words, naturally thinking from the opposite of his meaning. Supposing it was merely a stagnant pool, tossing large stones into it wouldn't produce waves. On the other hand, only an ocean is capable of turning disturbed waters into perilous waves in a storm.

It was clear that General Falkenhausen was slowly coming back to life.

He was still grasping, but that didn't seem to matter. He would slowly come along. Even though he didn't want to hear Qian Xiuling talk any more about that nonsense, she didn't take offense. But she reminded him that that woman was always thinking of him and pacing outside of the high walls of the prison and that she was not only somebody he had saved, but that she was also his most powerful supporter. She was using the limits of her own powers to tell others who didn't know the truth all about the things that this genuine anti-war warrior had done for the people of Belgium.

Qian Xiuling had a new way of interpreting Cecile Vent's appearance after all of this — in a woman's life, it was extremely difficult to run into someone who truly stirred her soul. Cecile Vent had of her own volition knocked on the door of life to see how she could as a woman throw open the rusted doors of death onto new life. She awakened a heart that had once died within her to activate another soul on the brink of death. How was this not a kind of mutual salvation?!

Falkenhausen let out a long sigh, expelling years of pent-up frustration and emotion that had been swirling around inside his chest, consuming all of his energies and slowly reducing him to a walking corpse. He exerted a massive amount of energy and finally expelled it all out. That wave of air and energy swirled around in the cramped prison cell, finally coming to rest where it hung for a while overhead like a heavy cloud.

His body seemed to relax tremendously.

"Pardon me, but can you help me open up this window?"

Sadly, that pathetic little window hanging on the wall of his prison cell was too high for Qian Xiuling's little stature to reach. Maybe the window wasn't meant to be opened at all, which is why it had been placed so high up in the first place.

"Huh ... Until today, I really didn't know that there was a window in this cell," he said, somewhat embarrassed.

As she was parting, he mentioned once again, "Please don't bring up that woman any more with me, alright?"

Qian Xiuling understood what Falkenhausen was trying to say, since his first wife had passed away, he had left his affections buried in the grave with her.

Nonetheless, their meeting had given Xiuling a strong sense of accomplishment.

When she met again with Cecile Vent, Qian Xiuling recounted events fairly cautiously and solemnly. She wasn't going to exaggerate any of the "success" she had sensed, but she also wanted Cecile to feel that there were some glimmers of hope. Luckily, Cecile wasn't one to give up easily. She knew this was going to be very difficult, so she remained quite dignified. This was Falkenhausen, after all — a true and loyal man. Cecile had time, and she had even more patience. From the moment she stepped into Qian Xiuling's house, she had set her foot on a one-way path.

The key phrase that followed was, "Let the court proceedings commence."

From September 1950 to January 1951, within the span of four months, the highest court in the land held 56 court sessions to try Falkenhausen for his crimes.

The tide of controversy almost capsized the entire Belgian nation. The mainstream desire to execute Falkenhausen argued forcefully and with conviction, drowning out every other voice.

On the other hand, the voice in defense of Falkenhausen was quite small. If you didn't carefully incline an ear, you almost couldn't hear its feeble sound. Its resonance was not enough to win over an audience. However, when that storytelling Asian woman began speaking, the entire room fell silent.

The royal couple, prime minister, trusted aids and ministers from above, and the common people of Brussels from below all knew that this Chinese woman had received the National Hero medal of honor. They fumed with rage when they realized that she was the one who had spared no effort to defend the German war criminal.

However, the most dismaying thing was that the entire situation was a bit chaotic. The clamor was almost entirely lopsided. Everywhere, constituents were gnashing their teeth, aligned in hatred to exact revenge upon a common enemy. Heroes, victims and their family members, bit players, politicians, speculators, the employers of the former puppet regime all wanted to use this opportunity to clear their own names. If they didn't execute Falkenhausen, how would they be able to purge themselves of hatred and revenge and reestablish peace in their nation?!

The unanimous position seemed to be that the people of this once vassal state of the Nazis actually had some fire in them all along and that they were now standing up out of the ruins of their collective injuries. They needed a guillotine to offer a sacrifice to all the innocent victims and to assert their dignified selflessness and honest courage.

But that guillotine shouldn't be used on the head of somebody who did their best to help and to rescue brave hostages on the precipice of death, otherwise the act would become a new disgrace for the Belgian nation.

Qian Xiuling took those words and wrote them into Falkenhausen's defense. Dr. Gregory believed her approach was too extreme. She needed to temper her rhetoric a bit. But Qian Xiuling insisted on her point of view. There was a constant vague ringing in her mind. It wasn't an alarm, but rather the funerary knell of a poor soul who had been unjustly treated.

Fortunately, her defense was not the write-up of a solitary defendant's personal opinion. Every point was backed up by discoverable supports. She had gone to Ecaussinnes and tracked down one by one every single hostage that Falkenhausen had saved and asked them to sign their name to the document. She also went to Herbeumont where Roger's entire family solemnly added their names to Falkenhausen's defense. There were also other survivors, whose names she couldn't remember, who had come in from the surrounding area asking her what she needed them to do, or offering to testify at the court proceedings. "If a good person who saved our lives was being vainly sent to his death, then this truly is the disgrace of Belgium, and our own disgrace too!"

The day of the last court session was quickly arriving. Qian Xiuling and Cecile Vent received permission to go to the prison for a visit together. She noticed that Cecile was quite nervous, like a young maiden who had never fallen in love before, going on her first date.

She walked sluggishly behind Qian Xiuling. They registered their IDs, passed through inspection, and then waited for their notification to meet with the prisoner. When she walked up those ice-cold granite stairs, turned down a long hall, passed through a long tunnel, and finally entered that low and dark cell, Cecile Vent received a shock to her system. Her heart began to pound and her body convulsed, sweat pouring down her entire body. Then, she froze in place. Qian Xiuling was scared at first, but she took Cecile Vent by the arm and helped her lean up against a wall. She was about to call for someone but Cecile Vent stopped her. Cecile calmed down and said, "I suddenly felt like I was returning to the past, the nightmare of my former life, where every minute was filled with torture. Everything about this place feels exactly like where I was locked up."

She said that she didn't want to meet General Falkenhausen that day. She would just terrify him in her present state.

"But the general is expecting you today. The prison has already informed him of your visit. Let's just rest a bit before we go on. We'll delay the meeting for a half an hour. I'll explain things to the prison guards."

"No, no. I'm really not in good shape. I beg you. I promise it'll be better next time."

She seemed like a drowning swimmer grasping for life. She tightly gripped Qian Xiuling's hand, her eyes helpless and mournful.

Qian Xiuling couldn't help but support her, walking outside the prison walls one step at a time. The air outside was heavy. Cecile Vent was as fragile as a sheet of paper, and cold to the touch. This always confidently outspoken — practically overbearing — woman had suddenly turned frail right before her eyes. It was an incredible thing to witness.

Abandoning their visit midway revealed something to Qian

Xiuling: Cecile Vent and General Falkenhausen would someday be together. They both had brushed shoulders with death a number of times, but what was similarly different about them that also illuminated their relationship? For a time, she had a hard time expressing what it was, but she could distinctly sense it. She believed that if she could get the two of them to grasp hands and walk toward a free and blessed earth, it would be one of her greatest accomplishments and satisfactions in life.

Decades later, Qian Xiuling's nephew, Qian Xianhe, the son of Qian Zhuoru, recalled the following:

> My aunt seldom talked about it, but one time she mentioned running around to defend General Falkenhausen. At the time, she had already prepared herself for the worst, like maybe being stripped of her national honor, or being sent to prison. But she wasn't frightened in the least. She said, "If Falkenhausen is put to death, then the scales of justice have lost their calibration. I'm the kind of person that lives by their convictions. If my values are stripped from me, I would turn into the walking dead."

January 27th, 1951.

When that final court session began, nobody could tell what was going to happen to Falkenhausen. But those in the know had an inkling. The endless court sessions had already begun to wear down people's hearts. It was extremely rare in Belgium's history that a four-star general from an invading nation had been killed. If they dispensed with his life, it could in one fell swoop rouse the nation and heal their rancor.

The atmosphere in the courtroom that day had completely

changed. There were a ton of people, and a lot of new faces. They say that they had rushed in from Ecaussinnes and Herbeumont and other places. There was an old christian priest seated in a wheelchair as well. It wasn't easy for him to move about, but he insisted on making his way there, and he was holding a placard he had made himself in support of Falkenhausen with his own signature: Father Stefan. There was a young man who was pushing his wheelchair. It was his son-in-law, Roger.

When Falkenhausen was brought in, he hardly drew any attention from anyone. It was because the scenario wasn't at all impressive; in most people's estimation, Falkenhausen was merely a broken body struggling with its final breaths of life. He trembled as he made his way forward to the defendant's seat. He then sat down and gently closed his eyes, not moving at all, as if he were meditating. Afterward, he told Qian Xiuling that he felt absolutely awful that day. He could already see that hangman's noose swinging before him on the scaffold. All of those prior court sessions had little by little sapped him of his will and determination, obliterating that little accumulated pitiful light he had stored in his heart. Just let it all come, then! Death wasn't really the thing he feared, it was that so many Belgians would never understand what it was that he had done. That would be the sole regret that he took with him into the next world.

The attendees ignored the tediously long court process to fix their gaze upon that yellow-skinned, black-haired, white-toothed Asian woman, Madame Qian. Her tall husband was sitting next to her. He looked completely calm and composed, but his forehead was glistening with sweat. Qian Xiuling sat upright, exactly at the center of the defense team. She was wearing a black and white jacket, and had a simple Asian woman's ornament in her hair. The folder in her hand was thick with documents. The crowd noticed that her confident expression seemed mostly to come from those documents, despite the fact that from beginning to end, she rarely had need of them. When those words of testimony had matured in her heart, the folder became more of a decoration than anything else.

The high judge called the defense's Mrs. Gregory Perlinghi, Qian Xiuling, to make her final remarks. The courtroom went silent, like they'd stepped into a lonely valley.

One couldn't just stand up there and tell stories: these people had already lived through the war, so no matter how fantastic the tale, it would surely fall on deaf ears. Qian Xiuling knew all this too well.

As a result, Qian Xiuling chose a scenario where she wouldn't take on the tone of a storyteller, but one that would lead the listeners into a memory, the final time that she went to beg General Falkenhausen at the break of dawn to save those 96 hostages. She explained that General Falkenhausen was risking his life by signing the pardon of those hostages teetering on the brink of an execution order. The Gestapo had a wiretap next door and he was clearly aware of his situation, but he didn't hesitate for a second.

> I saw those shadows swaying outside of the General's office. I found out later that they were in possession of a personal order from Hitler, permitting them to arrest him at any moment. General Falkenhausen could have sought a way out for himself, but I saw with my own eyes how he stayed there until the last possible moment, stalwart and fearless.
> He told me I needn't thank him but that it was he who needed to thank all of those brave resistance fighters. Since 1933, he had been a part of the anti-Hitler faction. What those hostages did at risk to their lives was identical to what he too wished to accomplish.

Afterward, she read aloud the document jointly signed by the rescued hostages. As she read each name, a person slowly stood up in the courtroom, making themselves known to all in attendance.

Following the reading, all the witnesses filed in front of Falkenhausen and reverently bowed before him.

Qian Xiuling was stunned ... This was not something she had planned. Nobody could have rehearsed such a display.

Falkenhausen lost control of his emotions and broke out in sobs.

Commotion took over the courtroom as journalists surged forward to snap their photographs and the bailiffs struggled to hold them back. A number of people applauded, although not with much enthusiasm. The sacred high judge was also a bit moved by all this. The jury's dignified faces were now flushed — emotional moments could be quite contagious.

It was indeed a fine display, but it was no Hollywood production, rather a genuine and contemporary Belgian saga. The people dimly reviewed that when their government was in exile in England, their people used their own methods to resist executions, while the highest officer of the occupying forces disregarded his own life and safety by repeatedly rescuing the lives of selfless resistance warriors.

Originally, they had thought that when Falkenhausen arrived at court that he would act just like the former German Viceroy dispatched to Netherlands, Arthur Seyss-Inquart, pleading and weeping as he was sent off to the hanging post. But, the plot had taken an unexpected turn: not only were the testimonies given true and reliable, they were also irrefutable. That dual PhD of chemistry and physics, Qian Xiuling, had never studied law, but her skillful use of evidence to make her case was unassailable.

The honorable judge had to declare a short 15-minute recess.

Cecile Vent kept her eyes fixed on General Falkenhausen. She wanted so badly to walk over to him and give him a handkerchief, and to pour him a cup of water. Though the honorable judge permitted nobody to approach him, Cecile was still enjoying the aura of his presence. Her heart was beating furiously, her blood racing through her body. Qian Xiuling's argument and the arrival of the witnesses on the scene to testify and perform their coordinated bow followed each other like waves on top of one another, crashing into the stagnant waters of General Falkenhausen's heart and reactivating his will to live.

Cecile Vent requested to make the final statement as a witness. Her tone was mild and serene, not one would expect from a witness at the trial of a war criminal, but more like from a performer reciting Shakespearean sonnets. It didn't resemble her usual way of speaking. Nobody knew how much she had painstakingly prepared for this moment. She was laying herself bare instead of putting on a brave show. From her tiniest corner of the room, she expounded on her admiration for her rescuer, emphasizing how General Falkenhausen gave her a second life, bestowing her with light and warmth, bestowing her with courage to live on. Returning innocence and freedom to General Falkenhausen was the only way to demonstrate the power of justice in this civilized world.

> When I was released from prison, for a time, I was lost in a fog of depression. I even contemplated killing myself. The only power that helped overcome my sickness and my own self was that one person who extended his hand to aid me. I originally thought that his name was only a symbol to me, a metaphor for the benevolent hand of the Lord. I never thought that he was an obscured and deeply aggrieved man — worse yet a man who had been subjected to inhumane

torment for a long time, and yet was still tenaciously holding onto life. I had assumed in the past that if I lived well that would be the best way to repay him and show my gratitude. But when I discovered his circumstances, I suddenly realized that every day I continued to live while my rescuer suffered was torture to me. I had never seen him before, but I imagined what he was like. Today, in this court, I have finally laid eyes on him. He truly is a pitiful creature! If the court really wishes to condemn him to death, then fairness and justice will topple into the fathomless abyss. I use my feeble voice to beg the court — your Honor, this distinguished jury — that if this dignified institution insists on executing the defendant that they allow me to take his place. I wish to make it crystal clear once more that a man who has given so many a second chance at life should be deemed innocent.

She choked with sobs, her body convulsing as she failed to complete her statement. She leaned against the banister of the witness box, insisting on finishing the final words of her testimony, her face streaming with tears.

Qian Xiuling's eyes welled up with tears as well. She looked at General Falkenhausen, whose face was glistening in the light. His crooked back straightened up as Cecile Vent spoke.

The courtroom filled with intense applause. The jurors, who had for a longtime remained haughty and aloof, were suddenly marginalized and estranged by this most fundamental expression. A reporter on the scene, Staff, recorded this in his "A Witness in the Courtroom":

That day in court, the jurors added physical movement to their repertoire: applause for the defense Mrs. Perlinghi Madame Qian Xiuling, and its witness Ms. Cecile Vent This was an aberrant and unfamiliar labor for them — they'd never clapped before in court. But watching them applaud, you would think it was perfectly natural to them, apart from their flushed faces. They looked like they had just come out of a luxurious theatre following an incredibly convincing Shakespearean performance that had swallowed them up in its drama.

When the hearing adjourned, Cecile Vent rushed over to Qian Xiuling and apologized profusely. She felt like she had stolen the show and upstaged Xiuling's defense, drawing everyone's attention to her.

"But I didn't mean it! I am with you — I only wanted to save him."

Qian Xiuling embraced her, "You dummy, who did you upstage?! You won over the jury! Did you see the tears streaming down the general's face?!"

The next day, every major newspaper in Brussels put out photos of the court hearing. In addition to a weeping Falkenhausen, two other ladies' photos appeared: Qian Xiuling's and a smaller picture of Cecile Vent.

The Final One O'Clock Times reported the following on Qian Xiuling:

> She solemnly performed her role as the executive producer. She easily ran away with the script prepared by the judge, calmly manipulating the rhythm of the entire scene. The arrival of those witnesses gave that thick folder before her

an irrefutable power. But her final strike was not hers — the most arousing 145 seconds of the hearing came from the mouth of an unknown woman, a certain Cecile Vent, once condemned to death, but whose life was owed to General Falkenhausen's intervention. Her testimony became the most powerful support in Madame Gregory Perlinghi's defense.

Waiting on the news was torturous.

Qian Xiuling and Cecile Vent were still quite optimistic. Although that trial on January 27th had twisted General Falkenhausen's fortunes, the challenging verdict was not entirely what they had hoped for.

Falkenhausen had been sentenced to 12 years hard labor.

The phone call came from Cecile Vent. She had caught a cold, and her nose was stuffed up and her throat a little hoarse. Though the decision wasn't especially bad, it was still worse than they had hoped for.

They originally thought that Falkenhausen would be declared innocent and set free. In fact, though, there were some machinations behind the scenes that Qian Xiuling had no way of grasping. Sometimes the honor of a nation works exactly the same as the honor of a person. The kingdom of Belgium could never in any case let an invader walk away so innocently and easily, not to mention the fact the countless attacks against Falkenhausen for being an invader and causing all that injury to Belgium had never let up. He was, after all, answerable for that destruction. Every voice emitted by the national machine had to be steady and cautious, not a disgraced footnote. As a result, a 12-year prison sentence was issued after the appropriate high-level figures took everyone's demands into account. They believed it was a rather suitable price to pay. As for whether a 73-year-old

Falkenhausen could make it through 4,380 days and nights in a dark and gloomy prison was a mystery for fortune to tend to.

Qian Xiuling still felt dismayed about the sentence. She hosted Cecile Vent at her home again. She had just returned from visiting Falkenhausen. She had become quite the celebrity — everyone in Brussels knew her, and everybody in the prison was quite lenient with her, given all factors. She mentioned that Falkenhausen's spirits weren't nearly as bad as she imagined. He was eating three meals a day, a few slices of bread with some caviar and sausage. The prison had, in fact, improved his diet. They were also permitting him to read the daily news, *The Fimal One O'clock Time*.

"I can wait for him until he makes it out of prison. Then, we'll grow old together. I tell him that he needs to walk 1,000 steps every day when he goes out into the yard. And I do the same. From this day forward, I'm going to begin jogging, otherwise, what am I going to do to occupy myself while I wait?"

Qian Xiuling pitied the straight-talking Cecile as she shared this news with her. She had noticed that Cecile was wearing athletic wear and a pair of running shoes. Her energy seemed nothing like before, either. People could truly be molded by one another; Cecile Vent's second spring had already begun.

She felt gratified. Even Dr. Gregory felt a sense of success.

During an interview held two weeks later, Qian Xiuling decided to pay a visit to Falkenhausen with her husband. They prepared to bring some things with them, too: a towel, soap, toothpaste, underwear, etc. The always attentive Gregory also brought a magnifying glass with him. Before they set out, the phone rang. It was Cecile Vent.

"He's been released!"

She then burst into tears of joy!

How could this possibly be? They stared at each other, wondering if Cecile was suffering a hysterical episode.

They rushed to the Prison. A prison guard familiar to Qian Xiuling told her, "Our cute little nation has already made peace with Germany, so that German general you've come to see has already been released."

Tears poured down from Qian Xiuling's eyes. She embraced Gregory, "My darling, please tell me I'm not dreaming!"

CHAPTER 15

People Come When They shouldn't, and Leave When They shouldn't

They had to leave. Falkenhausen and Cecile Vent were first driving to Wiesbaden, the capital of Germany's black forest region, and then continuing on to the small village of Schoenfield. That was where Falkenhausen's first wife, Wedderkop, was laid to rest. Cecile Vent had prepared fresh flowers and a little evergreen sapling. They were going to pay their respects to her and tell her all about what had happened since her passing.

Their final stopping point was in Falkenhausen's hometown, the small border town of Nassau, Germany.

During the farewell, Gregory noticed the sadness in his Asian belle. He gently leaned into her ear and said, "We must be happier! Could we have imagined a result any more perfect than today's? The old man is free, and he found love to boot! The Lord has rained his grace down upon this old man," he said, looking up at the drizzle falling from the sky.

"Are you envious?" She looked at him and responded half-jokingly.

"To be honest, maybe a little ... But, I am still very happy for them."

His sincerity and earnestness made Qian Xiuling smile.

They saw the two of them off that day, Qian Xiuling, Gregory and their youngest daughter, Yadana. She was a super cute, mixed-race child with fair skin and golden hair. Falkenhausen picked her up the moment he saw her and carried her around, telling her little secrets until it was time for him to climb into the car.

Cecile pulled Qian Xiuling to the side, "He loves children. Sadly, he never could have his own in this life. He wanted me to pass on to you that you should have another child — you and Dr. Gregory should have five children."

Qian Xiuling laughed. She turned around and saw Falkenhausen and Gregory whispering to each other. She then saw him open up his palm and lift up five fingers. Gregory let out a pleasant laugh.

Qian Xiuling knew what they were discussing.

Falkenhausen embraced the couple. He couldn't stop huge teardrops from flowing down his shriveled face. Perhaps he felt like this farewell was occurring at the ends of the earth, that he didn't have many years left and wouldn't be stepping onto Belgian soil ever again.

Qian Xiuling raised her hands in a gesture of prayer as the car's exhaust billowed out, mouthing quietly, "Be at peace, good people."

She wrote Zhuolun a very long letter that day. She believed that he would be thrilled to learn the news that Falkenhausen had obtained his freedom. But two weeks passed and she still hadn't received a reply.

One evening, she suddenly received a long-distance call from Zhuolun in Taiwan. He told her that there had been an incident in the family.

What was it?!

In April, 1949, Qian Zhuolun had unexpectedly received a call from Jiang Jieshi's second wife, Song Meiling. She chatted with him about mundane family affairs, as well as some things she had learned from experience. Then she told him something crucial,

"The old man says that when we get to Taiwan that I need to continue my studies with Mr. Qipei. I shouldn't be carelessly fiddling around with calligraphy like I've been doing."

Qian Zhuolun remembered their studies together — it was such a long time ago. But old things were now being revisited. He grasped the implied meaning of her words.

He was nothing more than a vice admiral — by no means an intimidating title. Why was the Lady making a personal phone call to him? It was because he still owed her a favor. It was also because Jiang Jieshi feared that he might have been drawn in by the Communists. He had asked his wife to call him as a way of honoring him and ringing an alarm bell.

They all needed to go to Taiwan. The Lady was hoping that Zhuolun would clearly state his position.

Thus, during their call, Zhuolun shared his thoughts and affirmed his loyalties, saying that he would definitely bring his entire family to the island of obscure fortunes. There would be no hesitation or regret.

Although the detail that Falkenhausen had disclosed to him all those years ago was enough to overturn his so-called "leak," most of the time, Zhuolun just accepted it all as a mistaken communication. After all, he had been with Mr. Jiang for so many years that he assumed the general must still regard him as a loyal supporter.

Taking stock of his family situation, Zhuolun had four sons and two daughters with his two wives. His eldest was Xianzhang, known as Keshun, who had been serving in the Nationalist army for quite some time, and by 1948 had reached the rank of lieutenant colonel. His second eldest son was Xianming, known also as Kexian, who, after graduating from Fudan University's news department, worked as a journalist on the *Mopping-Up News* for the Nationalist army and then went to Taiwan to be a journalist with the Central News Agency. His wife Wang Yaojun was a former colleague of his, and was also from Yixing County, China.

Zhuolun's second wife was from Suzhou, who gave him two daughters, whom he doted on terribly. His military peers all envied the full house of children he had fathered.

From May 1949 on, the Nationalist army retreated in succession from Shanghai, Qingdao, and Fuzhou. The United States issued a white paper, declaring their abandonment of the Republic of China. Next, the army retreated from Guangzhou and Xiamen in October. The lesser Zhuge, Bai Chongxi, and the notorious "Anti-Communist Great Wall," Hu Zongnan, went on to suffer defeat after defeat, as well, losing central China, northwest China, and southwest China. In December, Zhuolun followed the government apparatus in its retreat to Taipei.

When they arrived in Taipei, housing for a time was strained — life had been turned completely upside down. According to his military rank as vice admiral, the Department of Defense provided him with a large home that looked quite spacious, but because of the size of his family, it was actually insufficient. Some of the generals secretly went among the inhabitants and purchased homes. At the time, the citizens of Taiwan were rather poor, and their houses weren't

Qian Xianming and Wang Yaojun as a couple

that expensive. Land in the outskirts of the city was even cheaper. Some high-ranking generals enclosed their own land and constructed their own housing, which, compared to purchasing a ready-made home, was a great deal cheaper. When Jiang Jieshi discovered this, he flew into a rage. Qian Zhuolun knew the general had a jealous and sensitive heart. At any and every occasion, he would stress over and over the need to take back the mainland while his officers were all building homes and putting down roots in Taiwan! In order to preserve peace in the family, Zhuolun had difficulty in trying to convince everyone that they must overcome hardship and continue to live cramped in the quarters that the Department of Defense had assigned to them. He and his wife's master bedroom had only one bed and one table, and measured only a few square meters.

One time, an older subordinate came over to visit him. He sighed deeply as he explained the treatment that subordinate officers had to endure, "This is too difficult to bear! All our family members who migrated from the mainland have no place to live. The most they can do is split bamboo and weave walls, cover them in lime — they call it 'bamboo bones and mud skin' — and then salvage a sheet of galvanized metal for a roof. Because it rains so much here, the metal roof rusts right away, causing rust residue to drip into our dinner bowls! Wives and children all squeeze into a single-room home with a door, but no windows. In summer, it's like a steamer basket, and then during the monsoon season, you have to close your doors and then run the risk of poisoning."

Qian Zhuolun used this description to encourage his family members. Compared to the visitor's conditions, theirs seemed pretty good. At the same time, he understood the declining morale of the soldiers.

At one meeting for high-ranking officers, as Jiang Jieshi was raining curses upon all those generals who had purchased their own houses and property, he suddenly turned the conversation to Zhuolun: "Comrade Qian Zhuolun has 20 mouths to feed in his family. They're all crammed into a Department of Defense living quarter and he has never once complained. He lives the Huangpu Academy spirit and understands the revolutionary sensibility, choosing to sleep on sticks and drink vinegar for the cause ..."

Qian Zhuolun was alarmed. Cold sweat dripped down his back.

After the meeting, his old classmate General Chen Cheng, then serving as Premier of Taiwan, sent him some rather subtle musings, "Brother Qipei, though the Chairman is burdened with a million worries, he still seems not to have forgotten you!"

He grasped the subtlety of Chen Cheng's meaning, but pretended not to understand. This vice admiral of 24 years for the Republic of China hadn't made any forward progress in rank for 15 full years. If you know somebody's backstory, you know where their sore spots were too. Not long after arriving in Taiwan, there was a massive reshuffle in the Department of Defense. Zhuolun was no longer serving as a provincial head, but was promoted to the position of Director of Senior Staff. After a number of years, his eldest son Qian Keshun wrote the following in his paper, "The Life of My Deceased Father Qian Zhuolun":

> On the first day of the third month of the 39th year of the Republic, after having reviewed the ranks and examined matters, President Jiang moved my father to take over the Department of Defense's directorship of senior staff. In order to take back the mainland, he was to act according to the orders and research of Japanese forces and mobilization,

to organize the mobilization research team and the Japanese record instructional consultants, to research Japanese records and the Eighteen Year Ground Forces Plan Order, and finally to formulate the mobilization of Chinese ground forces and every rule pertaining thereto.

In short, he seemed to be quite busy. But everybody knew that the principal work of this hollow position was to supply Jiang Jieshi with the basis for every kind of decree associated with taking back the mainland. Within its hollowness was something not so hollow, but inside that not so hollow, how great was the hollowness!

Keshun had been enlisted in the army for a number of years and had already achieved the rank of colonel, and was serving some role in some unit. He didn't often return home. Kexian, his second son, the journalist, ran around everywhere for his work and often had a great deal of free time. He would return home to drink tea with his father and prattle on about this and that. He would always inadvertently tell his father about all the chatter happening on the mainland, most of it elevating his emotions.

For example, that one old classmate of his, Song Guozhong, the one who had saved his life while swimming, and had come over to chat and drink with his other friend that one evening that led to Zhuolun's panic and terrible luck. He had taken up the position of deputy commander of a PLA unit, and then later died in battle at Taiyuan. His other classmate, Liu Shizhao, the one nicknamed Liu Big Pants, had become part of a diplomatic military attaché somewhere in eastern Europe.

In his regret, Qian Zhuolun felt greatly astonished. Those two fellow students who had gathered around his hearth, were, in the end, part of the Communist Party. He employed his skill for meticulous thought to probe deeper into just why and how they had so perfectly set him up in his home, waiting for him to return from his meeting, and then using their old ties and drinking habits to pry open his mouth and with hardly any difficulty extract the intelligence they needed and walk away without a second thought?

The answer was like a super thin sheet of paper — one poke and it was punctured. In the end, he had to stop himself from probing too deeply. His heart was too heavy and tense.

The news that Kexian brought him also included information from the time before the Nationalists withdrew from the mainland, regarding the whereabouts of those high-ranking officers who had defected to the Communists: Cheng Qian, Chen Mingren, Tao Zhiyue, Dong Qiwu, etc. In Kexian's dramatic retelling of affairs, those officials who had finally "seen the light" had all been treated well and been given important positions by the Communist Party.

Father and son were extremely close. At first, Qian Zhuolun made no effort to take precautions when speaking with him, but as time slowly went on, he began to sense that his son was coming to him with prebaked topics and scripted approaches to get at something.

He sensed the point was to show him a pathway to return to the homeland and seek asylum among the Communist Party. Kexian wanted him to understand that the Communist Party treated well loyalists who turned over a new leaf, regardless of whatever they had said or done before.

For the Communist Party, taking Taiwan was like shooting fish in a barrel. When they would do it was just a matter of timing.

This kind of talk continued for a while.

He discovered that there was somebody else behind his son. It was his daughter-in-law, Wang Yaojun. She was also a journalist. They rarely were at home together as a couple. In fact, she seemed busier than his son. Qian Zhuolun's sense of his daughter-in-law was that she was quite filial, considerate, and loving towards her children. On the other hand, though, she usually spoke very little. Her voice was gentle and her words were rare as gold. She never carelessly expressed her opinion on a topic, but when she spoke, it was 1 is 1, and 2 is 2, and you would need to prick your ears to hear it.

He asked his son, how a bold man that him ended up finding such a stable and dependable wife?

Kexian replied that he'd met her at college. It was fate. Marriage to her was inescapable.

From his tone, it sounded that this was not the usual case of Kexian relentlessly pursuing and then forcefully striking his target, but rather the marriage came from the actions of his counterpart.

But there was loving affection between the couple, almost like that kind of affection between sister and brother. Qian Zhuolun always felt that his daughter-in-law was much more mature than his son.

One time, father and son were having a drink. They were eating some appetizers and drinking Jinmen Sorghum wine with a high proof. Kexian was rambling on a loop about stuff happening on the mainland. Zhuolun purposefully asked, drooping his face, "Have you been sent by the Communist Party to incite your father to defect?"

Kexian seemed to guess his father would ask this at some point. His response surprised Zhuolun, "Actually, Dad, you should've realized a lot earlier that it was I who poured your tea when Song Guozhong and Liu Shizhao came to eat with us."

Qian Zhuolun slammed his cup down to the side, the wine sloshing onto the tabletop.

"I did realize it! My crime against party and country was severe. You degenerate little imp! You destroyed my reputation and career!"

From the sound of it, it was time to draw pistols — at the very least someone should've shouted, "Somebody, quick!" But though their words were harsh, there wasn't that much rage in their faces, just the defrosting of facial expressions from all the excitement, muscles trembling in their cheeks.

"From this day forward, I don't wish to keep you in the dark any more, Dad. I am a member of the Communist Party, and I have been so since my freshman year in college. Think about it, why did Jiang Jieshi's forces totally fall apart? It was because that party, that government and troops were thoroughly corrupted, sinister, and working at odds with the will of the people!"

"You needn't instruct your father!"

"Furthermore, Dad, that so-called 'leak' from long ago was a fiction through and through. That was always one of the General's old tricks — he would use any and every method to test the loyalties of those closest to him, and you were only one of a countless number of sacrificial victims!"

"That's enough!"

Qian Zhuolun stared blankly, chilled to the bone from his disappointment. That little suspicious "gift" Falkenhausen had given him years ago had now been confirmed by the Communist Party.

He threw down his cup and left. Fortunately, he was already in his own home.

The two had laid all their cards on the table, and stormed away on bad terms.

However, from that moment on, whenever Kexian would stay out all night, Zhuolun would ask someone in the family to call him and track him down. Their tea and drinking time together always occurred under the cover of darkness after everyone in the family had gone to sleep.

In the past, during those long nights, Zhuolun would always grab a lamp and read, or practice the calligraphy of Wang Youjun or Sun Guoting. But now when the curtain of dusk fell on all sides, he anxiously waited for Kexian to bring his wife home with him early. Unconsciously, he feared that something might happen to his son, and inwardly hoped to hear him share more about the figures and events regarding cross-strait matters.

That verb "to defect" was taboo to him. The concept needed time. There was one viewpoint that he and his son were close on, though, and that was Jiang Jieshi's insistence on retaking the mainland — it was a pipe dream, and a self-delusional deception. The Americans had already lost hope in him. If the Communist wanted to recover the island of Taiwan, it was only a matter of time.

There was one more point, he also admitted that — yes — the Nationalist Party was completely corrupted, and the will of their military was slackening. How could they possibly continue fighting?

But it was just that he personally had been following Jiang Jieshi for so many years. At least before the "leak" incident, Jiang treated him quite magnanimously. Since ancient times, the monarch always had a jealous heart. Now Jiang had fallen into dire straits. Abandoning his master and defecting, from the perspective of morals and conscience, was not a threshold he was willing to cross.

One evening, his daughter-in-law returned home earlier than her husband. She was carrying with her a big bag of groceries. She stepped into the house and rushed directly into the kitchen. She spoke with Chen Ma, one of their maids, saying she wanted to make a regional dish herself.

Kexian returned, holding a lamp in his hand.

The sumptuous dinner contained a few delicious Yixing local dishes. One of them was a stewed fresh-water mussel tofu. He thought it was strange that being so near to the ocean they would have fresh-water mussels. Another dish was pickled bamboo shoot soup, with shoots from Alishan. The shoots were different than the hairy bamboo shoots from the mountains in Yixing. These ones were tender with a natural freshness, while the latter were a bit tougher. The ham was, in fact, very authentic, ordered from Jinhua in Zhejiang province. There was the mustard sauteed shredded pork as well. He praised Yaojun's cutting skill. The shredded pork was as thin as bean vermicelli. Their taste buds were the first to be titillated, followed by the natural rejoicing of their stomachs.

The family gathered around the lamps, gorging themselves on the feast, lifting their spirits more than they usually did. During the meal, his daughter-in-law used the serving chopsticks to offer food to her father-in-law, asking, "Is the taste to your liking — too much salt? Does it taste anything like Yixing cuisine?" When she laughed, it made you feel the honesty and warmth deep inside her bones, like there was no distance between her.

Qian Zhuolun put his chopsticks down and sighed, "Each place nurtures its own people. Ever since enlisting in the army, I haven't been able to spend much time in my hometown. The smell of that local cuisine was only something that appeared in my dreams. Ahhh, if only I could go back in time …"

Yaojun looked at him and smiled, "Don't say that, father. The proverb goes that no matter how tall the tree grows, its leaves always fall back upon its roots. You're still in such good health. Let's keep on hoping that we can return with the younger generation to your ancestral home!"

As she spoke, She coaxed Kexian and her son to stand up and offer him a toast.

In that kind of atmosphere, it was natural to have a few drinks.

But after draining three cups, Kexian put the bottle of wine away: "It's best for Dad to drink sparingly. Drinking too much isn't good for your health."

With his acute agility and smarts, Qian Zhuolun knew that tonight was the real moment of truth to lay all their cards out on the table. The moves of his opponent weren't original, by any means. To play the family card, one started at the taste buds and then proceeded to the hand, activating the opponent's homesickness — cities rise and fall at the tip of the tongue. Nostalgic things are merely signboards — leaves falling upon roots, returning to one's land of origin are all false attacks. Employing alcohol helped with the assault. He surmised that their trump card would be revealed during after-dinner teatime.

He didn't feel any aversion to this, though, but simply reaped the benefits as if he were a willing fool. These two children were still a bit naive, pushing things a little too quickly. Perhaps this was their superior effort. In his estimation, family affections were real — his son and daughter would not harm him, this he firmly believed. But he did have his regrets: how could he have possibly raised a member of the Communist Party? And as for the role of his daughter-in-law, she seemed even more intense about it than his son. Maybe they had already discovered his trump card way back when his two Communist friends dared enter his house, searching for intelligence on the Nationalists: his loyalties ran deep — he would never injure a friend, no matter what their party affiliation.

There was one point that he hadn't thought of. The lead in their discussion was not Kexian, but his daughter-in-law, Wang Yaojun.

To be more exact, not only was Wang Yaojun part of the Communist Party, but she was one of her husband's superiors.

Speaking with her father-in-law, she made sure to refer to him as father, using a familiar tone. Her husband sat by her side, not interjecting a single word.

She was the representative of the Communist Party organization, of which there was no doubt. Her attitude was serious, but her gaze was still warm. She said that the high officials on the mainland had earnestly investigated Qian Zhuolun's background and viewed him as a hero of the Northern Expedition and a famous general in the War of Resistance against the Japanese. Despite the fact that he had followed Jiang Jieshi all those years, they believed that the people's blood was not on his hands. Those many years ago, at great peril to himself, he refused to track down his two classmates affiliated with the Communist Party. Furthermore, on the eve of the fall of Nanjing during the War of Resistance, he stuck his neck out by issuing an order to commandeer two military steamers to ferry refugees across the river to save their lives. More than 100,000 people were saved in the process. During the War of Resistance, he also resolutely dissuaded his father from taking up a post as a puppet county commissioner for the Japanese. On every occasion, Qian Zhuolun proved himself to be a patriotic soldier of the highest integrity.

"So, my party deeply respects you. It is our earnest hope that you will return to the mainland, and return to the bosom of your people."

There was a fervent look in Yaojun's eyes as she spoke. Her tone was confident — every word leaving its own sharp footprint.

Qian Zhuolun sighed and then asked Yaojun whether Kexian had already become a member of the Communist Party, or she was the one who introduced it to him. Yaojun hesitated for a moment and then replied that, no, that was not how it happened, and that she had been a party member for longer than him. But none of that was important.

Qian Zhuolun asked her another question, "If I do not conform with your request — if you walk away from me empty-handed, will your organization punish you?"

Yaojun laughed, "Father! We believe that you will, in the end, walk the same path with us."

Though they didn't arrive at an agreement, the atmosphere was quite pleasant. That peaceful evening was going perfectly. But then Keshun abruptly returned from outside at around 10 o'clock. He had his key and opened the door without a sound. Since he was very little, his steps had been very quiet, so nobody ever noticed him entering. At least, that was until he suddenly appeared in the small study.

Usually there was nothing awkward about this scene — he was a member of the family, after all. If it were like all the other times, Keshun would've pulled up a chair, drank a cup of tea, and then gone about with his business. But this time he didn't say anything when he showed up. He just blended into the cold, stiff atmosphere, like he was an uninvited guest. He seemed to be enveloped in a cold aura. Even Keshun himself sensed that. He stammered, trying to tell his father, little brother and sister-in-law that he needed to leave tomorrow for a business trip, so he was hurrying to gather some things.

There seemed to be something off in his explanation. Ever since he had been promoted to the rank of colonel, he'd been given a spacious, new house. He had moved his things there already more than half a year ago.

The two brothers, Keshun and Kexian, fundamentally got along well. It was only the very different nature of their work that put such distance between them. Keshun had to conduct himself quite dependably in society. He had never been very courageous as a lad. It stood to reason that he should have become a teacher. But he enlisted with the army at a very young age, passing through hail storms of bullets to arrive unscathed at the rank of colonel. Then there was Kexian, the hyperactive, mischievous one, who liked to play swords, and when he grew up insisted on becoming a journalist. Qian Zhuolun knew that his boys had very different ambitions, and were at odds on a whole host of things. Though on the surface they seemed to be close companions, on the inside they were normally divided.

Wang Yaojun put on another pot of oolong tea to steep, and invited Keshun to take a seat and drink some hot tea. But Keshun declined. He exchanged some pleasantries and then promptly left.

In the past, he would have had a lot to talk about. But this time he didn't follow up with anything.

Qian Zhuolun had a subtle premonition that something was off. He knew that in this period the news of a wave of "banditry and spies" was sweeping through the town.

He repeatedly urged his son and daughter-in-law to take extra precautions for their safety when going outdoors.

Before three days had even passed, something happened to Kexian and his wife.

They had gone to attend a wedding feast of a friend at Taipei's largest restaurant, when a group of plain clothes officers barged in and arrested them.

Qian Zhuolun got word of this. He, of course, was shocked, but not entirely surprised.

The first thing that came to his mind was the spectacle of Keshun barging into the little study late at night.

There wasn't much time to ponder the situation — he hurriedly put a call through to Chen Cheng. Unexpectedly, after hearing Qian Zhuolun's urgent explanation, Chen Cheng flatly refused. His reasoning was that he had just resigned as commanding officer of the provincial garrison — that responsibility no longer fell upon him. Taiwan's new "Chair" was actually just a hollow shell.

It was like a bucket of cold water being spilled on his head. This old classmate had never acted like this before. Perhaps there was something troubling him he couldn't share? Qian Zhuolun played it cool for a moment, and then called the mayor of Taipei, Wu Guozhen.

Besides Chen Cheng, his peer Wu Guozhen and he enjoyed a good relationship. Wu had studied abroad in the United States and was rather frank in his expressions. While he was the mayor of Shanghai, they had occasion to associate, and Wu helped him arrange some personal affairs.

When he finished speaking, Wu Guozhen categorically affirmed that he was absolutely not the one who had performed the arrest.

He warned Qian Zhuolun that the current intelligence system all reported to the "crown prince" Jiang Jingguo, the son of Jiang Jieshi. Taipei city was under the jurisdiction of Peng Mengji. Peng was only a vice admiral. Although he was charged with the command of the Taiwan garrison, he wouldn't dare cross the "crown prince." He personally delivered the message to Jiang Jieshi, who in a self-deprecating fashion claimed this was a heavy burden he wouldn't shoulder, recommending a more virtuous person take up the responsibility: it would be best if the talented and capable Jiang Jingguo took lead on the case.

Jiang Jieshi had always had it in mind to transform his intelligence agency, condensing all of its disparate branches and pressing them into a single "political action committee." Peng Mengji asked to resign, which played into Jiang Jieshi's hands as Jiang Jingguo promptly assumed the responsibility of shoring up the new agency. After he took control of Peng Mengji's authority, he immediately changed the name of the committee to the Presidential Department of Special Affairs Information Group. In spite of it being a tiny "group," its authority reached into every special department of the Taiwanese party and government apparatus, especially the intelligence agency following its unification, placing every unit within his grasp.

Qian Zhuolun's heart sank. He knew that something terrible had happened.

So many years spent by General Jiang's side, he came to know the "crown prince" quite well.

Insiders all knew that the "crown prince" was on the throne with absolute influence. His past record in Shanghai of "fighting the tiger" was vividly on everybody's mind. Things had changed since then, though. In those days, they faced apparent and secret obstacles, but nowadays the party's old guard had all been marginalized. Not a single person could stick a needle between all the things he wished to control.

Pondering on it for a while, there was only one person that maybe could intercede.

Zhuolun called the President's Official Residence at Shilin and asked for Song Meiling. The original aide-de-camp assigned there had been replaced. The new attendant said that the Lady was currently outside of Taipei. As for where exactly she was wandering, he wasn't entirely sure. Supposedly, this former "calligraphy teacher" had already acquired some undeserved fame. After arriving in Taiwan, Song Meiling studied ink landscape painting with Huang Junbi, and Zheng Manqing taught her how to paint flowers and plants. She hadn't resumed her calligraphy lessons, though, her former contacts had naturally been cut off.

Rolling through her acquaintances' notifications, Song Meiling still remembered her friend from yesteryear, and agreed to meet with Zhuolun the next afternoon at the Jade House on Sun Moon Lake.

Sun Moon Lake was located 240 kilometers south of Taipei. Qian Zhuolun hadn't brought a driver or even a guard with him. He departed at 3:00 am the following morning. The rainy mountain road was difficult to navigate. A stretch of it was full of potholes and the car tires sunk into the muddy holes a few different times. He had to get out of the car and help to push it, getting covered in mud over and over again.

The moment he saw her, he jumped right to the main topic, pleading with the Lady to intervene and save his son and daughter-in-law.

The Lady was not one to pass the buck. She asked to hear about their circumstances, muttering to herself for a moment. Then she stood up and made a phone call. At first, she put on a happy face, but the moment she hung up the phone, a dark cloud came over her expression.

"This thing has Jingguo's hands all over it." She said this, and nothing more.

Everyone in the upper levels of the Nationalist party was aware of the Lady's subtle relationship with Jiang Jingguo. It wasn't one based on old scores, or non-blood relations, but just the resentments that naturally come from a step-mother being 13 years-old than the "crown prince" that can't be ignored. The crucial point was in the 37th year of the Republic of China when Jiang Jingguo was in Shanghai "fighting the tiger," which involved the Song and Kong clans battling for advantage, bitterly opposing each other and not giving an inch. At the time, Jiang Jieshi saved his wife's honor and reputation. The Song and Kong households dodged a bullet, and the impetuous Jiang Jingguo had to wind down his campaign and retreat from the battlefield.

The Lady gave Qian Zhuolun a bit of advice, "Go find the old man. You're his old subordinate. And if he reprimands you, at least you know he'll give you a way out."

Those words did not come easily for the Lady. She wasn't a fan of politics, ordinarily devoting her time to charity and aid projects. Their friendship was still there, but they followed the rules of propriety superbly. Qian Zhuolun knew the exact weight of her words.

However, getting in to see Mr. Jiang was no easy task. The present circumstances were nothing like they used to be. Moreover, Jiang often acted erratically now. Qian Zhuolun wasn't able to grasp how to ask him for this favor. But in order to save his son and daughter-in-law, he was ready to try anything and risk his skin once more.

It was Wu Guozhen who stepped in for him, first explaining to Mr. Jiang the full extent of things. It was a bold move! Everybody knew that Wu Guozhen and Jiang Jingguo's relationship had stiffened. When he was the mayor of Shanghai, he had some very strong opinions about Jiang Jingguo's "fighting the tiger" activities. He thought that he was being impractical and rushing things too much. He couldn't stand his arrogance and condescension, especially when he arrogated the power of the mayor to himself! The reason why Wu had gained Mr. Jiang's admiration had everything to do with his background studying in the United States and the deep ties he still maintained within the highest levels of the American government. At the same time, Wu had never formed his own clique, demonstrating his utmost loyalty to Jiang. As a result, his recommendations and opinions were always welcomed.

Wu Guozhen was a true friend to Zhuolun and speedily brought the matter to Mr. Jiang. His attendant informed him that while meeting with Mr. Jiang, he sensed things might take a turn for the better.

There was no small talk. Immediately he unleashed a fierce reprimand, using his Ningbo dialect to curse Zhuolun out — "You little fuck!" Mr. Jiang was furious! Besides scolding him for raising his kids wrong, sparing the rod and spoiling the child, he cursed him for being so depressed and sloppy in his duties in recent years. His thinking was flawed and malignant, his heart and body had grown apart from the party and his nation, etc.

"Inside the house of a vice admiral spring two members of the Communist Party — it's unheard of!! If this had happened in ancient times, your entire family would have been executed and all your property repossessed, spreading out to nine generations of your clan line, for God's sake! You need to shut yourself in and think long and hard about what has happened, and stop running around like an idiot!"

The scolding was harsh, but Qian Zhuolun felt somewhat at ease inside. Everyone who was close to Mr. Jiang knew that they were generally all his beloved generals and favored ministers. Like Dai Li of old, in his earlier years Jiang could instantly flip from nothing but kind words to rebukes and curses — even punches and kicks! Dai Li always very much enjoyed these types of "privileges." On the contrary, if Jiang suddenly became coldly polite and formal with someone close to him, treating them with the utmost respect, that someone was surely doomed.

Jiang told him to "stop running around like an idiot." But was the meaning behind this that things had already reached their end, and that he needn't go out and cause a bigger scene, or, on the other hand, was he telling him that things were now out of his control?

Sure enough, the following day, Jiang's attendant returned to him with some news. Zhuolun was permitted to go that day to the Machang ding Special Prison near the Taipei Zoo to pay a visit and declare the following order from the Chairman, "I hope that Qipei will place righteousness before family, and convince the two detained criminals to publish openly their misdeeds and turn over a new leaf. They must also hand over a list of names from their organization, and then their lives will be protected."

Qian Zhuolun's vision went black. He almost fell over.

It was only then that he understood that the "honor" Jiang was offering him was just the chance to see his son and daughter-in-law one more time before they were killed. As for protecting their lives, there were two conditions. As he understood things for his son and daughter-in-law, there was little chance that they would "publish openly their misdeeds," and it was pure fantasy to imagine that they would "hand over a list of names from their organization."

Interpreting these few words of Mr. Jiang, disasters came in series. If he failed to convince them to give in, it wouldn't just be that their lives would be unprotected, but that the lives of his entire clan would suffer by association.

His limbs went cold and he suddenly felt terribly weak. Although in the past he had experienced storms of fire and bullets, he had never given that much thought to life and death. But now, it was more than just his son and daughter-in-law's lives being thrown into the mix, it was possibly those of his entire clan!

Keshun didn't return home at all during that time. Zhuolun called, but the person who picked up said it wasn't a good time to talk, and the call was cut short. In the end, they found out that since the day of Kexian and Yaojun's arrest, Keshun had been placed under house arrest.

One possibility was that Keshun was completely innocent — that he hadn't sold out his brother and sister-in-law. But there was definitely that other possibility that in order to protect Keshun, the authorities intentionally shut him away in his house.

Zhuolun was upset and confused. He had never been so agitated in his entire military career.

When he went outside, he noticed some suspicious-looking types moving around nearby. He knew that he was being watched ...

He was allowed to see his son for a fixed amount of time. Although it had only been a few days, Kexian was already badly beaten up. His skin was split and his two eyes were sunken like dark caves.

It was challenging for him to speak Mr. Jiang's two conditions. He tried his best to make the delivery mild and restrained, but Kexian coldly laughed before he could finish, "Dad, although you and I each have our own beliefs, would you ever receive a traitorous son who betrayed his organization?"

Qian Zhuolun knew there was a tapping device in their room, "You need to think about your own son and daughter for a moment! This isn't just about your own life!"

Kexian smiled painfully,

"Ever since we entered the organization, Yaojun and my life stopped belonging to us."

For a time, there wasn't much else to say. He couldn't get out any more convincing words. The Qian family carried deep within its bones the inherited genes of its forefathers, that is their crucially timed resoluteness and firmness, and an uprightness wrapped in gentleness.

He held back his grim tears, and sighed deeply, "My son, your father has failed you and Yaojun. I cannot save you!"

Kexian suddenly fell down onto both his knees and choked on his sobs, "Dad, we cannot repay you the kindness of having raised us. There are children now that you must care for, Dad. We have failed you. Please, you must take care of yourself."

He lifted his son up with both of his hands and hugged him one last time. Kexian's body was trembling terribly. The warmth of his body was the last memory he left with his father.

When he saw Yaojun, it was in a small conference room. There was a sofa and a side table. And there was a teacup there, as well. It was clear that the prison knew of her rank and importance in the Communist Party.

When she came into the room, she was staggering somewhat. She had clearly been tortured as well, but at least things didn't look too bad for her on the surface. Qian Zhuolun knew that the authorities had much higher expectations for her.

They started talking about a few family affairs. Yaojun's mind was crystal clear — she knew that they didn't have much time and she wanted to explain to Qian Zhuolun the things he didn't know from before, for instance: which bank her and Kexian's savings were deposited in; where the passbook was; some documents related to their insurance; some former financial dealings with friends, who lent them money and who still owed them, etc. She was afraid he might not completely remember the children's birthdays, so she reviewed those with him one by one.

Then there was also the matter of her own father and mother. She entreated him to send word to them as well that she was devastated to have failed in seeing them through their old age.

She hoped that her father and mother could also share the burden of caring for children who had lost their father and mother.

As he listened, two hot streams of tears flowed down his cheeks.

How could he possibly try to convince them to give in?!

"Dad, there is one more thing I beg of you: if you ever are able to return to your homeland, please take our ashes there with you."

Her final words were, "Father, I will still be your daughter-in-law in the next life."

He broke down and couldn't speak.

He understood what she was hinting at. They both knew that there was a tapping device in the room, but she was still trying to get him to return to the mainland.

He knew that in the room next door, a group of people were huddled over their tapping devices waiting for him to say those words to convince her to give in.

But he didn't say anything. He knew what the consequence would be, but he still didn't want to say anything. At this juncture, he wasn't going to help them out anymore, and he wasn't going to add any more unpleasant feelings to his son and daughter-in-law who were staring death in the face.

Yaojun's face was pale, but her manner was serene. She had said what she wanted to and was happy. She smiled. Then she stood up, made a deep bow before him, turned and walked away.

That was the last time he saw Yaojun's smile — it looked as beautiful as always.

The next day, he received the news that Kexian and Yaojun were executed early that morning at Machangding Prison.

The prison coldly informed him to come and collect their bodies.

That day was his 63rd birthday.

While Qian Xiuling was hurrying to Taipei, the event had already occurred.

She wanted to see both of her brothers, Zhuoru and Zhuolun.

Zhuoru accompanied her to see Zhuolun. Their visit wasn't at home, but in the hospital. After taking care of his son and his daughter-in-law's funeral arrangements, he fell ill.

It goes without saying that this is how a family is destroyed. They had two sons and two daughters. The oldest was 12 and the youngest was only 6 years old.

Meeting under these circumstances, it was natural for tears to fall on both sides. However, Zhuolun had already climbed out of his abyss of sorrow. He strove to keep it together, but his soul had suffered incredible loss. It didn't end up breaking him, though.

His mind was as sharp and as clear as always. He was just suffering from insomnia.

Xiuling was boiling up a pot of rice porridge in Zhuoru's home. She placed it inside a thermos and took it over to Zhuolun in his hospital bed. She added some pickled veggies and dried carrots to throw into the porridge that Zhuoru's wife had salted herself. This was their standard breakfast growing up in their hometown when they were younger. He ate that thick, sticky porridge, and chewed on the crunchy dried carrot — it tasted just like it did at home. She stayed with Zhuolun, talking about family things as the time passed and the temperature gradually warmed.

Suppressed emotion settled deep inside his heart. When there was nobody there beside him, Zhuolun would spit out everything he was feeling to Xiuling, hoping she could help him sort it all out.

Xiuling always felt like there was a shadow hovering around the doorway. She would slip into their hometown Yixing county dialect, but she still felt that wasn't good enough. So, she called for a wheelchair, and would go downstairs and push her brother around the hospital lawn.

The weather in Taipei was humid all year round. The sky was always grey, and even in fall it felt like the height of summer. If you grabbed a handful of air, you could squeeze the water right out of it.

Zhuolun brought up the night Keshun suddenly barged into the house. He felt like that was a big mystery. He had asked their helper, Chen Ma, and she became nervous, saying that she had gone to bed earlier that night. Recalling it now, Keshun might have heard their conversation outside the door of the little study. Perhaps when he entered the study, he already knew everything.

Keshun was dedicated to the military, and he didn't take any bribes. The admonition to put national loyalty ahead of family was ubiquitous at all levels.

If it truly had been Keshun to denounce them, then it was a humiliating disgrace to the family. But, even if that were true, what would happen to him now? From the Nationalist's point of view, was Keshun wrong?

Whatever the case may be, the Qian family would never again endure a tragedy of losing young loved ones.

Qian Zhuolun's life had toppled into the deepest valley of despair.

Qian Zhuolun was still speaking with Xiuling, telling her how Mayor Wu Guozhen took a huge risk coming to see him, urging him to let it all fade from memory as quickly as possible, especially to let go of the desire to track down who turned them in.

Could it be that that was a kind of subtle hint?

Xiuling stayed silent for a long time, and then uttered the following,

"In my view, brother, you shouldn't go tracking down where Keshun is. Let it go — you needn't worry about it any longer. We don't bear grudges against others in the Qian family, least of all against our own! You have no evidence, so it's just pure speculation at the moment. I pray Kexian and Yaojun never return when they fly over Africa or some other ends of the earth. Brother, be at peace, they are together and won't be lonely. You have your granddaughters and grandsons and now need to care for yourself and live well. That is the best way to honor Kexian and Yaojun."

As the last words escaped her lips, she broke down and cried.

CHAPTER 16

Searching for the Wall with the Landscape Painting

On October 16th, 2018, we returned to Brussels from Ecaussinnes.

As scheduled, we arrived at St. Lambert Street to pay a visit to Qian Xianhe, Xiuling's nephew, and her grandnephew, Qian Weiqiang.

The first question was why, after helping General Falkenhausen to win his case in the 1950s, further adding fame in Belgium to her original title of "National Hero," did she not use that opportunity to return to KU Leuven and pursue her original "Madame Curie" dream? From what we learned of the situation, she had left the public's line of sight and opened up a restaurant with some Chinese friends. From that point on, she walked the path of the "Lady Boss Restaurant Manager." But why?

Qian Xianhe was a silver-haired gentleman of 82 years of age, a professor at Taiwan University, and an international expert on carbonate petrology. He was Qian Zhuoru's son. His father, along with his father's sister Qian Xiuling, had studied at KU Leuven. But that was a legacy more than half a century old. For the Qian family, Xianhe was the sole heir of that academic legacy. After his father completed his studies at KU Leuven, he returned to China, and then eventually moved to Taiwan. As a result, after completing his undergraduate studies at Taiwan University, his father approached him, hoping to help him fulfill a dream: to take the examination to become a KU Leuven paleontology research student, and then obtain his masters and doctoral degrees. He followed his father's admonishment and went on to don the doctoral cap. On the day he received his doctorate, Aunt Qian Xiuling appeared in her own splendid graduation robes. He got the impression that she was much more excited about the event than he was.

Qian Xianhe had this to offer for a reason why she opened up a restaurant:

> In 1951, after an introduction from her advisor, Dr. Wilson, Aunt Qian entered the Nuclear Engineering Research Institute in Brussels, established by the United Nations, where she worked as a research chemist. She did very well there, writing a number of very influential papers. However, in her second year, she became pregnant once more, so she had to leave her position and return to tend the home. When a woman returns to her home, it is very difficult for her to re-emerge. As for opening the restaurant, because of her wide renown in Belgium, a number of overseas Chinese sought her out for assistance. Some of them were living difficult lives and just asking her to lend them money. Being

the person she was, it deeply pained her to see those people struggling and not able to help them.

At the time, it was just her husband who was working. With five children, expenses were high. She met a Chinese couple from Anhui, a certain Father Chen and his wife, who had moved to Belgium from France. The two of them were gourmands, often preparing dishes for Xiuling. They realized that Xiuling was a great cook of Jiangnan cuisine, while Mrs. Chen was proficient in Anhui dishes. Idly chatting one day, somebody threw out the suggestion that they open a Chinese restaurant together. At the time, the idea inspired Aunt Qian — if they opened a restaurant, then she could eat Chinese food every day! Plus, she would get to know a lot more Chinese people that way and help foreigners to grow to like Chinese cuisine. The crucial motivation, however, was that it would bring in a little bit of money every day. With that new income flow, she could help out her overseas comrades facing life's difficulties.

In Qian Xianhe's recounting of it, at the end of the 1950s, on the rather tranquil St. Lambert Street in Brussels city proper, a restaurant by the name of "Confucius" gradually emerged into public view out of the depths of time. The exterior wasn't anything flashy, and the interior wasn't particularly spacious. The "Confucius" sign hanging above the establishment was written with Wang Xizhi type characters. On the day they opened their doors, the sun was unusually warm, and the visitors were numerous, particularly those from Ecaussinnes — even Roger from Herbeumont showed up with his children. From their familiar silhouettes, we can make out that Maurice and Old Raymond and his son were there, not to mention those who were not in the group photo of the 96 rescued hostages, Chinese friends, and Pastor Lu Zengxiang.

The restaurant setup was configured according to Chinese standards: an open hall in the entryway, a cheerful God of Wealth looking down on you from a wall, an antique table with an incense burner. Qian Xianhe explained that his father Zhuoru had sent these all to her. That large scroll painting hanging on the wall was imposing. Qian Xiuling said that mansions in the past needed to have their own precious treasures, and that that landscape scroll was the prop holding up the entire place. If it weren't for that painting, they wouldn't have been able to open up shop!

When first discussing it, Qian Xianhe couldn't remember the names of Qian Xiuling's restaurant partners. He only knew that they were from Anhui and had been living in Paris, France, before moving to Antwerp, Belgium, where Father Chen was then serving as a minister. It seemed like there were two types of opportunities for Chinese living abroad: work as a religious minister, where you relied on the skill of your tongue, or, open up a restaurant. Where else could foreigners eat that was so meticulous and particular about their food? From impressions, there were a lot of foreigners who loved to eat Chinese food.

One time in the Confucius restaurant, Qian Xianhe ate one of Mrs. Chen's stinky tofu. It was an amazing thing: she grew mold on the tofu, so much that it sprouted white hair. Then she tossed it in oil and fried it up. He remembers Dr. Gregory being very worried at the time — he said that that kind of rotten foodstuff could upset the stomach. In the end, everybody devoured it and not a single person had a problem. The next time Mrs. Chen made her stinky tofu, he gingerly tasted a chunk. "Not bad," he said.

That dish was understandably one of Confucius' signature plates.

Qian Xianhe ate a smelly mandarin fish there once, also an Anhui dish. You take the best mandarin fish, pile salt on top of it, and then seal it up in a clay jar for 6 to 7 days. You have to wait until it begins to stink, then you cook it up in a thick, oily red sauce, adding ginger and a healthy portion of cooking wine. Cooking that fish will make the entire room smell, but the taste is exquisite. Qian Xianhe remembers that one time after eating the fish, his aunt suddenly realized something, asking Mrs. Chen, "Where in Belgium can you find mandarin fish?!" Mrs. Chen just smiled back and explained that there was a very similar fish in Antwerp that you couldn't get in Brussels. They went to a food market and saw a kind of bream fish. Its meat was firm and fresh. They used that in place of the mandarin fish and its taste ended up working out as a substitute.

Of course, Qian Xianhe explained, it wasn't stinky mandarin fish or anything like that that propped up the Confucius restaurant. It was more dishes like Cantonese braised duck, Wenchang chicken, fried shrimp in crisp rice, braised pigeon, and a few other Jiangnan dishes that Qian Xiuling was adept at making.

One of the dishes that Qian Xiuling especially admired was called the "Jiangnan First Course." Actually, its original name was really the "Yixing First Course." In Belgium, the people only celebrated Christmas, but Qian Xiuling had strong attachments to the New Year's festival. When she was young, that was the first dish served at New Year's festival. When she was little, she just assumed that it was the same for every household.

People of all tastes could find something in that dish that they loved. It was made in high volumes and had all sorts of variety, so you needed a big soup bowl or casserole dish to eat it. When the plate touched the table, the New Year's ambience had arrived!

Qian Xianhe had heard his aunt say that the dish was called "First

Course" not just because it was the first to be served, but also because its ingredients were rich and it was packed with meats and vegetables. Everybody liked it, filling the home with an atmosphere of reunion and blessings.

Its ingredients were numerous: fried pork skin, pork belly, pig ear, fish balls, lamb kidney, black fungus, small dried shrimps, bamboo shoots, sea cucumber, big green garlic, all filling up a massive basin.

All of these things, except the bamboo shoots, could be found in the Brussels markets. Naturally, the most important thing was the big bone broth — it was the base flavor of it all. You had to have pure, hand-pressed sesame oil.

You could use mushrooms as a substitute for bamboo shoots. The large mushrooms in the Brussels markets were fresh and tender. Fried pork skin couldn't be found ready-made. You had to first sun dry the pork skin, then put it inside a fryer to cook. A piece of pig skin tumbling in a fryer quickly puffs up into a huge chip. You then remove it, let it cool, and soak it in cold water for a little while until its texture turns soft and loose. After that, you cut it up into little strips and fry it again so that the oil forms air bubbles inside the skin. Cooked together with the rest of the dish, the skin sucks up the fresh flavor of the broth, so that when it hits the tongue it's incredibly delicious — flaky, soft and slightly chewy.

The fish balls also needed to be hand-made. You selected a big fish abdomen with no spines, minced it with the back of a kitchen knife, and then added spices and let it boil in the bone broth until it formed little balls. This was all done pretty quickly in order to preserve the smooth texture of the fish balls.

Originally, this was a dish made by Qian Xiuling alone. She was completely happy to select all of the ingredients and boil the bone broth and everything else herself. It was like she was back inside the experimental laboratory completing a research study. Every step of the process had its challenges and interests. Afterward, she had the cook make it under her direction, adding her suggestions when she had the time.

Of course, Mrs. Chen was full of praise for the dish. She said, "The 'Jiangnan First Course' lived up to its name, and then some! And it's not just Yixing folk who come to eat it."

For that reason, they changed the dish's name to the "Jiangnan First Course."

Qian Xianhe remembered how he would go to Brussels over the weekend after school. The first thing he would do was to step into the Confucius restaurant for a meal and then go home with his aunt after closing.

Aunt Qian ate very simply, but was also very particular. She only ate two things: little wontons and spring rolls. She made the wontons herself, cooked in a bone broth. The spring rolls were stuffed with fresh vegetables and carrots that she minced or julienned herself. She would hum little ditties to her heart's content as she made the food. You would never be able to tell that this house wife was a dual chemistry and physics PhD.

When the restaurant first opened, they hired only a single cook, a Hong Kong man, originally from Guangdong. Everybody called him Mr. Wheat. He was very good at making Cantonese dishes: his braised duck was authentic and his fried pigeon with spiced salt was incredible. He was passable with Jiangnan cuisine — it was never quite as good as when Qian Xiuling would make it. It was perhaps because he never really thought very much of those homely dishes — they weren't worthy for the dinner table, at best they were appropriate as snacks for the household. Qian Xiuling said, though, "That's exactly the home-cooked flavor I'm looking for." She insisted that Mr.

Wheat begin to use his energies to cook well the Jiangnan cuisine she thought so highly of, including soup dumplings, sweet pot, and other kinds of snacks.

One time, two overseas Chinese living in Netherlands came over and exclusively ordered Jiangnan dishes. They had heard people talking about them — word of mouth passing the news from one person to another. One of them was from Wujin, Jiangsu, a place right next to Yixing. The other was from Taicang, Suzhou, another place where the Wu dialect was used. Their accents were similar and their tastes were about the same too. As they chatted about this and that, a steaming pot full of the Jiangnan First Course was brought in, smelling of scallions and sesame oil, caressing their noses. The one with the grey hair suddenly welled up with tears, "I just smelled the dishes my mother used to make me when I was a child."

The color and flavor were all excellent. In no time at all, they ate it all up. Qian Xiuling sent them an order of fried spring rolls, one with meat and vegetable stuffing, the other just with carrot strings. They stuffed themselves until they burped. They had that expression of utter satisfaction, like children doing something naughty. Another customer came in. He was bald and didn't say a word. After he finished eating, he asked for a pen and left them some words. Qian Xiuling slapped her head — how could she have forgotten the Guest Book?! She quickly had someone go out and buy one.

Ultimately, that bald guest's family had been private advisors to the old-style private school for generations. He wanted to leave a little poetic verse for the Confucius restaurant. His last name also happened to be Kong, his ancestral home being in Shandong — he was definitely one of Confucius' descendants. There were two lines in the poem that Qian Xiuling and Mrs. Chen felt were touching, invoking some nostalgia in them:

In a strange city, I taste home
My heart returns to Jiangnan, feeling mother's kindness

According to Qian Xianhe's memory, business at the Confucius restaurant seemed to be going really well with a stream of people coming in and out — it was a hot spot. But that didn't last very long, maybe less than two years before they had to close up the restaurant. The internal reason for that obviously had to do with earnings. They were losing money.

Throughout her life, Qian Xiuling was a lady and student — how could she know how to run a business? When they opened up their doors, there were plenty of friends that showed up and heaped attention on them, but Qian Xiuling felt awkward taking their money, so many of them ended up eating and drinking for free. Mrs. Chen didn't understand business all that well either, but seeing the carefree way in which Qian Xiuling ran things, she naturally felt a bit worried. She spoke to her a few times about it. Xiuling told her that when she was young and living in China, when any store opened, they would discount things for the first few days, even shipping things out. Friends from far, far away would make the trip to support them, some bearing gifts. How could she, then, take their money?

Time passed, but the problems slowly revealed themselves. The location they had chosen in Brussels was not necessarily removed, but it was by no means in the bustling heart of the city. Its clientele were middle to low spenders. Plus, their storefront was small and couldn't accommodate that many people.

The price of dishes was already quite a bit cheaper than your usual restaurant — Qian Xiuling insisted that they not inflate prices. She didn't want to make things harder for clients who were coming from far away, the majority of whom were their compatriots and getting along in their years. With their yellow skins and dark hair, it always felt like they were old friends from the same hometown, greeting each other with teary eyes. They would stick around all day, reluctant to leave, while Qian Xiuling kept them busy with chitchat. Some of them were veritable chatterboxes, telling them all about how they had been abroad for years working themselves to the bone. Qian Xiuling easily fell into their dramas, letting herself be moved by their bitter experiences. Sometimes, she couldn't help herself from opening up her own wallet and helping them out — their meals were obviously on the house. As this kind of thing continued, it was inevitable that they would lose money.

Could it also have been that Qian Xiuling and Mrs. Chen had overplayed the "Chinese" element, creating a barrier for foreigners?

Not necessarily. In Qian Xianhe's view, there were still quite a few foreigners who went to eat there.

However, it could have been that Qian Xiuling had overemphasized her own view of what the "Chinese" elements were, especially in how she attached herself to the "Jiangnan sentiment" and pushed Jiangnan cuisine. Though she received no small praise from the overseas Chinese, she was unable to make money from local Belgians. Europeans rather prefer foods high in calories, like chicken patties, beef steaks, red wine, coffee, etc. The Confucius restaurant had these as well, but Mr. Wheat's steak was nowhere near as good as his braised duck.

There was another reason for closing the restaurant that had something to do with Qian Xiuling and Mrs. Chen's cooperative relationship. They had no idea what they were doing at first. Most of the initial capital was provided by Qian Xiuling. But when it came time to share in the profits, Mrs. Chen's expectations exceeded what

Xiuling was willing to accept. Xiuling was the kind of person that didn't like to haggle over things with friends, but the restaurant was behind on its bills, a quite grievous circumstance. Qian Xiuling held on for a time, but couldn't keep it up in the end, and they had to dissolve their partnership.

Regardless, nothing bad happened between Qian Xiuling and Mrs. Chen. Mrs. Chen had given it her all and she and her husband had decided to return to Paris to stay with their children. They needed some money to settle down. Qian Xiuling took some of the initial capital and gifted it to her friend — easy come, easy go. Xiuling deeply appreciated their help, and their parting was hard to watch.

That landscape painting in the restaurant was originally lent to her nephew Qian Xianhe. However, when the restaurant transferred ownership, the new owner made a request that nothing be removed from the premises, including the two Guest Books full of names and messages.

Qian Xiuling felt like she had let her nephew down. She told Qian Xianhe, "What can we do? This was given to you by your father! We have some calligraphy hanging in our home painted by well-known artists. Go take a look at them and choose one. Consider it compensation for the landscape painting."

Qian Xianhe declined, of course. What was a painting worth when compared to the care his aunt had shown him?

In his view, his aunt treated him exactly as his mother did. When the weekend came, Aunt Xiuling would call him up and make him stay with them and serve him food. When he first began his studies at KU Leuven, all his classmates had field studies grants, the highest awards reaching $5,000 and the lowest $3,000. Qian Xiuling knew about this and helped him to go around looking for funds. In the end, she located an old study abroad classmate who had become a figure of some power at the time. The problem of a field studies grant had been resolved.

However, Aunt Xiuling made him apply for the lowest type of grant worth $2,500. She didn't explain why. Later on, Xianhe talked to that classmate of his aunt. He said, "Your aunt is just that kind of person: she's afraid of taking more than others. She only feels good if she takes less."

Afterward, Qian Xiuling brought up the painting a few more times. It was something she still felt bad about.

To our surprise, as we were hastily looking into the history of the Confucius restaurant, we unexpectedly came across one of those old Guest Books.

In our October 18th, 2018 Interviewer's notes, we wrote down the following:

> This afternoon, Mr. Peng Fei took us to a street in Brussels, where we located the first restaurant that Qian Xiuling and her friend had opened up together: the Confucius restaurant.
> The image of the God of Fortune was still there greeting us in the entryway, just as Qian Xianhe had described. Underneath the image stood a Ming-style antique table made of yellow poplar with a faint patina to give it an aged look. There was an incense burner in the shape of a gold ingot on top of the table. Ash had piled up as a few incense sticks were still smoldering. A blue-eyed foreign woman sat at the front desk, obviously an employee there. The owner, a Taiwanese woman, about 40 years old, warmly greeted us and boiled some oolong tea for us. We ordered a few dishes:

fried noodles, green peppers and potatoes, and tomato egg soup. We also wanted to order the "Jiangnan First Course." The watier of Vietnamese descent didn't understand the request. We asked for spring rolls, but he shook his head once more. Red-braised pork? He tapped his head, "OK!"
We looked around and saw other people eating in groups of twos and threes — there were actually quite a few foreigners there. Most of their orders were pretty simple: a cup of coffee, a few slices of cake, or a small beef steak or fish filet. Lifting my eyes up, I didn't see anyone eating any cold plates or stir-fried dishes.
It was no longer an authentic Chinese restaurant. Perhaps it had only become a mix-and-match place to eat in order to satisfy the requests of all of their diners in order to stay in business.
We searched for that wall where the landscape painting might have hung. The place had been decked out with all the European-style bells and whistles, nothing like the white-walled ambience required for a Chinese painting. A few third-rate, abstract oil paintings adorned the walls.
Unexpectedly, we discovered a back door that led out into a small courtyard. There was a large, tall sycamore there. In its shade was a circular clay desk and a clay stool. A set of tea instruments made in Yixing were sitting to one side. The bead style tea pot was still considered to be of excellent quality. It had obviously not been used for some time to boil tea. It was placed there merely for decoration. There was a bronze plate placed underneath the teapot. The craftsmanship was austere and humble. You could recognize it easily as the work of the potter "wise old

man" — a reference to the wise old man in the fable from "The Old Man Moves the Mountain," the one made fun of by a visitor watching him try to move a mountain. The ceramic manufacturer is poking fun at himself here, and we supposed he must be an uncommon person.

From the glaze on the ceramic table and stool, I was certain they were Junyou goods manufactured in Yixing, Jiangsu province. This discovery surprised me — I couldn't fathom how on earth they shipped these over remote mountains and seas to arrive here?!

I suddenly remembered a historical resource: at the beginning of the sixteenth century, a Dutch East India Company freighter made its first imported shipment of Chinese ceramics to the port in Amsterdam. Over 3,000 pottery vessels made the long journey. Ceramic desks, stools and the like were making waves across the world during the Ming dynasty. They were universally used. That ceramic teapot positioned atop the ceramic desk and stool would have been a naturally sophisticated pairing.

There were some chimes and a swing in the courtyard as well. These sentimental touches I wanted to believe were things that Qian Xiuling had left behind. In those brief moments between work, she would go outside and rest, or perhaps receive a visitor. And if the moon were out on a given night, the leaves of the sycamore tree would scatter the moonlight across the earth, sending warm feelings of comfort into her nostalgic heart.

The courtyard did make one's imagination roam ...

As we waited for our food, we struck up some casual conversation with the boss. We asked her if she knew who the original owner of the restaurant was. Without missing a beat, she responded with a proud expression, "Of course! It was Qian Xiuling."

A moment later she came back over with a black, laminated book. "This is the Guest Book she left behind all those years ago. Originally there were two. They say that one of them was signed by a high government official who brought friends with him to eat here. Because he left some words for her inside, it was purchased by an antiques collector. It certainly wouldn't have been sold off by Qian Xiuling. But I can't say for sure who it was."

This delightful surprise seemed to fall right out of the sky. We hurriedly cracked the thick book. Each page was protected by a plastic sleeve. The first page contained a short ditty written by an older overseas Chinese man:

In a foreign land I taste my home,
where sumptuous flavors are freely shared.
Across the world my yearning roams,
bow aiming at eagles through the air.
Honor to Confucius here I show,
White clouds above my longing declare.

Zheng Wanli
Singaporean Chinese

Flipping through the pages, there were messages left in English, French, German, Japanese, and Korean — Chinese messages aren't actually the most numerous. This discovery overturned my initial understanding of the restaurant. I quickly took some pictures and used WeChat to send them to a friend skilled in foreign languages.

There was one message that was very particular. The author had used a ballpoint pen to draw an American flag. Beside it, he drew the silhouette of a long-haired, Asian woman. Then he sketched a "thumbs-up" sign beside it, ending the inscription with "USA. L."

It must have been an American guest using comic illustrations to praise the beautiful woman he had met at the restaurant. Did this beautiful Chinese woman happen to be Qian Xiuling? It wasn't clear. But the author was certainly in a good mood when he drew it. With the American flag as a contrasting background, the culinary delicacies he enjoyed had set off his inspiration — there was no doubt about that. In other words, the Confucius restaurant clientele came from all corners of the globe, and most of them were actually foreigners. Thinking about it some more, that made sense since so many overseas Chinese had travelled abroad empty-handed, looking to make something for themselves. They were all workers, very few having obtained success. Eating out was, for a lot of people, quite a luxury. On occasion you would go out to eat. But when foreign tourists saw that name, "Confucius," hanging from the sign, it was like a Chinese person travelling abroad seeing the name of Jesus or Shakespeare. Curiosity compelled them to step inside and try it out.

For this reason, Qian Xiuling had originally selected the name Confucius. Overseas, that was the only name that could represent China — other names simply wouldn't do.

The messages I sent to my friend to translate returned to me one after another.

Some of the Japanese messages read:
I am far from Japan,
separated by a thousand miles,
living in Europe, a distant land.
I dearly miss my wife at home.
I experienced the tastes of my old home,
and how delicious it was!
That familiar smell,
how could I ever forget?

      43rd Year of Showa Period, Brussels
    Showa Electrical Stock Company Fuyuki Shoryo

This message was written with such sincerity and passion, but it also conveyed some news: this gentleman tasted flavors from his native home. In other words, the Confucius restaurant also prepared authentic Japanese dishes.

Then there was the matter of that message's date. The 43rd year of the Showa period was 1968. That time is much later than the Qian family descendants can remember. This also means that the period when Qian Xiuling was acting as homemaker to her husband and children lasted at least ten years.

A Korean message:
Hello! I am YangGuk from Korea.
The first time I saw the beautiful woman in the restaurant, I thought I had my mother here!
I am eating and singing here — I am so happy.
Wishing you prosperity!

There was a message in German as well — only one line long:

An Asian Goddess!
Love you
Erich and Johanna from Bavaria, Germany

From these little tidbits you can judge that the business and reputation of Confucius was good. It wasn't just the delicacies and service that motivated its clients to return, but the personal charm of its female owner. It seems simply unimaginable that it closed due to financial loss.

However, according to Qian Xianhe's memory, his aunt told him in all seriousness that Confucius shuttered its door because it couldn't turn a profit.

But maybe there is another interpretation: the reason Qian Xiuling started the restaurant was that she wanted to make and save money. As time passed, though, she wasn't treating it like a business. Her character had its bold and unrestrained side, and her affections for her comrades occupied a huge part of that. She could come up short anywhere, except with her friends, or her own heart.

So it was that Confucius honorably and unrepentantly went out of business …

CHAPTER 17

How to Measure Seawater

*T*hen, what?

Well, she opened up another restaurant.

If you assessed for a moment Qian Xiuling's social resources at the time, she could have easily obtained a dignified and respected post in high society. But, she decided to retire at the height of her fame.

Running a restaurant was actually quite tiring, but it was a beautiful thing in Qian Xiuling's eyes. Each day was full of challenges. From the looks of it, it was the outlet Qian Xiuling had been looking for to provide for herself, not, in fact, a way to retreat from society that caused others to forget who she was. At first, she put aside those possessions she once had. Moreover, her new life made her slowly fade from memories carved deep into others' hearts. She hoped to live a free life, floating gently along like thin clouds, without constraint.

She changed her location to a busy road right next to a large plaza in Brussels' city center. She also chose a new name for the place: Elegance Restaurant.

Was this a one-time shift in strategy for Qian Xiuling? We discovered from her change in name to her relocation in the city that Qian Xiuling's business sense had matured a little bit from before. She welcomed suggestions about this and that her friends brought up to her. That name, Elegance, was a rather popular term at the time. When Qian Xiuling was studying in Shanghai as a young girl, she liked the mood and tastes of the place. On the Bund in Shanghai, there was an Elegance Road, an Elegance Cantonese Restaurant, an Elegance Hotel, etc. Her impression was that the seaboard locations of Hong Kong, Taiwan, and Macau, all had restaurants and streets named Elegance. When she saw the word, her first reaction was that it felt very familiar. She believed that the Chinese with experience living in cities would have beautiful memories stirred by this word too.

The large plaza where they were located was one of the busiest locations in the Brussels business district. A large number of beautiful medieval buildings were preserved there. Wherever you looked was a dazzling, majestic sight. Every kind of small shop was stacked up, row upon row, people shuttling to and fro between them. Occupying a niche in an expensive district was no matter to trifle with. For instance, next to the most famous piece of medieval architecture, the city hall, was a restaurant called The Swan. A tiny sign hung over its door:

Karl Marx once lodged and ate here.

Qian Xiuling had arrived. Opening up a restaurant in this kind of place required spirit and ambition. Those were two things she had in her bones. She was up to the task.

We found the original site of the Elegance restaurant, on a street just behind The Swan. In terms of its size, it was a bit smaller than the Confucius restaurant. That "taste of China" approach had been completely obliterated — the cuisine was fully Europeanized. And we needn't bring up any kind of open and sunny rear courtyard. However, because of the support of the imposing atmosphere in the grand plaza, every inch of space felt strong and vigorous.

The restaurant had now been turned into a bakery. When we showed up there, they were in the middle of removing fresh waffles from the oven. The sweet smell enticed our nostrils and made our mouths water. We bought two of them and took them each from the hand of the madam behind the counter. The master baker smiled at us, reminding us that we should eat them hot. In all fairness, those freshly cooked waffles on the corner of a Brussels street overturned my previous perception of waffles. They were incredibly delicious! In a moment of weakness, I gulped down my entire waffle, chewing on a large piece.

Relying on Mr. Peng Fei's translation, we asked about the Elegance restaurant that had been there before. The baker shook his head. He didn't know anything about it. I mentioned Qian Xiuling's name. He turned to a short, old man, who I guessed was the owner, and mumbled a few phrases. The old man also seemed to be at a loss.

"Was there any Guest Book left by the former owner?"

"Huh ... No, I'm sorry, but we've never heard anything about that."

A line from a Tang Dynasty poem came to mind:

A Daoist Immortal has flown away on his yellow crane, leaving the Yellow Crane Tower utterly empty.

According to descriptions from Qian family descendants, Qian Xiuling wasn't in business for very long in that location either —

maybe one or two years. The story behind that has been swallowed up by time.

We lingered in the lobby for a while. We tried to imagine how many people could actually fit in such a narrow space — at most, you might have 5 or 6 tables. Rent here was undoubtedly expensive, but business would certainly be booming. Outside the front door of the restaurant, lined up in both directions, were rows of simple cafe furniture. This was probably their overflow seating. When things were busy, the customers could take a seat, drink a hot coffee or a chilled drink, and aimless chatter as they waited to be seated inside. Watching pedestrians with every kind of expression and posture rushing back and forth unknowingly melds one into the scene — it's truly a special kind of pleasure.

After a while, that female owner would come by with her conspicuous, winning smile and greet each one of her guests. While you spoke with her, she would pay extra close attention, making you feel like you were part of the family. She was good at understanding others. Sometimes there would be some language barriers between you in conversation, but the dishes and service at Elegance would make the diner feel that the food was much more important than language in this place. In other words, the warm environment was a lovely atmosphere, and the cuisine made it feel all the more rich.

When Qian Xiuling opened the Confucius restaurant, she unyieldingly stated that if the customer wasn't satisfied, they didn't have to pay. She didn't take a single thing away from that restaurant, except for that one rule. But would Elegance also have had a Guest Book like the Confucius restaurant? I would like to believe that it did, and that behind every message written was a stirring tale. Unfortunately, with the utmost regret, any such book has been lost without a trace in the fathomless sea of time.

Clearly, getting Elegance off the ground was not Qian Xiuling's ultimate goal. She was riding a wave, hoping to later move into deeper waters. The apex of her food and beverage journey was reached with the opening of the Jade Spring restaurant. That must have come about sometime after 1971.

In the broader context, China and Belgium had established diplomatic relations at the time. A door long sealed had finally been thrown open.

Her heart must have been deeply moved as she gazed up at the five stars on the red national flag fluttering outside the door of the Chinese Embassy in Belgium. Though she understood little about the Communist Party, and though for her entire life she and her relatives were more or less involved in political movements, a shadow must have still hung over her heart. However, in her mind, a person's fate and cultivation couldn't be wholly tied up with their motherland. Despite all that, seeing her country's new national flag for the first time must have made her heart skip a bit faster. It was true that she had obtained her Belgian citizenship, but, in the depths of her heart, her motherland would forever be her first home.

One day, a group of cordial Chinese customers came into the Jade Spring. They were officials from the Chinese Embassy. One of them was actually a fellow villager from Jiangsu province. They all amiably referred to her as Big Sister. The greeting made tears come to her eyes — her countrymen had paid her a visit. They were all aware of her influence in Belgium and praised her for her courage and fearlessness at the crucial moment when she undertook the task of saving those hostages. They also later expressed admiration for her modesty and independence. She never imagined that one of the guests who was a bit older than herself would actually be the first ambassador to Belgium, Mr. Li Lianbi. He sincerely thanked her and invited her to return to her hometown when the time was right. He also mentioned that with the reestablishment of China's official diplomatic relations with Belgium, she would see more and more Chinese visiting Belgium. Ambassador Li looked all around and humorously remarked, "Big Sister, you're going to have to expand your space here a lot more, otherwise there won't be enough room to hold all your countrymen!"

There aren't enough details to clarify, but Qian Xiuling once more migrated the location of her restaurant from the large plaza to Brussel's most famous street, Tervuren Main Street — equivalent to Beijing's Wangfujing. It inevitably had something to do with the embassy officials' visit to Jade Spring. From that moment on, the Chinese Embassy became a psychological mentor to her. This was a fact.

Shortly after opening its doors, a grey-haired woman walked into Jade Spring. She looked over 60, her face thin. She was looking for Qian Xiuling.

Coincidentally, Qian Xiuling was due to return from running some errands. The woman said she was happy to wait. She ordered an appetizer and slowly ate it in a serene manner.

It was her old friend, Cecile Vent.

The moment Qian Xiuling saw her, they rushed and tightly embraced. It had been much too long since they had last spoken.

She calmed down and told Qian Xiuling that General Falkenhausen had passed away. He had lived to the ripe old age of 88. In his last years, he spent a great deal of time remembering and reviewing his past, often unable to sleep well at night. Though he had permanently faded from people's view, his thinking was always very active. During those years, he intermittently wrote a personal memoir containing over 200,000 words. It described many cultural traditions of the German people, ruminations on ideologic forms, and especially why Germany had produced a war demon like Adolf Hitler. His reflections were painful. However, he would say, "We ponder pain when it is gone. That's when we can probe the source of the malady."

The book was entitled *Memoirs Outside of War*. It wasn't an officially published print book, but it had Falkenhausen's personal signature on the cover. Cecile gave it to Qian Xiuling.

"He was very tranquil as he approached his end. He told me that I needed to thank you one more time on behalf of him."

She held the thick tome in her hands. She was speechless, feeling too much. She did not know how or what to express. Cecile said, "You must read this very closely." She imagined that Falkenhausen's own spirit had merged with the volume.

She asked Cecile, "Are you going to return to Belgium to settle down?"

Cecile shook her head with a firm expression, "I will head back to Germany and live out the remainder of my days in his hometown. My own family still cannot forgive me for what I've done, nevermind reconcile with me. After I'm dead, I will be buried with him, forever resting at his side."

Qian Xiuling sighed, "After all these years, you haven't changed a bit. I admire you."

As they parted, Qian Xiuling gave her some money, but Cecile resolutely refused. Qian Xiuling said, "Take it! This is given in kindness — it will make me feel better. We're older now and always need money. If I can't help you, and you have no other way to earn an income, it'll greatly upset me."

She walked her out. Her heart was troubled for a long time after that. She knew that in this world good people were destined to exist, showering their light upon you, but you couldn't make those brief encounters with them last long. She believed that as General

Falkenhausen passed into the next life, he did so with little suffering because Cecile Vent was there by his side. If it hadn't been for her, he absolutely wouldn't have finished so thick a memoir. She felt extremely gratified about that. Maybe in his final years, his meeting Cecile Vent — such an honorable woman — was a grace shown to him by God.

So, what was the meaning behind the restaurant's name Jade Spring?

Qian Xiuling once told her nephew Qian Weiqiang that the name seemed pretty ordinary, but that it was very Chinese. Jade illustrated a noble quality — Chinese liked to talk about a "jade spirit." Then there was "spring", an ever-flowing water source, which conveyed the sense of something small that continues to flow forever.

Qian Weiqiang was considered to be the first descendant of the Qian family from China who "jumped the line" in Belgium, and it was without a doubt because of the guidance offered to him by his great aunt, Qian Xiuling.

> At the end of the 1970s, China's efforts to open up to the outside world increased, and the number of those travelling abroad grew. Aunt Qian went back to Shanghai for a visit and to have a reunion with us. At the time, we didn't know her work situation in Belgium. My grandfather was Aunt Qian's brother. Their conversations were sometimes conducted outside of the earshot of us younger kids. One time, Aunt Qian asked me whether or not I wanted to go back to Belgium with her and work in her restaurant. Her plan for me was first to study the food and beverage industry at her restaurant, and then go and open up my own place. That was the way most overseas Chinese

expanded their operations. At the time, I was working at a chemical factory on a three-shift rotation — a dry and mind-numbing job. I was thrilled that I might be able to go abroad with Aunt Qian. But my family and I were the same in thinking that it would take more than a year to complete the visa process.

Qian Weiqiang never assumed that in just a month's time he would receive a notification from the Belgium Consulate in Shanghai for an in-person interview. Following that notification, it was all green lights! The procedure for going abroad was quickly completed.

It was his impression that almost everybody at the embassies and consulates showed great respect whenever Qian Xiuling's name was mentioned.

He never imagined on his arrival in Brussels that he would see his Aunt's restaurant located on the bustling Tervuren Road. No more than 500 meters away was the 50th Anniversary Independence Monument, like Beijing's Monument to the People's Heroes. The large road was open and spacious and full of people. The location of Jade Spring was a premium site for making money. The entry to the restaurant was through a tunnel, bordered by plants on both sides. The sign was written in official clerical script, like a rubbing found on a Tang Dynasty stele, elegant, smooth and refined. There was a parlor just inside the door with a screen inlaid with ivory. It had a definite Chinese feel. Then there were 7 or 8 private dining rooms and a place for tables upstairs as well.

Qian Weiqiang would never have guessed that business at Jade Spring would be booming. It was ordinarily full, and the afternoon was no exception. Four waiters were usually always on duty, with the need for eight later on. There was fundamentally no time to rest.

Weekends were when the restaurant was most crowded. Throngs of customers would sit outside at the cafe tables, waiting for tables to free up and be reset with new tablecloths and settings. They truly had their hands full — they had to hire 2 or 3 temporary waiters just to handle the weekends. During Qian Weiqiang's first day on the job, Qian Xiuling sent him into the kitchen as a helper. She urged him to learn the job well, starting from how to chop correctly. There were four people in the kitchen at the time. The head chef was a Taiwanese man named Peter Chen. His Beijing Duck was incredible. Many customers rushed to their establishment just for his duck. They always ran out of the dish. Peter Chen normally thought very highly of himself. When he spoke to others it was always with a bit of condescension. But when he was in front of Qian Xiuling, he acted submissively. He had a mantra: "Only if you can make Big Sister tell me to."

As time passed, Qian Weiqiang learned that there was some history between them. Before coming to Jade Spring, Peter was working as a cook in another restaurant — a really awesome one. One time, he had some pressing business back in Taiwan and unexpectedly forgot to give his boss notice before leaving. It was a weekend and there was a big wedding reception being thrown by an old overseas Chinese man for his daughter. They had booked 8 tables for the wedding feast. When the crucial moment arrived, Peter Chen was nowhere to be found. The owner frantically ran around in circles, finally ringing Peter's phone. Peter had already landed in Taipei. How could this be? His boss almost fainted from shock. At the last second, she found some second-rate cook, who hurriedly threw the dishes together in a muddled manner. The old Chinese man was livid, so much so that he refused to pay. At that moment, the restaurant's reputation was ruined. The owner went to court to sue for damages, but the cook wasn't in the country — the court had no jurisdiction in

Taiwan. But Peter wasn't permitted to reenter the country.

Qian Xiuling didn't know about any of this. She had only heard others say that a certain Peter Chen's Beijing Duck was excellent. She found out that he had returned to Taiwan, so she called him up and asked him if he would like to serve as the head chef at Jade Spring. Peter replied that he wasn't allowed back into Belgium, that customs wouldn't let him through. Qian Xiuling said, "That's not a big deal. I'll just speak with them." As a result, Qian Xiuling gave the customs officers a phone call. When they heard that Ms. Qian would be showing up, they immediately responded, "No problem at all. He can come." In the end, Peter Chen ended up returning to Brussels.

Peter Chen hadn't been at Jade Spring for more than a few days before his original boss discovered it. He came around knocking on their door, wanting to denounce Peter but also to investigate Qian Xiuling's role in the matter. Until that point, Qian Xiuling didn't know anything that had happened between them. What was she supposed to do about it? Qian Xiuling wanted Peter to apologize to his former boss, and to compensate him for his losses. If he didn't have that kind of cash on him, Qian Xiuling said she was willing to lend him some — in fact, it meant that she would pay for his damages. After all that, Qian Xiuling also personally apologized herself, since she truly had no idea what the actual situation had been.

Because of that, Peter Chen behaved himself at Jade Spring. His former boss' restaurant had closed. He couldn't go on any longer with that damaged reputation. He came looking again for Qian Xiuling, and asked her for a job — any old job, just as long as it paid for his food. Qian Xiuling appointed him to the front cash register. At first, he was quite animated, but as time dragged on, his hurt feelings resurfaced and he would often complain in the dining room, poorly influencing the performance of other workers. Qian Xiuling took it all in and always used kind words to placate him, saying that if he opened up a restaurant again, she would surely support him. Her level of tolerance was really something that others couldn't match.

The staff at Jade Spring all worked very hard. One reason was because of Qian Xiuling's personal charm, the other was because of the distribution mechanism that existed. Qian Weiqiang discovered on arrival that the workers were paid every day for their work. Qian Xiuling had a rule: everybody counted the money, stacked it up into various piles, and then waited for Qian Xiuling to divide it up. She would grab an abacus — SNAP-SNAP-WHAP-WHAP — subtracting her overhead, wear-and-tear percentage, and capital accumulation. Then, with whatever was left over, she would pay each worker their wages according to their position, seniority, and share of work. She would even give those staff who had worked over three years with her a share in the business.

She felt that if somebody stayed at the restaurant for three years that they had become family, and should take part in the same blessings. Everyone's allotment was made in front of everybody else, public and transparent. Imagine for a moment these workers after a long day, returning home with bulging wallets and purses — what employee wouldn't be happy?! They worked especially hard during the day. Every single person felt like they were working for themselves. Qian Weiqiang said he had walked all over Brussels, and no other restaurant — big or small — had this kind of payment system.

She created a free and easy atmosphere, acting good-natured towards all. She could always be seen with a smile. You never saw her with furrowed brow or sour face. The staff all knew one of her famous phrases: a smile costs nothing.

There was only one time she got angry, but it wasn't even that much.

It was with Peter Chen's former boss again. After coming to Jade Spring, he was always constantly complaining and nitpicking, probably because he was no longer the boss. Qian Xiuling knew he was feeling low, so she was always giving him a break. She would also pay him more than the other workers. But he still was resentful of the amount. One time, right in front of the rest of the staff, he openly complained that his wages were too low, adding that hares may pull dead lions by the beard.

This happened during closing time when the staff was putting everything away. Qian Xiuling gathered all of the employees together for a meeting. At the beginning, she maintained a cool and calm atmosphere. When he had finished speaking, she didn't get angry. She merely said, "So, what would you like me to do? Speak up. How much more do you want me to give you?"

The untactful former boss unexpectedly answered with a demand that made the whole staff laugh out loud.

Qian Xiuling abruptly slapped the table, and leapt to her feet, unable to contain her indignation any longer, "Go all over Brussels and ask everybody how Qian Xiuling treats her people. I would like to help you, and hope you can make a comeback. We're both Chinese and it's not easy to do things out here. But, your conduct and deeds here are very disappointing. If I were to accommodate you, it would be an injustice to the rest of your brothers and sisters here."

The moment her voice stopped, the staff rose to their feet and applauded.

Qian Xiuling believed that acting kindly to those who behaved poorly only injured the good. If the scales were thrown off balance, her restaurant would start sliding down a slippery slope.

She asked that he promptly leave.

The man's attitude suddenly softened. He expressed that he

would demand nothing ever again, and asked for one more chance.

She just waved her hand, "Pardon me for not seeing you to the door."

After some time had passed, Jade Spring became part of the scenic landscape of Tervuren Road. For a local from Brussels, to be invited to dine at Jade Spring was probably considered a special honor. Whether a high official or a lowly commoner, all had high praise for Jade Spring. Every element of the place was brimming with allure: the cuisine, the ambience, and the service. Qian Xiuling would arrive every day one half-hour before lunch started. She would personally inspect every inch of the kitchen and private dinner rooms.

She showed interest in everything from the positioning of the flowers to the table settings and furniture placement to even aspects of hygiene. When an important customer would arrive, she would be there at the door to welcome them. Whoever she didn't know, she would go and meet, asking them if the dishes were to their liking. If they brought their children along with them, she would send them over a children's meal. And if it was somebody's first time at the restaurant, she would give them a new dish or soup on the house. That kind of atmosphere made all feel at ease.

Those customers who knew her would bring guests with them and tell them the story of how Qian Xiuling saved those hostages long ago. The guests would stop her and ask her if that was all true.

Qian Xiuling would just smile, "The past is the past. If you want to know who really saved them, it was my older cousin. He was the one who knew General Falkenhausen. It was those two who saved those people. I was just the messenger."

One time, a German reporter came to eat at the restaurant, asking her about the story of saving all those people back then. She said, "Oh, that was ages ago. I don't remember that anymore. It wasn't that big of a deal. It's like walking down a street; if you see a child fall down, you run over and lift them up — it's just that simple."

Qian Weiqiang sensed that his aunt had an extraordinary sensitivity to media types. She didn't want them hyping the story up, and really hoped to avoid being mentioned at all. She told Weiqiang, "What's the point in always bringing up ancient history? Whenever somebody asks you about it, just say you don't know."

When the restaurant's peak hours passed, she would take her lunch, usually with her husband. Dr. Gregory had already retired at that time, and his tastes had been utterly transformed by his Asian belle.

Little wontons and fried egg rolls were per usual the main dishes on their table. Qian Weiqiang thought that Dr. Gregory was a good man. He was reserved, tall and thin, meticulously graceful and poised. Whenever he would come to eat at the restaurant, he would come dressed in a suit and tie. Qian Xiuling would talk, while he listened and smiled. He seldom interrupted. Comparing both of them in conversation, it appeared that Qian Xiuling was the stronger of the two.

As she grew older, Qian Xiuling began mainly eating vegetables. Her wontons would be stuffed with vegetables and shrimps. Qian Weiqiang remembered she especially liked to cook one of her hometown dishes: fried cabbage and bean sprouts. She would use her own brined vegetables and sprouts she grew herself, adding tofu skin, golden needles flowers, and black tree fungus to the mix.

Qian Xiuling's house was only a stone's throw away from Jade Spring at the time. You crossed the main road, walked a few minutes, and you were there. They lived in a big apartment on the eighth floor of a luxury apartment building. After he arrived in Brussels, Qian

Weiqiang would follow his aunt home almost every afternoon after work. His aunt would prepare a pot of coffee for him and then sit down and instruct him in French with her own personalized lessons. She required that he grasp French quickly, otherwise it would be very difficult to gain a foothold in Belgium. This went on for over a year. Sometimes, she would stop, and tell Weiqiang stories from long ago in her hometown. She'd often bring up her father and how she believed she let him down. She'd go on and on until the tears started to come. Weiqiang sensed she was a tender-hearted, family woman.

Qian Xiuling and Gregory had five children together. They all married and settled down. One of them became a doctor, one opened up an art gallery, the others were businessmen. Some of them were a cut above the rest, and some were mediocre. In Qian Weiqiang's estimation, Qian Xiuling's favorite grandson was the eldest Jerome. During one of Jerome's birthdays, Xiuling went to a store to pick out a Leica camera as a birthday present for him. Every Wednesday, when school would get out in the afternoon, Jerome would give his grandmother a phone call and bring some of his friends to the restaurant to eat.

Jerome taught his classmates how to eat with chopsticks, then he'd order some of Jade Springs signature dishes like a seasoned pro. Qian Weiqiang always remembered how happy and enthusiastic they were while they ate. When Jerome showed up, Qian Xiuling was always especially happy. She really treated well the little guests he brought with him. It was as if she had returned to her youth as she chatted with them. One time, there was a particularly shy girl in the group named Masha. Qian Xiuling was over the moon! She quickly told one of the waiters to go to the store and buy a school supplies box to give to the little girl.

In private, Qian Xiuling told Weiqiang, "None of my

grandchildren have any feeling for China, except for this grandson. I had him eating Chinese food since he was little, using chopsticks. I also told him traditional Chinese stories, so now he likes Chinese food, which means he'll like China later."

One day, one of Qian Xiuling's old Chinese friends, Jiang Zhushan, brought his entire family to the restaurant to eat. Old Jiang was from Shanghai and had been in Belgium for a number of decades. His son and grandson couldn't speak any Chinese. Old Jiang just sighed, "Without that linguistic base, how can we get our children to speak Chinese? If you don't speak Chinese, how can you still be considered Chinese? In two more generations, they'll have completely forgotten their ancestors."

Those words stirred Qian Xiuling's soul. She replied, "Why don't we set up our own Chinese school? We'll make these overseas sons and daughters study traditional Chinese culture and remember where their roots are."

Qian Xiuling interviewed everyone in her Chinese friend circle. Practically every single person said that the second and third generations had become complete strangers to Chinese culture.

They all approved setting up an overseas Chinese school.

For a time, this made Qian Xiuling very busy. What she said she would do, she always put her full effort behind. A few of the more well-off Chinese gathered around her and elected to make her the first principal of the overseas Chinese school. They later found a school building, submitted their certifications, contacted qualified instructors, hired staff, purchased equipment for the facility, set up campus, organized the classrooms, and on and on. All of this was personally done by Qian Xiuling. Qian Weiqiang accompanied her on some of her errands — wherever they went, she was met with great reverence and respect. He asked his aunt why all these people were so accommodating to her requests. His aunt just smiled back, "How should I know? Maybe it's just because there are so many good people in this world."

Weiqiang still remembered a dialogue he had with his aunt. He had asked her, "Why do you want to establish this school? Isn'n it going to cost you a fortune?" Qian Xiuling explained that when she was young she wanted to be a scientist like Madame Curie, but fate passed her by. She had wanted many times to return to China to repay the kindnesses it had shown her, but those opportunities were all missed as well. Now that she had grown older, she no longer attached importance to a lot of things, but deep down in her bones she was still Chinese. That sat rested deep in her heart and was only growing stronger. She wanted to set up the Chinese school so that she could hear Chinese spoken and see more Chinese people around her. Seeing little Chinese children made her very happy. It would be an incredible achievement if the older overseas Chinese generation was able to retain its roots and ensure that they continued to grow through their children's and children's children's generations.

Besides that, what else can I do at this point?

Qian Weiqiang remembered that when she said that, her eyes were moist with tears.

With respect to money, Qian Xiuling said that in a person's life the struggle for money and its uses never ends. When money is earned, then it needs to be spent on something you like, like setting up a Chinese school — it was the thing that had brought her the most joy since she arrived in Belgium.

She turned into a ball of energy, spinning this way and that. Once people in the restaurant mentioned the Chinese school, chatterbox of hers would start popping away, her face lit up by an unusual vigor. There was a period when she rarely made an appearance in the restaurant. Her energies were all being thrown into the Chinese school. After a while, everybody knew she was either in one of three places: in the restaurant, in the Chinese school, or on the road between those two places.

One day, she returned unusually happy to the restaurant. She said that the cultural attaché to the Chinese Embassy had paid the Chinese school a visit. He had offered them many supportive and encouraging words. The Embassy sent over a load of books to the school, among them are *300 Poems of Chinese Tang Dynasty*, *300 Poems of Chinese Song Dynasty*, *Origion of Chinese Characters*, *A Dream of Red Mansions*, and more. She said it took her back to her youth when she saw all those books: "I grew up reading these books!"

My October 20th, 2018 Interview Notes:

> I arrived in Belgium almost two weeks ago. My tourist visa is about to expire.
> I finally was able to interview the two-days newly appointed mayor of Ecaussinnes city, Xavier. He was in his forties, tall and strong, with a full beard. A pair of aged jeans hugged his two long legs. He looked like a basketball star. This man had originally served as the vice-chair of a union for some middle school, but he had a passion for politics, and he had a rich and powerful boss-friend, Raymond Maucq's friend Nuer, boss of the local head economic and development office boss. He helped Mr. Xavier, who unexpectedly beat out the other 9 candidates and won the position. The opposition wouldn't accept it, though, gathering to protest in the plaza every day. At first, Mr. Xavier politely

refused an interview, but when Nuer stepped in, he finally consented to meet with us.

From his appearance, it didn't look like he had taken on the role of the city mayor yet. He seemed to be a bit heedless and indifferent in his reservation. He kept on rubbing both of his hands together, constantly looking at his watch, like he was almost urging me to hurry and wrap things up.

I asked him only one question:

"Are there still people in Ecaussinnes who remember Qian Xiuling? After taking office, will you do anything to help disseminate knowledge of Qian Xiuling's deeds?"

Mr. Xavier's response was very honest:

"I am a native of this city. Ever since I was little, I listened to my father tell stories about Madame Qian saving those hostages. Now, there are truly few people younger than the middle-aged who know anything about Madame Qian. This doesn't mean, however, that time has forgotten her. History has marked her virtue and achievements. In my view, if, in our normal life, somebody saves another person, everybody thinks it is a great feat. Then there's Madame Qian who, during the war years, saved over 100 souls — that's truly incredible. After taking office, I'm going to have the stories of Madame Qian written into students' extracurricular books in order to help them know that there was once such a magnificent woman, who in a distant era did a good deed that is worthy of our eternal commemoration."

I gave Xavier a Yixing pot as a gift. He gave us a common coffee cup wrapped in beautiful paper, saying, "Ecaussinnes is a romantic city. Many young people when they marry choose to come to Ecaussinnes for their wedding ceremony and their honeymoon."

Looking back on it, my biggest regret was that we didn't interview Qian Xiuling's eldest son, Timothy. We trusted Qian Weiqiang to set it up, hoping he could secure a meeting for us, but Timothy always had some kind of excuse to put us off.
Qian Weiqiang believed that he had never been to China and lacked understanding of it, especially in 2002, when CCTV was promoting their TV soap opera *A Chinese Woman at Gestapo Gunpoint*. He watched it and saw that some of the plot points weren't accurate enough, getting quite angry, in fact. There was a lack of communication between them, and from that point on he distanced himself from Chinese people.
They say he is now 83 years old.
But Qian Xianhe revealed to me that Aunt Qian Xiuling had secretly told him a detail years ago. While she was still in Herbeumont, Timothy was hurt by the phrase shouted at him as a child: "Chinaman." No matter how many times Qian Xiuling tried to console him, there was still a cloud left hanging in his immature soul. "China," in his estimation, had a dark feel to it. And after he grew up, he watched all those relatives and friends seeking help from his mother, living in their home, working in his mother's restaurant, struggling to make money. He saw how his mother treated them even better than her own family members, and it threw his heart off balance.

Qian Xiuling disciplined her children rather severely — a completely traditional Asian way of raising children. However, after the kids went to middle school, high school, and college, they learned other western ways of thinking. "Rebellion" broke out as a result. All this, for Timothy, congealed into ill will and coldness towards China.

CHAPTER 18

Ashes to Ashes, Dust to Dust

Dearest Xiuling,

You know everything from my previous two letters. For three months now, chills and fever have riven my body — this sickness is unceasing and my convalescence has not yet delivered its result. For this I am deeply regretful. Your humble brother retired from the military last December, removing his armor and returning home. My heart has returned to Taoyuan, no longer involved in the world's affairs. Distancing oneself from a certain person is like splitting a mountain pass. The government is still pursuing its labor of many years. The Ministry of Finance has hired me as a consultant for the Chinese Weaving Construction Company. It is an empty position, with no need to punch the clock in the office every day. It pays for meagre meals for me. How embarrassing!

I have accumulated stores of pain, not the body's manifestation of inner ills. Only you, my dearest sister, know your brother these many decades. Since last year, your brother and sister-in-law have converted to Christianity, going to Church to pray night and day. The radiance before my eyes gradually expands. All sorrows and joys alone depend upon Heaven. I wish you and your excellent husband, Ge Lixia, conjugal happiness and health!

Your brother Qipei
May 15th, the 13th Year of the Republic

This letter was written in 1954. Although it is a common letter, it reveals a part of Qian Zhuolun's emotions and frame of mind in his later years.

From his own words, we know that he finally retired and settled down. That phrase "meagre meals for me" referred to the salary he received from a state enterprise under the Ministry of Finance. The so-called "certain person," should be clear to the reader. In the end, Jiang Jieshi couldn't send him to the fields of death — Song Meiling most likely had a big role to play in that. Jiang also knew that Qian Zhuolun was mourning his son and sister-in-law in his old age. That was a tragic misfortune in anybody's life. Hatred born from his son's execution must have created a deep ravine. An utter stranger could understand this. He stripped him of his military ranks and honors, and left him with a meagre stipend. It wasn't a way to end things for him, but a way to recognize his loyalty over the years. And Qian Zhuolun's reference to converting to Christianity came from the needs of a tortured heart — a way of protecting himself.

The Qian family letters were that rare ray of light warming their icy hearts. Over the decades, the ray of light shone through the correspondence between brother and sister. Those yellowing pages reflect the extraordinary times of their ordinary days. The letters left so many memories for their descendants.

> My December 5th, 2018, Interview Notes:
>
> A special visit to Taipei.
> At two o'clock on December 4th, at Dante Cafe on the first floor of Taipei First Hotel.
> I was finally able to secure an appointment with Qian Zhuolun's grandson, Qian Yuxuan, his daughter's son, Shen Yijiang, and a rather old Qian Xianhang, Qian Zhuolun's second eldest son.

I had so many questions I wanted to ask General Zhuolun's descendants.

Firstly, did Qian Xiuling often visit Taiwan during the 1950s and 60s? And when she met with her elder cousin, did they ever talk about the rescue of the hostages in Belgium?

Qian Yuxuan had a head full of white hair. He was 71 but his body was robust, and he had a healthy red color in his face. When his father, Qian Kexian, and mother, Wang Yaojun, were executed, his elder sister was 12, he was 10, his younger brother was barely 8, and his youngest sister was only 6.

He responded to my question like this:

> Before, I had never heard about the matter of Aunt Xiuling rescuing hostages in Belgium. Before that CCTV series, none of us knew anything about it. Of course, we were all very young back then. Our aunt did come to Taiwan to see our grandfather. They talked as adults did, avoiding us children. But my grandfather also never mentioned this matter either. I think that for them this was just a small thing — like raising a hand. It wasn't worth putting into words, especially for us little ones.

Qian Xianhang was Qian Xianhe's younger brother, Qian Zhuolun's second son. He was 80 at the time of the interview. He was the eldest in the family, a generation older than Qian Yuxuan.

> Aunt Qian came to Taipei to visit my father and Uncle Zhuolun. I was there a lot of the time. When they got together they would chat a lot, share things about their families, children, and talk about old friends from Yixing, their hometown. I never heard her mention anything about rescuing hostages. I don't think my father or Uncle Zhuolun ever talked about it either.

"In other words, if it weren't for CCTV broadcasting their series *A Chinese Woman at Gestapo Gunpoint*, Qian family descendants would still know nothing about Qian Xiuling's saving those hostages."

> This isn't difficult to explain, since they didn't think of what she did as a big feat. A lot of folks in their generation would live for the country or their beliefs, abandoning their

families and children, offering up their very own lives and those of their entire clan. So, saving people, in their view, was like greeting an acquaintance and asking for a favor. What was the big deal?

That was Shen Yijiang's view. He spent his childhood years at the side of his grandfather, Qian Zhuolun. He remembered that when Aunt Xiuling came to the house, they spoke mostly about their children, her own and everybody else's.

So, what was General Qian Zhuolun's mental state in his final years?

In the few materials of Zhuolun's sent to us by Qian Yuxuan, there was an article written by Zhuolun's eldest son Qian Keshun entitled "My Father's Life." In it, he speaks of his father's final years:

> Father, in his later years, and my stepmother, were devout followers of Jesus. Every morning and evening they went to pray, loyally attended all their meetings, spread the gospel, and participated in the Lord's work rain or shine. From that point on, smoking, drinking, and all such amusements came to an end. Father's affection for his homeland was deep. Early on during his time in Nanjing and Chongqing, he would maintain contact with his peers from back home, initiating the establishment of Yixing Townsmen Association. The Nanjing Plum Blossom Yi Xing Hall was single-handedly created by father. After arriving in Taiwan, he and Zhang Yulin, Xie Shaohong and various old businessmen organized the Taipei Yixing Townsmen Association, and published the Yixing Hometown News. The masthead calligraphy was done by Father as well.

Mr. Zhuolun's descendants tell the stories of the old, hunched, thin man holding an umbrella in the hot, violent rains of Taipei, fading away under the shade of tropical vegetation. A head once full of dark, thick hair, had turned white and thin. His gaze had lost its light. When he looked at people, he reacted a bit slowly, though warmly, and his once straight waist and back had hunched and bent his frame. His friend circle shrank through the vicissitudes of time, but he always knew himself. Smoking and drinking no longer touched him, but tea was hard to give up. Living alone, he drank boiled water. At home, he also wore old clothes. He would write letters to his friends and stuff them into old, torn envelopes that he flipped over and pasted back together. The friends he dealt with all knew his simple life: "The three points that form the line." He would move from his home to the Christian chapel to the Yixing Townsmen Association Hall.

He resolutely distanced himself from that former circle of friends — he didn't listen, didn't inquire, and didn't associate with them. He used what mental and physical efforts he had left to focus on doing the things he liked.

When a person grows old, they gradually begin to see certain things as less important. Every time he got together with his Yixing friends, he would always talk nonstop about the good old days in Yixing. At that time, cross-strait relations were completely cut off, both sides still had their guns aimed at each other, and almost no information was being exchanged. Sometimes, his fellow Yixing friends would gather and pool together whatever crumbs of news they had learned about their hometown. It was vague and unclear, but it was better than nothing.

While in Nanjing, Zhuolun was the director of the Yixing Townsmen Association. He arranged to have the society meet in a hall in a spacious, classical courtyard on Plum Blossom Lane in Jinling old city. Its bustling atmosphere and august company was still vivid in his mind. During the War of Resistance, they moved to the provisional capital in Chongqing, where the society's activities resumed just as before, once more guided and perfectly organized by Zhuolun. When they arrived in Taipei, moods gradually turned darker as homesickness grew worse. They were able to gather on and off to reminisce about the past, wishing for those simpler times on the mainland.

In his hands, the Taipei Yixing Townsmen Association went from nothing to something, building it up brick by brick. In just one year, it had greatly expanded its reach. Though the association hall wasn't set within the classical architecture of Nanjing, it was still an exquisite place of respite from the city's noise — a garden of old pines and green bamboo with winding pathways and abundant tranquility. Zhuolun took the role of the director general and launched the Yixing Hometown News, serving also as its chief editor. Zhuolun threw himself selflessly into the work, helping him to recover his spirits and bringing a bit of peace to his household.

Shen Yijiang remembered how, for a time, his grandfather stayed inside and called a list of his friends to ask them to submit articles. He had said that running a publication was like opening a restaurant: you needed abundant products that dazzled the eye in order for business to take off. The Yixing Hometown News published a season's worth of issues before going defunct. There weren't enough people to submit pieces, so articles grew scarce. There was nothing to be done about it. He was forced to go back into the writing battle, taking the pen name "Perimeter" and creating a new column called Memoirs of the Homeland. Its first article took the revolutionary forces' first uprising in Wuchang as its backdrop, recounting the precursor to the Xinhai Revolution, the process of recovering the old city Yixing. The language was clean and succinct, its materials complete and accurate. There was a section that recorded how the great changes in the Xinhai period reached Yixing, and how he as a young man at the time once participated in the events:

> My hometown is located at the crossroads of Suzhou, Zhejiang, and Anhui provinces. This strip of land is backed by mountains and faces the water, and has always been exposed to banditry and invasion. Plagued by misfortunes over the years, this land has also produced a host of gifted and visionary individuals. In order to think up ways to stabilize society and protect the people, they invited Xu Gong to write a letter inviting Mr. Zhang Huanqi to take up the post as their leader and devise a strategy for self-defence. Mr. Zhang Huanqi had already passed the imperial examination and served in an official post with the court. After serving in faraway places, he had returned home to rest, showing little interest in outside affairs. However, given the difficulties of the times, he resolutely and righteously stepped forward to answer our call and assume the burden of leadership, establishing the Peace Preservation Association and Peace Preservation Corps, along with other zealous local figures, to use military force to defend their homes.
>
> At the time, all students learning out of town left their studies and returned home, subsequently called to join the ranks of the Peace Preservation Corps. All associations and organizations were set up in an empty hall at the back of East Pearl Alley. They employed Wu Yumo to serve as their commanding officer and trainer, assisted by Cheng

> Hongxiang and Qian Zhuolun. These educated youth leapt at the opportunity to heed the call and receive their instruction. They formed various teams and performed their drills. During the day, they would train, and then at night they would perform their patrols. Meanwhile, businessmen travelled to Shanghai to purchase firearms and buy military uniforms in bulk. In just under one month, the Peace Preservation Association had become a dignified and strong military unit, taking on the duty to defend its land.

The writing style was gentle and simple, concise and comprehensive, and free of pretension. In the end, he wrote over 60 historical pieces reflecting on his hometown. For him, the process of writing was a way to journey back to his hometown. Sorting out these historical tales was also a way for him to return to his own spirit.

His younger cousin Zhuoru was working in a coal mine. He also had a family with a dozen mouths to feed. Zhuoru often came to see Zhuolun. Sometimes, Zhuolun would be able to get a nugget of information from Zhuoru about their hometown. He would keep Zhuoru for a while, eat with him and then remember the good old days back on the mainland.

One day, while drinking tea with Zhuoru, Zhuolun let out an odd sigh:

> The past cannot be retraced, and how can the so-called future be known? The only thing a person can possess is the present. Any person, whether rich or poor, lives their lives today, not yesterday, and not tomorrow. The only thing that can be taken away from you too, is today. If you

comprehend this truth, there will be nothing to lose, and nothing to be gained. A long life of 100 years and a short life of a premature death, how are these not the same?

Zhuoru seemed puzzled and asked, "Brother, what do you mean?" Zhuolun smiled faintly, but didn't explain further.

Zhuoru later understood that he was reconciling things with himself. His thoughts had changed his spirit, gradually making him indifferent to the world — he had no regrets, nor did he have any attachments.

On another day, Zhuolun's grandson Qian Yuxuan staying at a boarding school, received a phone call from home. His grandfather had fallen seriously ill and they hoped he could go as quickly as possible to the hospital.

In his opinion, he and his grandfather seldom met. He was just 10 years old when his father and mother perished. He remembers two coffins appearing in his house with photos of his parents sitting in black frames. It was frightening and he grabbed his head and cried. His grandfather came over and embraced all of the children as their tears rained down.

Later on, he and his sisters and younger brother went to live with their grandfather and grandmother on their mother's side. It was only during the New Year's and other holidays that they got together with their other grandfather. He remembered the kind eyes and warm speech of his grandfather, but there always seemed to be some distance between them. Later on he discovered that his grandfather was actually always being watched. They couldn't actually live together and were estranged a bit. Besides family reasons, grandfather did this to protect their safety.

He was participating in the last day of his National Entrance Exam that day. He hurriedly finished up his last section and raced to the hospital and entered his grandfather's sickroom. He was laying on a bed, his face wasted away and his body pierced with tubes. When he saw his grandson walk in, a smile instantly spread across his face. He mustered up all his energy and called loudly for the nurse to come and pull out the tubes from his body. He wanted to eat.

He discovered that grandfather hadn't eaten soup in a number of days. It was his grandson's arrival that revived his final life energy. That so-called last flash of light needed a close relative to activate it. His final breath refused to be cut off, waiting for its time.

He held up the bowl and fed his grandfather the soupy porridge. He watched as his grandfather struggled to swallow. His grandfather paused for a while, took in a big mouthful of air, and then slowly leaned into his grandson's ear, "Little Xuan, you look the most like your father."

When he finished speaking, huge teardrops gushed from his blurry eyes.

He sadly turned away a few times.

> Today, I am favored to be called back to my eternal home, happy and content, happy and content.
> You must devoutly serve and patiently wait for him, rest in peace, rest in peace.

These were the final characters grandfather wrote, a couplet he composed himself.

There is a deeper layer of meaning behind the couplet, something Qian Yuxuan came to understand later. From what Zhuolun understood of Jiang Jieshi, after he died, Jiang would dispatch his people to deliver an elegiac scroll. This was a conventional honor Jiang performed for his subordinates when they passed away, a kind of "norm." Zhuolun requested his family to only lay his own couplet over his grave.

This was his final account.

How could he lay all his burdens down? In his final moments, he still had his worries.

On March 5th, 1967, Qian Zhuolun passed away in Taipei from diabetes, heart disease, and a thromboembolic complication. He had enjoyed 77 years of life.

My December 7th, 2018, Interview Notes:

> We went downtown in the afternoon to buy fresh flowers, accompanied by Qian Yuxuan, then went to Yangmingshan to pay our respects at Qian Zhuolun's grave. Halfway up Yangmingshan, there were gravesites everywhere. We crossed the road, and walked through the tombs of high-ranking officials from the Republican period: Sunke's grave, Chen Cheng's grave, Yan Xishan's grave, Yan Jiagan's grave ... Reeds and flowers formed little clumps, sprinkled across the slope in verdant mounds. The mountain wind blew, brushing against the vegetation, making the white blossoms nod and blurring their outlines, like clouds floating along through the mountains.
> We bowed at the waist in front of the gravestone, then laid flowers down. The grave was extremely simple, no bulge or curve in the mausoleum, only an unadorned, granite stone laid flat on the ground. On both sides of the stone were engraved lines from his poetic couplet. The characters were written with a clear and vigorous hand in the green and

white granite, firm in their suppleness. You couldn't help but feel sorrowful reading the poem over and over.

A fine drizzle began to fall, slanting with the wind and adding a bit of coolness to the scene. Through the sound of the falling rain, we could hear Qian Yuxuan say:

Grandfather understood Jiang Jieshi too well. He knew that Jiang would send his people to give the family a large elegiac scroll. So, he anticipated this by writing his own elegiac couplet and had it engraved in his headstone. As expected, on the second day following grandfather's passing, people arrived from the Presidential Palace, bearing Jiang's own handwritten inscription. But, the elders in the Qian family let them know that their grandfather had already had his own poetry engraved on his headstone. This was tantamount to a polite refusal. The dispatched men said nothing, only placing the inscription down and promptly leaving."

"What does the inscription say? Did you keep it?"
"It was thrown away a long time ago."
Regarding the prolonged surveillance of his grandfather by the authorities, Qian Yuxuan believed that Zhuolun knew nothing about it. But, he let go of everything — he truly didn't care about it all anymore. There was only one thing that maybe wasn't so clear to him: not only had the authorities been tracking him for a long time, they had also always been closely monitoring his descendants, almost every single one of them. Qian Kexian's children obviously bore the brunt of all of this. In his forties, thirty years after his parents' execution, Qian Yuxuan one day was

unexpectedly visited by a stranger, calling himself an officer of the national security division. He told Yuxuan that from that day forward they would be releasing him and his brother Qian Yucheng from their monitoring.
This drawn-out, astonishing chapter of their lives had dragged on for 30 years!

My grandfather's biggest grievance in life was that my mother and father were killed by Jiang Jieshi. He reflected on this a great deal in his final years, and even left some words written down about it. But on the brink of death, he committed his thoughts to the flames. He thought that if his words were read, it would cause us problems later on. With respect to my father and mother, the Communist Party confirmed that they were martyrs to the cause. You can go to the Beijing Xishan Unnamed Martyr's Square Website and look. Among the 1500 plus covert Communist agents martyred behind the lines in Taiwan, you will find the names of my father, Qian Kexian, and my mother, Wang Yaojun. In the Xishan Revolutionary Martyr's Public Mausoleum, there is also a gravestone for my mother and father, but they're not located together, since names are organized according to the stroke order of the characters."

The account was sober, bobbing along on the great waves of past events, with only the faintest hint of bitterness.

I silently used my cellphone to look up the Beijing Xi Shan Unnamed Martyr's Square Website hosted by the China People's Liberation Army's Political Division. Sure enough, I found Qian Kexian and Wang Yaojun's names separated in the 32nd and 38th groupings.

CHAPTER 19

An Unpayable Debt

One day out of the blue, she told Jerome that she was going to make a trip back to China.

That year, she was turning 66. She didn't look old at all — still vibrating with energy, head to toe. She didn't even look like she was 50 yet.

That's right, she would fly back to China to visit her hometown. It sounded simple, but it would take 20 hours to get there. It was those 20 hours of distance that had made her wait half a century to return. How many times had she dreamed of going back there? But it was no dream this time. It was a truly real journey. On her ticket was written "May 3rd, 1979." That day became extremely precious to her.

In the past, she would accomplish a lot of meaningless tasks as she pondered returning to China. Gazing back along the path of her nostalgia was like tugging on a distant kite with a broken string

— neither near, nor far. Searching in the boundless realm of her expectations, she ultimately always came up empty and frustrated.

Was Gregory going to go with her?

She thought about it a good deal but said that he would wait until the next time around. There would always be another opportunity.

When all was said and done, Qian Xiuling had some misgivings about the trip. There had been massive changes in the past half century, and the ways of the world and its people were erratic. She could bear any misfortune thrown her way, but Gregory was not the same. His impressions of China had all come from her own portrayals and narrations. Decades earlier, he had formed a vision of that distant nation as beautiful as a flower and as precious as jade.

Knowing that she was to depart, her friends at the Chinese Embassy hurried to help her. They completed every procedure. Formerly, she had brought up many times her desire to return to China, but her friends at the embassy were reluctant to assist, saying that "official policy" had not yet opened things up for them. But since 1978, they reached out to her to set her feet on the path. Big changes had occurred in China and they hoped that she would return to see them for herself.

She knew the shifting stars of world affairs. Every news source was reporting that huge transformations were occurring in China. The clamor of "reform and opening to the world" had reached across the Pacific and touched Belgium. She discovered that even the spirit and appearances of the embassy officers had greatly changed.

Preparing to leave, her mind would sometimes abruptly wander back to the Wang Po Bridge she knew long ago, a gloomy scene of dark clouds and rain. Her father, mother, brothers and sisters, were walking towards her one by one. She suddenly questioned her own sense of growing old.

She first flew into Shanghai, where she reunited with cousin Zhuochai's family. Then, one of her nephews accompanied her to Beijing to do some sightseeing. They then spent a half day along West Lake in Hangzhou and then transited via bus to Lin'an. She wanted to go there to pay homage to the remains of their great ancestor Qian Liu. This had been the cherished dream of her elder cousin, Zhuolun, as well. He had fallen seriously ill one year, and she had flown to Taipei to pay him a visit. He shared a lot of things that had been on his mind, one of them being a visit to their great ancestor Qian Liu's tomb in Lin'an. He had only heard about their forebears spoken of in the past, but he had never had the opportunity to go to Lin'an to pay a formal visit and light incense to them. Zhuolun shared mournful words with her, which she had always remembered, "I can never go back there in this life." If she ever had the opportunity to return to China, she must remember Lin'an and go to the mausoleum of their ancestor to pay their respects, and to kowtow and light incense there on his behalf.

When they reached the small town of Lin'an, nobody really could tell them clearly where the tomb of Qian Liu was located. So, Xiuling found the local historical preservation office, where the deputy director, also named Qian, received her. He happened to be a descendant of Qian Liu as well. When they mentioned their great ancestor, it triggered a rich conversation. In that tiny town, there were no public means of transportation, so the deputy director had to volunteer to take them around himself. They rode around on a clinkety-clank, beat-up bicycle, with Xiuling sitting on the rear seat. This was the first time she'd ever ridden on such a contraption, and yet she leapt up onto it without hesitation, "That's pretty comfortable!"

She gazed at the scenery as they went along. The commercial area of the town was bustling, and though all the houses on the street were gray and dilapidated and its people dressed in sullen black and white hues, the smells coming from the market were a warm welcome to the senses. Director Qian brought her to King Qian's Mausoleum to pay her respects. What met her eyes was a ruinous site — piles of debris were everywhere, as well as trash accumulated over a period of years. Director Qian explained that a hurricane had swept through, and that they hadn't yet had time to clean up the area.

She was speechless. Director Qian whispered that it was not an easy thing to preserve the mausoleum of their greater ancestor. But things were improving.

Xiuling went to a nearby small shop to look for a pair of incense sticks that she could light in succession in front of the tomb.

Director Qian was puzzled, and asked her, "Why would you burn two incense sticks, since it's only you here?"

"It's for my older cousin," she said, and left it at that.

She raised her hands to her solemn face in a gesture of prayer, silently mouthing words of gratitude. Remembering those of old, tears streamed from her eyes.

Director Qian also took her to visit King Qian Temple, where she also saw many valuable relics. Now she knew why the world called Hangzhou and Suzhou "Humanity's Heaven on Earth." All its ornaments and delicate workmanship were originally established by their great ancestor, Qian Liu. In his hands, the West Lake was expanded three times, its scenic preservation and beautification beginning with backbreaking work and hardship, until it became a cultural treasure. The gardens at Suzhou were also undertaken by his son at his father's behest. They took many years to build. Later generations had very little recollection of this.

On an ancient stele in different hands were carved the various wishes of Qian Liu:

> For many generations, may this family live on the embroidered city wall, preserving the pines and catalpa of its high ancestors. Today, the family is thriving and prosperous, having become its own kingdom. May its children and descendants never lightly abandon their forebears.

A weight lifted from her heart, as if the sun had pierced the rain clouds. She now believed that the words of recorded history could defeat time, passing on to posterity a kind of consciousness.

Now, she wanted to put her feet on the earth of her hometown. Her heart began to skip faster. Outside the car window, fields of golden, dark green, and violet flitted by in alternation. She knew that they were oilseed rape blossoms, wheat sprouts, and purple muscovite. She remembered how, when she was young, she named the purple muscovite "the lotus boy," and pulled up a powdery, tender bunch of them, mixed them into a distiller's grain and then fried them up to eat. They smelled exquisite.

> South of the five ranges, cut off from the words of family and friends, I suffer through winter and on through spring. Approaching the village, I grow timider, not daring to inquire of the man coming toward me.

It was as if Mr. Gao was right there in her ear leading them all in the recitation of that Tang Dynasty poem. The Qian family Ancestral Hall had faded into the abyss of time. Even the small stalk of grass on the windowsill distinctly waved in her direction.

As originally planned, the person who was to receive her was a grand-nephew named Jiaji. She knew that because of recent history he had changed his last name. He might have changed his name, but his heart hadn't changed. He was still a part of the Qian clan. His family nevertheless called him by his original name, Jiaji.

At that time, Jiaji was serving as the Finance Section Chief of the local Yixing hotel. He appeared to be the only one of the Qian clan working in the governmental section. One of the reasons most certainly was because he had changed his last name. Locally, he was surprisingly a figure who "changed pockets." In order to welcome Xiuling, Jiaji used his own network of contacts to procure a week early a minivan from the county supply store. Unfortunately, the minivan was severely broken down — it needed a complete overhaul, not to mention it had no gas. But Jiaji had his ways: in just under a week, he not only had the minivan repaired, but he'd managed to get his hands on 200 liters of gasoline.

When they met up, Jiaji left very early in the morning, following the vehicle toward the local scenic spot, the Shan Juan Caves, to wait for Xiuling. Her arrival was a major event for the Qian clan. Mr. Jiaji still remembered that moment perfectly 30 years after the fact:

> At two o'clock in the afternoon, I stopped my car at the front gate parking lot to the Shan Juan Cave, holding up a sign: "Aunt Qian Xiuling." About half an hour later, a middle-aged woman, perhaps in her fifties, walked towards me, dressed very peculiarly. Her hair was permed in large waves, her face only lightly touched by makeup. Her skin was especially fair, and she was wearing lipstick. At the beginning of May, the weather was still fairly cool. She was wearing a long, dark green gown, decorated with golden

thread. It looked expensive. On her chest, a diamond broach glittered. Her legs were covered in pantyhose that ended in a pair of milky white high-heeled shoes. Such a display was a rarity in domestic China. She smiled, saying in pure Yixing dialect, 'You must be Jiaji!' I called her aunt and she gave me a big hug, saying nothing more. I noticed tears trickling down her face.

As the car pulled into Yixing town, Qian Xiuling suddenly remarked that she would like to go for a walk to see the changes that had occurred in the Yixing old town. Jiaji never supposed that her walking would abruptly attract a throng of people around her. The stretch of road from Taige Bridge to the Yixing Hotel seemed like the liveliest strip in town at the time. This small town in Jiangnan hadn't het opened up to the world. Its streets and alleyways were narrow, but also closed and protected. There had never been a woman bedecked with glittering jewels that had strutted through there before. A growing line of curious onlookers trailed her from behind.

She smiled as she greeted all those stunned and curious observers surrounding her. And even though some of the more impulsive gawkers pressed close to her face, she still repaid them with a gracious smile, even extending her hand in greeting. As a result, everyone was exhilarated, many of them thinking that a film was being made and that this must be the celebrity Baiyang. Others clamored that it was Wang Danfeng! Jiaji loudly spoke and explained, "She is not a film actress, she's an overseas Chinese woman. And she's one of our own from Yixing! Please, everybody, help us out and let us pass through."

Qian Xiuling asked Jiaji as they walked whether the school house that previously was not even a kilometer south of where they were headed was still around. When they passed the entrance to a certain alley, Xiuling suddenly stopped and said, "This was the northern entrance to the Shuyuan Alley. Zhuolun's family lived here, house number 5. Is his house still here? Who lives there now?"

She asked him a string of questions along the way. Jiaji couldn't answer them all. Some didn't have convenient answers, either. At one point she seemed to understand and stopped asking.

They came to a level, cement bridge in the center of town. She looked left and right, hesitated for a moment, and then couldn't help but ask, "Is this the Jiao Bridge? It was the tallest and biggest stone arch bridge back in the day. There were stone lions on top. We would climb up it and play on top when I was young."

Jiaji replied, "It was torn down and rebuilt during the 'Cultural Revolution.'"

She looked at the river, "The river is low, too. The water was so clear before. It looks like the river has been opened up a bit."

In short, it was exhilarating, but also at times undeniably sad. They went along at a stop-and-go pace until they finally reached the Yixing Hotel. Inside was a spacious, well-lit entrance hall. The walls were decorated with political slogans of the day, such as, "Crush the Gang of Four," "Emancipate Your Thought," etc. There were also various silk banners and ribbons, all red. Jiaji told her that as the biggest hotel in the town, its standards were naturally the highest. However, they hadn't yet adopted the "private quarters" concept. The welcoming banquet being thrown for her by her relatives would be arranged at the southernmost end of the hall on a lower level, where there was a large enough circular table to accommodate 12 people.

The hour arrived for Xiuling's reunion with her relatives. She never anticipated in her tears of joy the cautious expression of happiness on everybody's faces. Uncle Xi, is what the younger generation universally called her. The youngest of them called her

Aunt.

In the surging commotion of the scene, as people were introducing themselves to one another, Xiuling suddenly recognized some of the features of certain young nieces and nephews, who looked remarkably like their parents. This triggered emotions within her. Passing out gifts finally broke the veneer of their cautious expressions with sudden ruptures of delight. Now and then, a burst of laughter would cover up the sad topic of relatives who had passed away. Truthfully, there was not a single person from the older Qian generation still alive. Qian Xiuling knew a little bit about their fates in a tumultuous world. She didn't dare inquire about the circumstances of their passing, however. Of those brothers and sisters of her generation, some were no longer living in their hometown, and others, for some reason or another, had left this world prematurely.

Most of the family members she met were nephews and nieces. They all appeared fairly reserved. When it was time to be seated, they suddenly realized that there was little room for them around the table — barely a drop of water could be squeezed between them. The servers could hardly push through to deliver the dishes. Jiaji discussed the matter with the hotel manager on the spot, getting the accounting office on the second floor to move them at the last minute to the banquet room. Consequently, the entire group moved upstairs. Qian Xiuling kept her smile up, "Why are we moving? It doesn't matter to me." All the Qian relatives helped to move the table and chairs. Every motion seemed nimble and rehearsed. Though the reunion dinner went more than half an hour over than planned, Qian Xiuling was ecstatic when the fragrance of that Yixing First Course hit her nose. She happily exclaimed, "Now that is what the First Course should smell like!" Tear drops plopped from her eyes.

According to Jiaji's memory, the dishes from that night's banquet were prepared with the utmost care. The head chef and grand master's name was Ye Zuren. He had travelled far and wide, and whenever an important leader came to Yixing, he always served as their cook. That day he brought all his outstanding skills to bear, choosing the freshest ingredients in season in Yixing to make local dishes, per Jiaji's request. He wasn't interested in appearances, he just wanted to cook up the best homestyle dishes he could: Coiled Dragon and Silly Tiger, Gingko Shrimp, Sweet and Sour Mandarin Fish — all traditional staples of the local cuisine. He only used local Yixing stoneware pots, filling those precious white cauldrons with bamboo shoots, little floral mushrooms, chicken-fir fungus, and porcino mushrooms. The broth was strong but not greasy, containing chicken, dried scallops, ham, dried shrimp, etc. He put the soup on low heat and cooked it for most of the day. His freshly roasted eel spine and whitebail fish soup were fresh and crisp, smooth and exquisite. The garlic shoot stir fry with fava bean seeds, glistening jade green, was somehow both limp and crunchy, transporting Qian Xiuling back into the countryside of your youth. Each time a new dish was brought out, Xiuling had to admire it for a moment, followed by her accurate announcement of its name. She tasted the dishes, then praised them unceasingly. Their final dish of the night was a Hengshan fish head soup. The chef used an especially large earthenware pot, filling it with a milky white soup, emerald green cilantro, black ear fungus, mushroom sheets, and floating bamboo shoots. It was utterly captivating. If this fish head soup had been served in Belgium, it would have caused a sensation across the entire city of Brussels!

Halfway through the meal, Qian Xiuling stood up and asked for some pen and paper, saying she wanted to record all the dishes she was eating so she could cook them later upon her return to Belgium. Jiaji had already prepared a menu beforehand and handed it to her. She took it and smiled gleefully as she hurriedly placed it into her hand bag. She took it out again as they were finishing the meal. She wished to see the head chef and grandmaster, as well as visit the kitchen to look around.

At once, Jiaji called Ye Zuren into the dining room. Qian Xiuling bowed to him, "Master Ye, your food was exquisite today. I am someone who has been away from her home for decades. This dinner has filled that decades-old gap in my heart."

Ye Zuren was only in his thirties and didn't know quite how to take such a compliment from a superior.

She asked Master Ye what his monthly salary was.

Master Ye truthfully responded, "32 yuan."

Qian Xiuling replied, "How would you like to work with me in my restaurant in Brussels? I will give you 3,000 yuan in salary each month."

Ye Zuren was struck with fear. 3,000 yuan was the equivalent of his 10-year salary in China. He didn't know where Belgium was, though he did know it was far, far away in Europe. But he was someone who had never left the provincial capital. A very practical problem suddenly came to mind. He couldn't help from blurting it out, "That sounds nice, but I have not yet completed my dozen years of service for seniority."

"Seniority?" Qian Xiuling was puzzled.

Jiaji explained the concept to her. She understood and said, "Don't worry about that. I will take care of your pension and old-age insurance. I will take responsibility for all of that."

The people on site had no idea what the terms "pension and old-age insurance" meant.

Ye Zuren was on the verge of breaking into a sweat. He raised his hands to Qian Xiuling, and quickly asked her to forgive him for withdrawing.

Xiuling's regrets that day were not only limited to Chef Ye's decline of her offer. What she couldn't understand was that whenever she brought up wanting to go to Wang Po Bridge and the old Qian estate to look around, almost every single person urged her not to go. On cue, everyone seemed to utter the same thing: There was construction on the road and cars couldn't get through. But she just replied with "Well, we'll just take a boat." When she was young, she would often go into town with her father on a canopy speed boat, admiring the beautiful scenery on both banks. She had Jiaji book a boat for her right away. But Jiaji said that the river was being dredged and wasn't passable by boat either. She observed everybody's dismayed faces, unable to figure out what the hidden backstory was. She asked them, but they all said there was nothing more to tell. For a time, they all felt a bit awkward. There was much they wanted to say, but they all swallowed their tongues. Xiuling couldn't bear it — why were they being so difficult?

She wanted to tell them that she wished to return home to visit the graves of her mother and father, as well as her ancestors. "I dreamt that they are waiting for my return!"

Jiaji was an intelligent fellow, though, and ultimately brought her some relief as they walked along:

"Aunt, this is only your first preparatory visit back. Our nation is in the process of reforming and opening up to the world. Our situation will only improve. The next time you come back, the Wang Po Bridge will certainly be restored to its former size and quality, and at that time, I will definitely take you by car to go and visit your old home!"

Eight years later, when Qian Xiuling stepped foot onto the soil of her native home once more, she saw how much China had truly changed.

Yes, the outer roads had been widened, buildings built higher, and clothes were brighter and prettier, but also people's facial expressions had transformed. The former anxiety and reservation on the faces of her relatives and the aloof and inflexible attitude of local officials was no longer apparent. It was as if everyone's countenances had been smoothed out and opened up. Every bit of news casually delivered made her feel extremely pleased: some of her relatives had passed their college examinations, some had become factory directors in local enterprises, some were running supply chains, attending night school, or testing into professional positions. All were busying themselves. She had brought Gregory with her on this visit, as she had promised earlier. Gregory was much more excited than she was. Usually taciturn, Gregory had turned chatty, asking about this and asking about that. From the time of their departure, he had been taking sleeping pills. From the first moment that everybody saw his tall, slim figure, and scholarly, easygoing manner, they instantly liked him. They called him Uncle Xi — it pleased him tremendously. To everyone's surprise, he could speak a few lines of Chinese too, beyond just the usual "Hello," "Thank you," and "Delicious. He said, "Ge Lixia is but my Chinese name!"

Qian Xiuling counted on her fingers for a second, faintly saying that that name had been selected for him 50 years ago. If it hadn't been for all those wars and misfortunes of history, he would've already become a proper Chinaman.

Surprisingly, on this trip, she received quite a lot of attention and preferential treatment.

The agency responsible for handling Qian Xiuling was the Emigrant Affairs Office under the Yixing County Government,

Qian Xiuling and her husband in Yixing

referred to simply as the Qiao Wu. One day, their unit suddenly received a red-letter document forwarded to them from the provincial level that had received it from the central emigrant offices of the state foreign ministry. The letter said that they had received an official communication from the Chinese Embassy in Belgium, stating that a certain Qian Xiuling, an overseas Chinese, was planning to pay a visit to China within a month. Her main itinerary was through Jiangsu's Yixing county. Qian Xiuling was one of Belgium's "National Heroes," who had saved over 100 anti-war hostages from execution during World War II. It was an outstanding achievement that enjoyed immense acclaim in Belgium, particularly among the overseas Chinese. The document requested that as the Yixing government interviewed her that they warmly receive her and make the process convenient.

As a result, the government dispatched vehicles to pick her up, assigned the county commissioner to host her for dinner and had an activities specialist accompany her, as well as ensured that there were people to plan and see to her needs for lodging and food.

This was something that Qian Xiuling was not accustomed to, though. She felt like her first trip walking among the simple folk of Yixing suited her vision of what she wanted. Besides visiting with some friends and relatives, she didn't really wish to be a bother to anybody else.

At daybreak, following an autumn rain, a minivan took her and Gregory to Wang Po Bridge. They exited the vehicle and stepped onto the muddy ground. They walked around a few newly planted electric poles, and walked towards the bridge. They lifted their gaze to see that the fields had just been harvested, leaving stalk stubble behind in damp pools of water, like flowing juice. The sweet fragrance of rice still lingered in the air. The vasty, empty fields exercised a kind of enchantment on a person to loiter there. Xiuling heard on the edge of hearing the faint sound of a bird call, like the accumulated mournful cries of past generations: her father's sighs, her mother's admonishments, Mr. Gao's recitations, even the sounds of her and her brothers' and sisters' footsteps. She suddenly froze, unable to move forward. Her gaze was calm, but in a flash she felt that this was her former life, no longer relevant to her present existence.

Gregory had already heard his Asian belle tell the story of Wang Po Bridge a thousand times. And he still liked it. That stone bridge's patched composition looked like an old, weathered man just creeping along. On both sides of the bridge, reeds were growing unchecked. In the wind, their graceful white fluff was sucked into the air, floating until its seed became formless. It was beautiful to behold. Gregory asked, "Ling, what kind of flower is that?" Qian Xiuling replied, "Reed flowers." At that exact moment, a boat emerged from underneath the arch of the bridge, its rear oar pushing it along — swish-swish. Gregory thought it was a splendid sound, beautifully syncing with the sway of their postures, and the flow of the limpid, suave river. The simple hues of the criss-crossing footpaths on both sides of the river were simply enchanting.

Qian Xiuling spoke up, "Back in the day, I would sit in a sailboat with my father. It was a bit smaller than that one, but it was fast. We'd ride it into the city."

Gregory said that standing there reminded him of Herbeumont village. But Herbeumont didn't have such a beautiful river. "You never mentioned this river. We should've come here a lot earlier!"

Those last words struck her like a drum — BOOM — knocking on her heart.

The feeling she experienced entering the village was better than she had ever imagined. Fifty years apart from the Qian estate village had brought a greying decline upon the place, but its style was still warm and welcoming. There were some new, upstart buildings there as well, their fancy roofs poking out above the low-lying homes. They exuded a satisfaction with progress that made the old buildings look ruined and abandoned. The sounds of human voices, dogs barking, and birds chirping all sounded so familiar.

The nostalgia turned dense everywhere they looked. Some of the older folks recognized Qian Xiuling. They embraced her, their dark, chapped palms holding her for so long it made her heart beat fast. She was speechless. The muddy roads in the village, where you step down and can't pull your foot back out, delighted Gregory. His pair of leather shoes turned into a pair of mud-caked loafers, but he thoroughly enjoyed it. He said that he would love to open up a clinic in this village and care for the health of the humble farmers. Xiuling responded to him on and off as she anxiously searched for the gate to her old home. She wanted to find her family's ancestral hall, but she couldn't seem to locate it.

"Where is our house?"

She looked in every direction, confused.

Her relatives accompanying her said that over the past decades there had been some huge changes to the village homes. Some older homes were torn down, their foundations ripped up and converted back to farmland — all in response to some policy. Her home, including the Qian Family Ancestral Hall, had been reduced to a rice paddy.

An unsuppressable sadness overcame her for a time. She wanted to follow up with a question about the location of her parents' cemetery, but as the words reached her lips, she swallowed them back down. However, as they walked through a small alley in single file, they came up to a fenced courtyard. There were a few somewhat uniformly arranged homes blocking the outlet. One of her nieces pointed to a half-decaying old home: "Uncle Xi — look! There's still one old home they haven't completely torn down yet."

Xiuling looked up and studied it closely. Finally she recognized the home — it was her father's old study!

Her home originally had three courtyards front to back. The study was located to the right of the second courtyard. The lady's chamber was situated right next door to it. But presently, all other buildings had been completely obliterated. If nobody had pointed the place out, she could have stood there all day and never recognized it.

Her father's small study room was the heart of the home. So many decisions, including the one to send her to Belgium to study abroad, were made in that little study.

Today, though, it served as a warehouse for a large manufacturing team, where agricultural chemicals, fertilizers, and other sundry items were stacked up. The front door was locked. The doorman was nowhere to be found for a time. Qian Xiuling stole a look inside through a glassless window.

What she briefly saw made her heart hurt. "Let's go," she decisively declared.

Her words were pronounced rather loudly.

Everybody sensed a change in her mood. Their silence seemed to express their regret.

Xiuling suddenly felt remorseful for the tone of the two words she had just spat out.

Who was she, anyway? A deficient deserter who never returned home; a hurried traveller just passing through. The destiny of this village and its homes was tied to the ups and downs, prosperity and decline of an entire nation. What was once stormy weather might at any moment turn to sunny skies. She hadn't taken shelter from the rain. All living things moved to and fro, making their own progress, sometimes fatigued, sometimes striving, without her intervention.

She felt deeply remorseful. Why couldn't the hands of time just roll back and restore everything to how it was decades ago? She had to face those two words, and for her that meant escape. In the end, there was no way for her to compensate for her deficiency, and that realization felt like an ache boring a hole through her heart.

In that tremendous, stagnating silence, she and Greogry left the village.

A short while later, Xiuling made a request to the director of the county emigrant office accompanying her. She wanted to purchase a plot of land to build a cenotaph to the ancestors of the Qian clan.

The request was carried out in short order. The county's civil servants joined in, actively coordinating on the project. A day later, Qian Xiuling returned once more to the Qian estate village. She settled on a south-facing slope just outside the village, currently used as a farmer's private plot. A good price was quickly agreed upon. That same day, work began on the monument. Within the cenotaph were placed photographs of her mother and father, and other elders. For those without photos, objects were chosen from their life, perhaps a cigarette holder, or a thimble for needle and thread. Afterward, they went in search of an old stonemason, and then selected quality stone. That very night they began to chisel the monument, carving the names of the Qian deceased according to their rank and seniority in the clan. Finally, she brought back all the relatives that she had spent the day with earlier and guided them to the tomb to offer sacrifices to their ancestors.

It was then that she fell to the ground and cried loudly, tears gushing forth like the Yangtze River.

On the way back, she told Gregory that she had only felt this type of pain twice in her life. The first was when her father left this world. She was living on the other side of the globe and couldn't return. She immediately cried and her heart was set at ease.

She took a small bottle and filled it with dirt from the tomb site, and then placed it inside her pocket, without saying a word.

Her niece, Qian Tangna, remembered the scene like this:

> There was a firm aspect to Uncle Xi's character. Whatever she did was done decisively, like when she constructed the Qian family cenotaph. The whole process took only a few days, start to finish. When the tomb was finally completed, her mood improved greatly. She then talked to us about her children in Belgium. She was in a very good mood. Nevertheless, she never once spoke about her saving the hostages in Belgium while we were in the village. We had no idea that she was one of Belgium's "National Heroes."

Her grandnephew, Jiaji recalled:

> She spoke with some of us from the younger generation: "Would you like to go with your aunt to Belgium for a quick visit? Young folks needn't cling to the door in their homes — you need to have higher aims and ambitions. Now that the country has opened up, you all should get out and have a look, see what the world is like." In her view, whoever wanted could go with her to Belgium and work in her restaurant, study cooking, and then set off on their own and settle down. If they didn't open their own restaurant, they could just as well open up a take-out place — those made money too. And when they returned to China, they would have gained immense experience. Sure enough, a lot of my

relatives later took her up on the offer. Her Jade Spring restaurant turned into a "Huangpu Military Academy" for cultivating new chefs and take-out owners.

When the tomb was finished, an official walked into the village and invited Xiuling and Gregory to tour a fire-resistant clothing factory run by the village. On the way, the official mentioned that his father had studied with Xiuling in the Qian Family Ancestral Hall. They were from the same family as well. The official shared more about the history of the Qian Family Ancestral Hall over the years: "Back then, during the Cultural Revolution, it was like a hornet's nest! This teaching was all considered part of the 'Four Olds,' so the hall was torn down and a warehouse put up in its place. Who knew that the world would change so drastically into what we have today!?" His thoughts would come and go. Sometimes he seemed to be mocking himself even as he tried to explain what had happened. Qian Xiuling listened quietly, not responding. Under the guidance of the factory manager, they visited a number of workshops and the products they produced. Naturally, they were all to be praised. Qian Xiuling marvelled, "I really never imagined that a factory of this scale would ever be set up in the village — it's pretty amazing!" The official explained that these factories were being built everywhere. Nobody sat idly at home in the village anymore.

They filed into the factory director's office. They sat down on the leather sofa and sipped some tea. The director somewhat embarrassingly grabbed a huge pear and said, "I just sent someone to go and buy fruit, but they're only selling pears at the moment."

"Woah! That pear is massive!" Qian Xiuling laughed.

She turned to Ge Lixia and explained, "There's a Chinese tradition you don't know about: pears can't be divided, so you can't cut them."

"So, what do you do?" Gregory asked, splaying his hands.

"You're the first visitor here, so you need to eat the entire pear."

Gregory replied, "Why don't we break the standard and unleash its curse? We'll split it up and eat it, and then we'll each be able to enjoy something sweet, right?

Incredible! That usually taciturn Gregory can suddenly surprise you with a string of flowery words. It made even Qian Xiuling feel a bit surprised.

As a result, that 500-plus gram pear was sliced up into eight pieces.

Everybody ate the pear and said it was very sweet.

CHAPTER 20

Was My Grandma a Hero?

On September 4th, 2000, the Ecaussinnes media published a piece conferring upon Madame Qian Xiuling the title of "Honorary Citizen."

She turned 88 that year.

A lot of things happened that year, but things were forgettable. Only those things that are etched into one's bones and heart have staying power and are not easily forgotten.

In the spring of 1995, Gregory departed this life, having enjoyed 86 full years. His mental state had been troubled for quite some time. He had difficulty remembering things. And when he was clear-headed, he would constantly suffer a poignant sensation of pain. Qian Xiuling understood that Gregory was going to be the first to go and find a place to rest and wait for her. She could distinctly hear his call. "My dearest, I know," she said.

Half a year later, their little boy Nicolas died an untimely death. He was only 51.

Karma stands behind the impermanence of human life. If you go early, you go. If you leave later, you still go. This is what she said to soothe herself. In this life, she had already seen too many partings by death. Learning how to arrive together and to separate was the entirety of human existence. But when a loved one truly let go and moved on, Xiuling felt like a part of her own heart had left with them.

Ecaussinnes always remembered her, and this still made her very happy. Every time she went there, she would visit with old friends. Their friendly mayor, Ron Dutailier, came by a number of times to discuss the formal awarding of an honorary citizenship to her. He called her "mother", even omitting her last name "Qian." If it hadn't been for her saving his father during the war, he wouldn't be around today. He was right about that, but Qian Xiuling could never accept that way of seeing things. As she grew older, she wanted less and less to discuss those events from the past, not least because she had already truly forgotten some of the details.

Her eldest son Timothy accompanied her on the day she received her honor. He had become an outstanding doctor, taking on the mantle from his late father. They enjoyed the reverence and welcome of all in Ecaussinnes. They each perceived things differently during the event, however. Qian Xiuling didn't understand why so many people were still keeping alive the memory of the things she did so long ago. Only when something is recorded or sung does a person or thing transform into a permanent part of history. Things that aren't recorded, though, you just forget. That's not fair. But as she knew, the primary feature of this world was that it was grossly unfair. Many people fought for a single issue of justice, ending up sacrificing their lives for it. This is how righteousness is generated. Compared to those people whose names were engraved in the annals of history, Qian Xiuling preferred to be forgotten — completely and utterly forgotten.

She spoke these exact words during the award ceremony. Everyone was speechless, then they wildly applauded. The few hostage survivors still living, and their widows, and sons and daughters, all rushed over to embrace her, pay their respects, and take photos. Mayor Dutailier persisted in inviting her to be seated to accept her Honorary Citizen plaque, since it was rather heavy. He bent over and conferred the honor upon her.

The cameraman's lens froze that moment in time, capturing Qian Xiuling sitting on a chair and Ron Dutailier in the act of bowing as he handed her the award.

Ron Dutailier said, "History will remember the events of today. Ecaussinnes has already taken your name for one of its streets and added a word 'virtuous' to it. You know that in Belgium, a person's last name often has that word 'virtuous' added to it. It signifies majesty and dignity. 'Virtuous' pairs perfectly with you and Mr. Gregory Perlinghi."

So, the full title of "Qian Xiuling Street" would actually have been:

Mrs. Gregory de Perlinghi — Qian Xiuling Street.

Timothy's perception of the event was completely different. He was extremely proud of his mother. For others, it was unlikely that when a person did a good thing that everybody around them would remember it for decades. He was a doctor. Assisting the dying and healing the injured was the purpose of his occupation. Bringing a patient back from the brink of death was a common occurrence. Nobody was going to remember whom he saved, and he didn't make

Mrs. Gregory de Perlinghi Qian Xiuling Street

a big deal out of it himself. So, he always felt happy for his mother for receiving the honor.

He did sense that his mother didn't associate this with any sort of feeling of success. In reality, she looked down upon it a bit. She felt that that historical moment had already passed, and that anybody in her shoes would have done the same thing anyway. She had never once turned that event into a story to tell Timothy's brothers and sisters, despite the fact that she had shared a countless number of tales with them. Things concerning their mother's rescue of the hostages were narrated in succession to them from the mouths of other people. Her attitude in all of this had always been that she wished others, including herself, would just all forget about it.

He didn't have a clue what it was propping up her stance on this.

Ron Dutailier helped Qian Xiuling into her car as she prepared to leave Ecaussinnes. He whispered into her ear, "Mother, I will go to China very soon to pay a visit to your hometown."

Qian Xiuling responded, "You should do that. My townspeople are very hospitable and generous. You'll see when you get there."

She stretched her hand outside the window, and waved goodbye to everyone crowded around the car, tears welling up in her eyes. They drove for a bit, but her hand was still waving, and she was mumbling something softly to herself. Timothy stopped the car on the side of the road and leaned over the front seat. He finally understood what it what she was saying:

"My dear friends, please forget me."

Timothy was stunned. Why would she say such a thing?

He asked her, "Mom, would you like to go down that road and have a look?"

He was obviously referring to the brand new sign for Qian Xiuling Street with the word "virtuous" added to it.

"No. Let's go," she said.

She lifted her head, closing her eyes and resting her spirits. She said nothing more.

It was Timothy's impression that in his mother's later years, especially following the passing of their father and brother, she became more and more taciturn, always contemplating something.

Mayor Ron Dutailier returned from China, bringing Xiuling a bunch of news. He told her that her native place of Yixing had become a Sister City to Ecaussinnes. He had endless praise for her hometown cuisine, "Mother, how could you bear to leave your hometown?! Such a beautiful place, and the fine food is painful to leave behind."

She replied, "I do awfully regret leaving my home. I didn't ever do anything for it." She also told the mayor that her niece Tangna was the head of the local village clothing factory, and that she wanted to try and sell her clothes in Belgium. If he was interested, she would be happy to collaborate with him on a venture.

"I'll remember that, mother," he replied.

Ms. Qian Tangna still kept the three letters that "Uncle Xi" had written her. One of them read:

> Dearest Tangna,
>
> I just received your letter. Thank you very much! Within two or three weeks of my return, I requested strongly that a large catalogue of clothing patterns and two books of European skirt samples be sent to you. Have you received them yet? There are hundreds of clothing patterns inside. I think it's strange that I haven't heard any news from you about them. A Mr. Xing is returning to China, so I took the liberty of asking him to carry some clothing design magazines to you. Let me know when they have arrived.

And let me know if these materials have any reference value for you, or if you're able to use their patterns to make your own clothes.

I want to help business flourish between the fatherland and Europe, but I have absolutely no experience in international trade. I have no idea where to begin. For instance, Europeans love Yixing Ding Shan ceramics. If there were a market held here, which special Yixing products could we sell? If the opportunity arises, I'd be happy to pull some strings for my homeland.

There is a very successful businessman here who exclusively does business in China. He often comes into my restaurant. He has hosted a lot of Belgians who do business with the Chinese here. Whenever I get the opportunity, I will certainly bring up the idea. But, I'm not really sure how to go about bringing it up with him. Maybe I just start by talking about Yixing ceramics and imported clothing? If there's any good news, I'll let you know.

The Lunar New Year is coming fast. I wish you and your entire family a happy New Year. May all your hopes be fulfilled.

Love,

Aunt Xiuling

Qian Tangna recalled how she leaned on "Uncle Xi" to help connect her to Belgium's market to sell her clothing. Xiuling was enthusiastic about it, enlisting an official in the commercial affairs unit of the Chinese Embassy to write her a letter, telling her that when doing business with Belgians, it was always important to pay close attention to the item, what the requirements were, etc.

Not long after that, a representative delegation from Yixing arrived in Ecaussinnes, reciprocating the earlier visit by their mayor. They made it a point to travel to Brussels to visit Xiuling's home. They chatted in the Yixing dialect, all referring to her as Mother Qian. They showed her a picture of the ongoing construction in her hometown. She asked, "Is this the nightscape of Yixing? I don't know how I feel about this — it looks a bit like Hangzhou's West Lake!"

She felt especially happy that day.

One day, she hosted a female Chinese author, Zhang Yawen, in her home. When Xiuling discovered that the author had borrowed 100,000 yuan to travel to a foreign place all alone, where she didn't speak the language, to conduct her project, she took pity on her. The two of them hit it off right away. Later, CCTV adapted Zhang Yawen's novel into a television series, adding a bunch of its own details. The production team came to Belgium to shoot some footage, causing a lot of commotion along the way. At first, Xiuling felt uneasy about it. She felt like all those things in the past had been swept away with the winds of time — why should they bring it all up again? There were some details that she didn't even remember any more. However, when she talked about her older cousin, Brother Zhuolun, she quickly gained clarity and would talk at length. The most eye-catching parts of her home were decorated with Zhuolun's calligraphy. Commenting on his writing style, Xiuling would use this phrase to highlight his uniqueness: skeletal, pure and coarse. This scroll possesses the quality of someone with conscience, the original form of a cultured individual. As for herself, her often repeated phrase "I have truly forgotten" had already become a kind of personal mantra.

Quickly, the television series moved from China to a Belgian television channel. It was a hit! People from below her apartment would often come up to ask her about it, "Does that Asian goddess who saved the hostages really live here?" Media interviews became ever more persistent. Her quiet life had been disturbed. She wrote a letter to the relevant media parties declining all further interviews. This is how it was at the time.

During his interview with the Belgian media, the director of the TV series share his opinion:

> There are far too few who originally knew about her story. She was like Oskar Schindler, who became world famous because he had saved a large number of his own people, the Jews. Qian Xiuling saved Belgians, not Chinese, though. For that reason alone, I believe Qian Xiuling is worthy of much greater public praise. Her act has more international significance than Schindler's.

There are some things in the TV series that members of the Qian family don't agree with. The principal thing was that there was never any mention of General Zhuolun. In their view, if he hadn't been there, the entire thing would've fallen apart. Even Qian Xiuling herself felt quite disappointed by his absence.

> Although they were unsatisfied with the ultimate result of the series, "Uncle Xi" candidly confessed that she wasn't upset. In her view, whatever the team wished to film was within the rights of their creative license. Whatever goal they had in mind had already been decided much earlier, anyway. The older generation knew well the intentions and benefits behind the word "hero," and they could serenely handle all it implied. She said, "This is all merely a small

thing in my life. The past is just the past."

(Qian Tongxi, "My Great Aunt Qian Xiuling")

She perhaps knew and understood that there isn't an artist who intentionally wants to tell lies or to push out fabrications that violate reality. Within a fixed period of time, those challenging narrations always contain unavoidable compromises backed by decisions that artists likely secretly sigh to themselves over as well. Believe it that when a story is spoken, it cannot be retracted. But the existence of a story is always superior to its non-existence. Yesterday's tale helps people today to mend and correct things, allowing people tomorrow to continue to trace today's divergences back to their historical points of origin.

> One day, her granddaughter Tatiana accompanied Xiuling on a walk.
> "Grandma, why do you think they wanted to film your story?"
> "Because during World War II, a Chinese woman used the friendship between her older cousin and a German general to save the lives of captured Belgian anti-War hostages."
> "Do you still remember what you and they said about it?"
> "I don't remember …"
>
> (Qian Tongxin, "My Great Aunt Qian Xiuling")

As for some things, she truly didn't recall them. She wished that others would forget about them as well. There was one phrase she didn't like at all: "Never forget." And why not? How could you never forget? That would just be exhausting — the world would become too complicated. If you can forget, then let it go. Just enjoy the moment and free your limited life from all its hitches and weights.

Her granddaughter Tatiana was a documentary filmmaker with one of Belgium's television stations. Qian family members grew to regret having sparked her interest in the story, which morphed into a sense of duty for her. She was determined to give her grandmother another accounting. Her video camera captured a large amount of the conversations she had with her grandmother. In 2004, she brought along a film production crew to visit China a few times. They shot interviews with descendants of the Qian family and their associates. For a time, they embedded themselves in the Yixing village, hunting for material. On top of Wang Po Bridge during the blooming of the oil rapeseed flowers, Tatiana discovered her grandmother's keynote visual inspiration, a vista as open, pure, kind, and supple, yet firm, as her grandmother's very character. How similar in nature and origin their feelings were.

She realized what it was her documentary film was trying to tell people: her grandmother Qian Xiuling was in truth not a globally significant hero. She was simply a good and upright person. Others had always enthusiastically discussed that past achievement, but she had already forgotten about it long ago. She had never wanted what she once did to be tied up and placed upon a lofty pedestal to later be inappropriately and incessantly blown out of proportion.

She sincerely requested that she be forgotten, not have her name carved into stone.

Qian Xiuling's health began to deteriorate after the age of 90.

She practiced Tai Chi, sang, walked, and chatted with her grandchildren. She also liked to look at old photographs. Behind every single picture was a story. When she began to tell those stories, it felt like she'd been transported back to her childhood home, hearing the sound of her mother spinning thread.

Officials at the Chinese Embassy were constantly watching over her and often visited to check up on her. On each of her birthdays, a large bouquet of flowers, a cake, and beautiful wishes were sent from the embassy.

She loved to sing this old song:

> Fly, fly, fly, just like that, fly
> Slowly fly, this way fly, that way fly
> You want to ascend just lift your head
> You want to turn then move your backend
> You want to descend slant down through the sky
> Hey! Fly just like that, fly high
> ...

These lyrics were presented in Tatiana's document as Qian Xiuling sang them in the recording. Was she singing about a cheerful little bird in that song? Or was she envying the vast sky she possessed? Xiuling couldn't fly away, but she still had the strength to sing to a carefree bird soaring in the sky. At least in those rare moments her heart could flit after that little bird, flitting back and forth with it through the air.

> Out of the blue one day her children took her to a nursing home in the Brussels downtown area. We only heard that some contradictions had flared up between the children focused on "Uncle Xi's" inheritance. They had sold her residence. None of this could be confirmed, however. From that point on, she had very few visitors, and her complexion steadily deteriorated. However, my young uncle would

often deliver small wontons to her. She was still delighted to eat small wontons, my uncle told us.

(Qian Tongxin, "My Great Aunt Qian Xiuling")

One Sunday, Qian Xiuling's grand-niece, Qian Tongxi arrived travel-worn from where she was studying abroad in France to visit her great aunt in her nursing home on Otgon Boulevard in downtown Brussels.

Her back was turned towards the door and she was sitting in a high-backed, yellow chair with barriers around it to prevent her from falling. This was the loneliest rear view of anyone I'd seen in twenty years.
Seeing somebody come for a visit clearly brings happiness to the elderly. She was wearing a bluish-purple floral blouse, her full head of white hair had been brushed with extreme care. She looked emaciated but still attractive. She smiled at me. That was the warmest smile anyone had ever given me in twenty years. My uncle, who came along as well, as usual took out a bowl of small wontons he had prepared and fed them to her. She had much more of an appetite than I believed she would.
I saw that the blackboard in her room had some French words written on it, "Please bring some fruit, and if you can, some small wontons and magazines."
Her and her family's pictures were spread out in a jumble all over the desk in her room, including the group photo of her receiving the "National Hero" medal.
On the wall were hung pictures of her children when they were younger. Imagining how this old woman in the final

moments of her life had once contended with the Gestapo, experienced the vicissitudes of nearly a century, and now had finally returned back to the starting point of life brought tears to my eyes.

(Qian Tongxi, "My Great Aunt Qian Xiuling")

Her nephew Qian Xianhe recalled the following about her final years:

> It was an average to poor nursing home. To begin with, her children had told her that her home needed to be renovated and that she would just be staying in the nursing home for a little while. But after a few months, I went to see her and took her out for a spin in the car. Passing below her old building on the road, she suddenly asked, "When are the renovations going to be done on my house?" I replied, "What renovations? I haven't heard anything about that." She understood, and said nothing more about it, never bringing it up again. My great aunt was like that. She only spoke when she had good things to say, never speaking ill.

On August 1st, 2008, Qian Xiuling passed away in Brussels, Belgium, having lived a full life of 96 years.

Her burial was simple and solemn. Her coffin was draped with the Belgian flag. Among those who came to see her at the funeral home were representatives of the Ecaussinnes municipal government, the descendants of the underground resistance fighters, the children of the saved hostages, representatives of Belgium's national government, and representatives of the Chinese Embassy in Belgium.

In my notebook dated October 9th, 2018, I wrote:

> Under the guidance of Qian Weiqiang and his wife, I proceeded to the Wezembee-Oppem cemetery in the suburbs of Brussels to pay my respects to Qian Xiuling.
> The cemetery was quite large and spacious. It was late autumn, but the vegetation was still lush. We walked along, finally entering a crowded section of tombs. Some of them were dazzling, others looked like proper works of art, still others were quite ordinary and simple. Qian Xiuling's grave was situated in the third section of the grave area. It was shocking how plain her grave was — it was even smaller than the average grave there, without any adornments. There was no pathway beside the grave. It was squeezed up against other plots so that you couldn't even slip a foot between them. While laying flowers at the tomb, I had to stand on top of it and bend over. It made me feel sad. Furthermore, her plot was built for three people. Mr. Qian Weiqiang said that her son was placed at the lowest level. Her husband was laid on top of him, and finally Qian Xiuling was resting closest to the surface.
> On the lid of the grave, three people's names and dates of birth and death were recorded in French.
>
> Nikola D. Perlinghi
> 1944—1995
> Gregory D. Perlinghi
> 1909—1995
> and his wife Qian Xiuling
> 1913—2008

I had always believed that there might be an epitaph, or a seated Buddha image or something else there. There at least should have been an open green space in front of the grave plot. But, there was nothing…

We had supposed that when we arrived there there would be some sort of obstacle.

But it was just Qian Xiuling.

Mr. Qian Weiqiang said that his aunt didn't want to bother anyone. She also didn't want any flattering words written there about her. There were plenty of accounts told during her lifetime, and at the end of it she wanted to dispense with all formalities. She wished for her husband and her young boy cut off in his youth to be laid to rest together.

I stood there for a very long time, saying nothing. My heart was choked with emotion. I remembered that call from overseas 16 years ago: This appointment-breaker has finally shown up. My apologies, Grandma Qian.

"Ok. I'll be waiting for you in Brussels," she laughed in a clear voice, like she was speaking right into my ear.

As I bowed to her grave, a single tear drop fell upon it without my noticing.

A breeze blew, tossing a single maple leaf onto the grave. In the bright sunlight, the leaf looked as red as blood.

The author vistited Qian Xiuling's grave

EPILOGUE

Jerome Steps on Grandma's Soil

Jerome came to China again.

On December 11th, 2019, as agreed upon, I went to Shanghai to pick him. He hoped from the beginning to visit the hometown of his grandmother and see what it was like.

He went to his grandmother's hamlet on Taihu Lake. He was extremely excited. He said, "Yesterday, I dreamt I saw grandma. She said to me, 'When you arrive there, you must get down and kowtow to your elders.'"

Kowtowing must be done in the proper context to have meaning. When Jerome entered the village, a group had formed and was trailing him from behind — even more than had followed his grandmother when she first visited.

When the dogs in the village began barking in unison, he felt especially happy. It was as if they were an honor guard announcing his

Jerome at his grandma's place of origin

arrival. As a famous international filmmaker, he liked the style of the place: the unadorned farming homes, the various piles of items strewn across the threshing floors. The chaotic array of every kind of vivid expression around him kept his camera busy. He had purposefully brought that Leica camera with them that grandma had given to him as a gift those many years ago.

Standing together with the other Qian relatives on that particular day proved to be challenging for members of the Qian family. Many of them appeared somewhat cautious with the camera lens in front of them. They welcomed the warm sun rays of early winter. At that instant, he fixed in time an image marking the 91st summer since his grandmother left for Belgium for her studies.

He then went to an enchantingly beautiful cemetery. There, he saw the family tombstone that his grandma had guided the Qian relatives to construct for all of their ancestors. It had been newly built by descendants of the Qian family, an amends for the regret grandmother had deeply felt. The Qian family members wept as they watched him kowtow.

The master of the cemetery, a simple local man, unassumingly expressed a wish that they would select the nicest plot in the cemetery to erect a tombstone just for Madame Qian Xiuling. This would give those who wished to remember her a place to come and see her, and also establish a final resting place for her.

Jerome went to see the cemetery plot. On one side was a bright green hill, on the other was a small, gentle stream. It was quiet, peaceful and spacious, and shaded by trees on all sides. Under the blue horizon, the plot was gently breathing.

Jerome solemnly expressed his intention to return and discuss this with the older generation and his brothers and sisters. After a couple of weeks, his email message arrived:

I am extremely humbled and honored to represent the Perlinghi family as we agree to the proposal to erect a cenotaph in memory of Grandmother Qian Xiuling. It will be erected in her wonderful and stunning hometown. I offer my personal and sincerest gratitude for this gift.

—Jerome Perlinghi

He said that he hoped to return to Yixing soon and to stay for a while. He wanted to take at least 300 pictures of Chinese indigineous peoples and then hold a photography exhibition in his grandmother's old family village.

"Yes," he affirmed. "I will be back."

The author Xu Feng spent 16 years researching and preparing materials for this book, including visiting and interviewing Qian Xiuling's descendants, old friends, and the only hostage still living today. With the exclusive details of stories once forgotten and rescued and precious historical materials lost in time, he has recreated an engaging historical moment, brilliantly conveying the turbulence of an era through which the valiant qualities of Qian Xiuling shine.

About the author

Xu Feng (Chinese: 徐风) is a distinguished Chinese writer of novels, prose works and biographies. He has published 17 works with a total of 5 million words, including *Buyi Huzong (Chinese Ceramic Master: Biography of Gu Jingzhou)*, *Hua Fei Hua (A Flower in the Haze: Biography of Jiang Rong)* and *Jiangnan Fanhuang Lu (Records of Jiangnan)*. He has won many prominent literary prizes in China such as the Chinese Good Book Award, Chinese Writers Literature Award, Chinese Biography Award, Bing Xin Prose Award, and many others.

www.ingramcontent.com/pod-product-compliance
Lightning Source LLC
Chambersburg PA
CBHW030106100526
44591CB00009B/293